West Bengal
and the Federalizing Process
in India

West Bengal
and the Federalizing Process
in India

BY MARCUS F. FRANDA

PRINCETON UNIVERSITY PRESS

PRINCETON, NEW JERSEY

1968

Printed in the United States of America
by Princeton University Press, Princeton, New Jersey

To Harry and Warner, and
especially to Milt

Acknowledgments

THIS BOOK is the result of field research carried out in West Bengal over a period of eighteen months (December 1962 to June 1964). Partial acknowledgment for my education in the politics of West Bengal during this time is made in the footnotes and bibliography of this work, and in the few sentences that follow, but those who are principally responsible for that education are the numerous unmentioned Bengalis who shared so freely their knowledge and attitudes about politics. Admittedly excluding a large number of people who influenced the study a great deal, I must mention six politicians (Atulya Ghosh, Promatha Nath Bisi, Nirmalendu De, Nirmal Bhattacharya, Rabindra Lal Sinha, and Asok Dutt), two journalists (Amitabha Chowdhury and Robi Chakravarty), and one very close friend and research assistant (Suhrid Kumar Chatterjee), all of whom were especially generous with their time. To most of the Bengalis with whom I talked, but to these especially, I owe a great deal for their willingness and patience in the education of a foreign scholar.

The study was also shaped, in a less tangible but very real way, by a number of fellow Americans who shared their Calcutta experiences with me: Ronald Inden, Leonard Gordon, Patti and Ross Brewer, Kathy and Wally Reed, Lorraine and Ed Dimock, and Frank Tysen. Much of the discussion, argument, and interchange of ideas that went on among these people, and in which I was fortunate enough to share, is reflected in the following pages. Most important in this respect was my wife, Vonnie, who also served as a sounding board for ideas, and as part-time cartographer, librarian, and editor.

Materials on which this study is based were made available to me by the library of the West Bengal Pradesh Congress Committee, the Sarat Bose Academy in Calcutta, the Asiatic Society of Bengal, the National Library in Alipore, the India Office Library in London, the Library of Congress in Washington, D.C., and the Columbia University Library in New

York City. Most of the written source materials for the study were gathered from the South Asian collection of the University of Chicago Library, so ably organized and maintained by Miss Maureen Patterson and her staff.

I owe a special debt to Milton Singer and the members of the Committee on South Asian Studies at the University of Chicago during the period when I was associated with the Committee. The influence of Professor Myron Weiner on my own scholarship has been far greater than that of anyone else, and Professors Edward C. Dimock, Jr. and Somdev Bhattacharji were responsible for my initial interest in Bengali literature and language. The ideas of Professors Grant McConnell, James Q. Wilson, Bernard Cohn, Stephen Hay, W. H. Morris-Jones, and the late Morton Grodzins had a much greater impact on the study than any of them realize, as did the dialogue with three fellow graduate students, now Professors Francine Frankel, Baldev Raj Nayar, and Paul R. Brass.

Those who read all or parts of the manuscript and made helpful suggestions and criticisms include Professors Lloyd Rudolph, Leonard Binder, and David Greenstone at Chicago, and Professors Karl Deutsch of Yale University, Wayne Wilcox of Columbia University, and Richard L. Park of the University of Michigan at Ann Arbor. William McClung, the Social Science Editor of Princeton University Press, and especially the readers for the Press, were helpful in suggesting final revisions.

I wish to thank the editors of *Asian Survey* and *Pacific Affairs* for permission to use material from my articles which first appeared in their journals.

Field research for the study was made possible by grants from the National Defense Foreign Language Program, the American Institute of Indian Studies, and the Ford Foundation Foreign Area Program. Funds for secretarial and other research costs were provided by the Committee on South Asian Studies at the University of Chicago, the Colgate University Research Council, and the Center for International Programs and Services of the State of New York. None of these institutions, of course, are responsible for any errors contained in this work, nor have they sought to determine in any way the content of the conclusions and interpretations presented.

Contents

Tables

Figures

West Bengal
and the Federalizing Process
in India

Introduction

WHILE there has been a growing interest in Indian federalism in recent years, it is surprising how little we know of the political dynamics of India's federal system. Some of the factors that affect and condition the operation of a federal arrangement have been quite thoroughly studied—the rise of nationalism and the growth of regional independence movements, the evolution of a constitutional system through the periods of British rule, the creation of the present constitution, and the development of constitutional law, all of these are well represented in the literature.[1] But the largest gaps occur at the center of our interest, in those areas that involve center-state political relations and questions of political integration. We want to know the ways in which central and state leaderships have evolved, and are evolving, working relationships one with the other, and the effect of state and regional political, economic, and social conditions on the evolution of center-state behavior patterns. We want to know the relationships between party and administrative structures at different levels of government and the ways in which they behave. In short, we seek to expand our focus from a narrow concern with legal and formal federal arrangements to a larger area that places the federalizing process in the political context.

A number of difficulties confront us when trying to answer the questions involved here, many of which are inherent in the very subject we wish to study. Not only is India large and diverse and rapidly changing, it has also encountered federal-

---

[1] An excellent bibliographical essay on Indian federalism is available in T. J. Leonard, "Federalism in India," in *Federalism in the Commonwealth: A Bibliographical Commentary*, ed. William S. Livingstone (London: The Hansard Society, 1963), pp. 87-145.

izing problems (language differences, to mention only one) of a magnitude unprecedented in history. Moreover, Indian political leaders at Independence generally felt that federalism was "'not a definite concept' and 'lacked a stable meaning,' with the result that they have, since 1947, generally pursued 'the policy of pick and choose' to see [what] would suit [them] best, [what] would suit the genius of the nation best."[2] The result has been a federalizing process that combines, modifies, and transforms many of our established ideas about federalism, a process that cannot accurately be described by any single appellation or phrase that we have used in the past.

This study is an attempt to cope with the complexity of India's experience by focusing on center-state relations as they affect one Indian state. It was assumed that, since detailed studies of state politics in India are almost nonexistent at this stage of our research,[3] it would be impossible to describe or to compare all of the various kinds of relationships that are developing in all seventeen Indian states (much less to analyze the emergence of such relationships). It was also as-

[2] Quoted from a statement by L. K. Maitra in the Constituent Assembly by Granville Austin, *The Indian Constitution: Cornerstone of a Nation* (Oxford: Clarendon Press, 1966), p. 186. Austin's commentary on the federal provisions of India's Constitution (Chapters 8 through 11) is the most valuable discussion available on the development of constitutional federalism in India.

[3] This gap in our research has been rectified somewhat by the collection of eight studies on Indian state politics, *State Politics in India*, published by Princeton University Press in 1968. The volume is edited by Myron Weiner, and my chapter on the politics of West Bengal has been used as the basis for discussion of the subject in this study. A number of other studies that do not deal directly with center-state relations provide insight into the politics of particular states. See especially F. G. Bailey, *Politics and Social Change: Orissa in 1959* (Berkeley: University of California Press, 1963); Paul R. Brass, *Factional Politics in an Indian State: The Congress Party in Uttar Pradesh* (Berkeley: University of California Press, 1965); and Baldev Raj Nayar, *Minority Politics in the Punjab* (Princeton: Princeton University Press, 1966).

sumed that, if only because of the magnitude of governmental involvement, it would be impossible to study empirically the federalizing process by reference to even most of the possible contacts between the center and a given state. What is attempted, therefore, is a limited inquiry.

Essentially, this is a series of three case studies on the development of working agreements between the Government of India and the Government of West Bengal. Each of the case studies was completed before 1967, during a period when the Congress party was in a majority in both state and central legislatures. In the case studies the focus is on the role of party and governmental leaders, as well as political groups, in developing working agreements on broad matters of policy. While each of the cases is written in such a way as to be understandable by itself, the two chapters that follow the cases do attempt to summarize the generalizations evolved during the course of the study, and to make them relevant for others interested in research in Indian federalism.

Although the ordering of the cases could have been done in many different ways, it was decided to take up the study of the cases in the order in which they were most directly concerned with inter-state relationships and the integrity of the single state. Chapters II and III are concerned with the reorganization of the boundaries of West Bengal; Chapters IV and V with the creation and maintenance of the Damodar Valley Corporation (which involved both West Bengal and Bihar); and Chapters VI and VII with the development of land reform legislation in West Bengal. These three cases were selected for several reasons. First, since they involve central legislation, center-state cooperative legislation and administration, and state legislation respectively, they concern three major types of contact between state and central personnel. Second, they represent most clearly the goals and actions of the present Indian leadership, and not those of the British in India, since they all trace the development of policies that have been implemented after Independence. Finally, they deal with major aspects of governmental involvement; they all concern policies that have required heavy investments of time, money, and skilled personnel. They are, therefore, cases that have been seriously considered by Indian leaders, and their development has been the result of the most careful consideration for future consequences.

The evidence from these case studies indicates that political leaders and groups in West Bengal were not constrained to accept central government decisions concerning either state matters or constitutionally central matters, even during that period when the Congress party was in power at both central and state levels. Some central leadership groups at times made national plans, or sought nationally standardized policies on some issues, but the plans and policies that were adopted in many instances were substantially the same as those that were submitted to national planners in the initial stages of national planning by state leadership groups. While West Bengal politicians were encouraged to bring policies into conformity with those of some central leaders and with the policies of other state leaders, they also had considerable freedom to formulate their own plans on the basis of regional considerations, and to reject or negate unacceptable plans, programs, or policies. When central political leadership groups found it necessary to interfere in direct clashes between West Bengal and other states (or between individuals or groups of individuals within West Bengal), they preferred to act as arbiter or referee in such instances. Rather than attempt to impose their own solution, or to accept the solution offered by either of the disputants, actors at the center preferred to bring disputants at the state level into agreement by the proposal of measures acceptable to all who were involved—or, in case this was not possible, to postpone the decision.

In the case studies, policies were decided through a process of hard competitive bargaining, between a divided central leadership on the one hand, and, on the other, a divided state leadership. Running through the cases is a picture of an unusual and perhaps characteristically Indian interpenetration of participants from one government into the work of the other (in administrative, party, and other governmental bodies). In this milieu, each case was disposed of, not with reference to formalized or constitutional procedures, but rather by a bargaining process which reached a conclusion only after each set of "deciders" had found out, through elections or agitation, what the unknown state of public reaction was likely to be. Party politics and political mobilization, therefore, became exceedingly important for the operation of the federal system.

While the cases in this study are limited to an examination of the behavior of political leadership as it affects center-state relations in West Bengal, an attempt is made in the last chapters to suggest contrasts between the federalizing experience of West Bengal and that found in other Indian states. It is obvious that we will be unable to develop a comparative analysis of India's federalizing process for all areas, or to identify all of the significant variables that impinge on that process, until such time that sufficient data is available for other Indian states. The present study, therefore, does not offer any general theories as to the federalizing process for all of India, but it is hoped that it will in some small way eventually contribute to a larger study.

States Reorganization: The Development of State Demands

IN THE Indian Constitution, the authority to redraw the boundaries of any state, or to simply abolish or create any state, rests clearly and unmistakably with the central government. Moreover, according to Article 3 of the Constitution, revision of boundaries need not be done by amendment, or by any other elaborate or complicated procedure, but can be effected by an ordinary act of Parliament. The Constitution does provide that the President of the Union shall ascertain the views of the states concerned before submitting a bill to Parliament, but it is also clear that the President is under no obligation either to accept these views or to obtain the consent of the states to a contemplated reorganization bill.[1] The following chapters, however, point to an inability or unwillingness on the part of central government leaders and agencies to use the sweeping and specific powers granted by the Constitution when redrawing the boundary that divides West Bengal and Bihar. At the same time, it indicates the important role of party structure and political mobilization in West Bengal in shaping the nature of center-state relations.

The provincial and state boundaries that were in existence when India achieved Independence in 1947 were a result of the political events that occurred during the more than two hundred years of British rule, and of the concepts of administrative convenience that had prevailed among the British and Mughal rulers of India. In the 15th and 16th centuries, the Mughals had divided northeastern India into three *subahs* (or provinces): Bengal (which then included most of present-day Assam), Bihar, and Orissa. It was these three *subahs*

[1] Trimbak Krishna Tope, *The Constitution of India* (Bombay: Popular Prakasan, 1963), pp. 11-12.

which subsequently came to form the Bengal Presidency of the British East India Company when Shah Alam in 1765 granted the *diwani* (or right to collect revenue) to the Company's soldiers. While administration of the provinces was initially difficult because of the size of the original units, it became even more so during British rule when the Company proceeded to conquer inland and to add newly acquired territories. By 1810 the Bengal Presidency stretched up to Delhi and beyond to the Sikh frontier.[2]

An attempt to reduce the size of the Presidency was thus initiated in 1833 when the Charter Act provided for the separation of the areas north and west of Bihar from those areas east and south of the United Provinces of Agra and Oudh. Bengal then became once more confined to the area that had previously been included in the Mughal *subahs* of Bengal, Bihar, and Orissa, and the remainder of the Presidency was grouped together to form the North-West Provinces. In 1874 the Bengal unit was again reduced in size when Assam was separated and placed under the control of its own Chief Commissioner; and in 1905 it was further reduced when Assam was united with Chittagong and fifteen districts of Bengal to form the new province of Eastern Bengal and Assam. Although the "partition" of 1905 was later revoked (in 1911) the size of the Presidency of Bengal was reduced still further when Bihar and Orissa were separated from the Presidency in 1912.[3]

The partition of Bengal which accompanied Independence

[2] The history of the boundaries of Bengal prior to this century is contained in Great Britain, Parliament, *Papers Relating to the Reconstitution of the Provinces of Bengal and Assam*, Cd. 2658, PP. 1905: LVIII; and Cd. 2746, PP. 1906: LXXXI.

[3] The partition of Bengal in 1905 and the revocation of the partition in 1911 are traced out in P. C. Chakravarti, "Genesis of the Partition of Bengal, 1905," *Indian History Congress Proceedings* (1958), pp. 549-53. See also Mahesa Narayana Sachichidananda Sinha, *The Partition of Bengal or the Separation of Behar* (Allahabad: Indian Press, 1906), pp. 1-41.

was thus the last of a long series of partitions that have left the state of West Bengal less than one-seventh the size of "Greater Bengal" a century ago.[4] Moreover, during the course of this partitioning, the boundaries of the Bengali linguistic and cultural unit have at no time coincided with the administrative boundaries of the unit known as Bengal. As a result of this anomaly, and as a consequence of the development of a regional consciousness in this century, the demand for state administrative boundaries drawn on the basis of linguistic and regional cultural factors had assumed prominent proportions in this area by 1947.[5] West Bengal thus shared in the general demand for the creation of linguistic states that was so prominent during the first decade of Independence.

The movement for the creation of linguistic states is one that was consistently and consciously supported by the Congress party during the course of the nationalist movement. Beginning in 1920, the Congress had organized on the basis of linguistic and cultural regions, despite conflicting British administrative patterns, and as late as 1945 Congress resolutions had advocated reorganization. The linguistic principle had been further supported by a number of Congress studies and reports, principally by the Nehru Committee Report of 1928.[6]

Because linguistic provinces had been so unanimously championed during the nationalist struggle, agitation for reorganization increased in almost all areas of the subcontinent with

[4] In the first Indian census of 1872, the area of Bengal was 248,231 square miles; by 1901 it had dropped to 189,837 square miles; by 1941 to 82,876 square miles; and by 1951 (after the partition of India and Bengal) to 33,524 square miles.

[5] For the growth of regional nationalism in Bengal, see Richard L. Park, "The Rise of Militant Nationalism in Bengal: A Regional Study of Indian Nationalism" (unpublished Ph.D. dissertation, Harvard University, 1950).

[6] Indian National Congress, *Report of the Committee Appointed by the All-Parties Conference to Determine the Principles of the Constitution of India* (Allahabad: General Secretary, All-India Congress Committee, 1928), see especially pp. 61ff.

the attainment of Independence. Congressmen from all parts of India were anxious to undo British imposed administrative boundaries and to reorganize on the basis of cultural and linguistic factors. In Bengal feelings of linguistic and cultural identity were heightened by partition (which split the Bengali-speaking area in two and divided it by an international boundary), by the influx of refugees, and by the communal riots that resulted from partition. While leaders of Bengal had themselves been a party to partition, the censure of the Bengali middle class was directed primarily at central leaders (especially at Gandhi and Nehru) and charges of "Hindi imperialism" were rampant. Indicative of the feelings that were generated at this time is the report of a large Calcutta daily written in 1948:

> . . . the Biharis have organised squads on the lines of Hitler's storm troopers and Muslim National Guards of pre-partitioned India. . . . They are inciting the Santals . . . to be fully mobilised for immediate action [against Bengalis].
>
> Has that class which gladly accepted the gallows to assert its claim become extinct? Why are not all the sons of Bengal combining to push on their cause? . . . To assert the claim of Bengal, we must raise a great agitation. Let the successors of Khudi Ram and Surya Sen rise up. . . .[7]

The agitation for the defense of the Bengali culture and language during these early years was not, however, confined to agitational movements, nor was it confined to the middle class of Calcutta and the opposition parties. A Memorandum calling for the inclusion of all of the Bengali-speaking areas of Bihar, Assam, and Orissa was submitted to the President of the Constituent Assembly by two of Nehru's early Ministers in the Central Cabinet—Shyama Prasad Mookerjee (then Minister of Industry and Supplies) and K. C. Neogy (then Minister of Commerce)—and similar memoranda were

[7] Quoted in India, Lok Sabha Debates, XIV, No. 15 (August 23, 1951), 1250.

prepared and submitted to the Constituent Assembly by the West Bengal Pradesh Congress Committee and the West Bengal Government.[8]

The Policy of the Center and West Bengal

At this point, however, the reaction of the Constituent Assembly and the Congress party high command to the claims of Bengalis and other linguistic groups indicated that Independence had caused a great deal of rethinking on states reorganization policy. In 1948 the Constituent Assembly appointed a three-man Linguistic Provinces Commission under the Chairmanship of S. K. Dar, a former High Court Judge, to examine the question of reorganization in South India. In a unanimous report submitted in December 1948, the Dar Commission rejected the principle of organizing states on a linguistic basis and advocated a change of previous Congress policy on the question. The Commission argued that linguistic provinces would lead to disintegration of the country, largely because they would bring into being "sub-nations":

> . . . the emotional response, which the sub-national sentiment will receive from a linguistic province, will always be greater than the one received by the national sentiment. The linguistic group, by being put into a linguistic province, may or may not become stronger; but it does not follow that by being stronger it will become more nationalistic in outlook. . . . In a linguistic province sub-nationalism will always be the dominant force and will always evoke greater emotional response; and, in a conflict between the two, nascent nationalism is sure to lose ground and will ultimately be submerged.[9]

[8] The content of these memoranda is detailed in *The Statesman* (Calcutta), August 8, 1952, p. 1, and August 31, 1952, p. 1.

[9] India (Dominion Constituent Assembly), *Report of the Linguistic Provinces Commission, 1948* (New Delhi: Government of India Press, 1948), p. 31.

The Commission argued that, instead of linguistic or cultural factors, administrative convenience should be the main criterion for reorganization, and that attention should also be paid to geographical contiguity, economic viability, and capacity for growth.[10] Above all else, the Commission argued, there should be a large measure of agreement among the people living within the borders of a proposed state, and new states should not be forced on unwilling substantial minorities.[11] On the basis of this analysis, the Dar Commission concluded that perhaps administrative boundaries should be redrawn at some point in the future, but that in the circumstances of the Indian polity in 1948 reorganization could only lead to great inconvenience, if not disaster.[12]

As a result of the Dar Commission Report, the Congress party Working Committee established a Linguistic Provinces Committee (LPC) of its own to inquire into the demands for linguistic states. This committee, consisting of Nehru, Vallabhai Patel, and Pattabhi Sitaramayya, submitted its report in April 1949, and voiced substantial agreement with the conclusions of the Dar Commission. The JVP Committee (as the LPC came to be known) argued that India's boundaries might indeed have to be redrawn at some point in the future, but that reorganization in 1948 was impossible. In the eyes of the JVP Committee, reorganization would be feasible only after (1) the various communities advocating reorganization had consolidated their programs for redrawing boundaries; (2) the Princely states had been brought within the Union; (3) the period of stress which characterized the Dominion period had passed; and (4) continuity of administration in the states had been achieved. In 1949, the Committee argued, "Formation of new provinces . . . would unmistakably retard the process of consolidation of our gains, dislocate our administrative, economic and financial structure, let loose, while we are still in a formative state, forces of disruption and disinte-

[10] *Ibid.*, p. 29.   [11] *Ibid.*, p. 2.   [12] *Ibid.*

gration, and seriously interfere with the progressive solution of our economic and political difficulties."[13]

On the basis of the reports submitted by both party and government, the Congress high command established a policy wherein reorganization of boundaries was postponed temporarily, while future reorganization was promised and room was left for experimentation. Following the divisions created by British rule, the Republic was divided by the Constituent Assembly into Part A states (corresponding to the former provinces), Part B states (comprising the former Princely states), and Part C states (consisting of smaller territories in the nature of enclaves). Provision for future reorganization was provided by the inclusion of Article 3 of the Constitution, which provided for a specific allocation of powers to reorganize boundaries,[14] and assurances of future reorganization were made in numerous pronouncements by central government Ministers and party leaders. The JVP Report, for example, stated: ". . . if public sentiment is insistent and overwhelming, the practicability of satisfying public demand, with its implications and consequences, must be examined."[15] Moreover, the JVP Report suggested that the demand of the Telugu-speaking

[13] Indian National Congress, *Report of the Linguistic Provinces Committee* (New Delhi: All-India Congress Committee, 1949), p. 9.

[14] Professor Alexandrowicz, in a study of the Constituent Assembly debates, has concluded that the powers in Article 3 were not designed to tilt the balance of the Union in favor of central dominance as some have argued, but rather to provide for an orderly states reorganization when it became necessary: "All the Constituent Assembly had been able to do was to enact the Fundamental Rights, to define the principles of Government and lay down a federal framework leaving the disentanglement of the regional communities to a later, more suitable moment. In other words, as constitution-making promised to be a speedier achievement than federation-making, it was resolved to complete the first and to delay the latter." Charles Henry Alexandrowicz, "India Before and After Reorganisation," *The Year Book of World Affairs*, XII (1958), 135.

[15] *Report of the Linguistic Provinces Committee*, p. 9.

population of Madras for a separate Andhra state be met, and the Working Committee in November 1949, also recommended formation of such a unit.

Despite the assurances of the high command at this time, the policy of the central government was not interpreted everywhere as being necessarily a temporary decision that allowed for the possibility of future reorganization. Indeed, in West Bengal the policy of the high command was viewed in many quarters as an outright rejection of the claims of West Bengal, and this feeling was expressed most vocally by the opposition parties in the state. The leader of the West Bengal Communist Party, for example, took the following position: ". . . we know that the Bengal Ministers have been very vocal with regard to the claim on Bihar. But unfortunately somehow or other the All-India Congress leaders are at the moment supporting not the Congress leaders in West Bengal but the Congress leaders of Bihar with the result that our Ministers have been times without number snubbed with regard to this claim."[16] Even the Congress party in the state was not willing to follow the injunctions of the party hierarchy to desist from agitation for boundary revision on the assumption that reorganization would come at a more suitable time. In 1951 a Congress MP from West Bengal moved a resolution in the *Lok Sabha* calling for an alteration of the boundaries of West Bengal "with a view to establishing contiguity between the detached parts of the State,"[17] and at the Bangalore Session of the Congress party in the same year the West Bengal PCC submitted a Memorandum to the Working Committee calling attention to the demands of West Bengal.[18] During the course of the next few years the West Bengal Assembly passed a resolution which claimed large areas of Bihar

[16] *West Bengal Legislative Assembly Debates*, III, No. 1 (September 16, 1948), 185.

[17] *Lok Sabha Debates*, XIV, No. 15 (August 23, 1951), 1254ff.

[18] *The Statesman* (Calcutta), February 1, 1951, p. 1.

as Bengali-speaking and therefore rightfully to be included in West Bengal, and copies of this resolution were submitted to the President of the Union, to the Prime Minister, and to the AICC. The state Congress resolution and accompanying Memorandum was subsequently adopted as the basis of the demands of numerous other groups—the Calcutta Corporation, the *Bangiya Sahitya Parishad*, even some leftist parties—and reaffirmed at each meeting of the PCC during 1952 and 1953.

In the face of linguistic sentiment in Bengal and elsewhere (it was especially vocal in South India at this time), the central government remained firm in its resolve to postpone major reorganization and to steer a course midway between coercion of provincial units on the one hand, and, on the other, concession to provincial demands. Nehru insisted that his government was not in favor of "imposing a solution," and argued that "it [reorganization] could be done only through peace and mutual understanding."[19] On numerous occasions—in Parliament, in public appearances, and in private interviews—he reiterated this stand:

> . . . what the Government has declared as its policy is that if there is this large and broad agreement brought about by the parties [states], Government would gladly take steps to finalize it, to further it, by appointment of Commissions and the like. . . . It is rather difficult to bring compulsion in this matter. In a desire to please one side, another side is displeased and the Government ought to come down with a heavy hand trying to compel somebody to agree and even if that could be done that leaves traces of ill-will born out of friction and conflict. The thing if it is to be done and successfully done should be done with a large measure of goodwill and agreement and so far as we are concerned, we are prepared to go ahead as fast as possible, but I do submit

[19] *Ibid.*, January 3, 1952, p. 1.

that the basis should be with a large measure of agreement and goodwill.[20]

Under the cloak of this broad policy, the actions of the center during the first three years of the Republic consisted essentially of censure of agitation,[21] especially when such agitation was led by Congressmen, while at the same time of refusal to coerce either the state Congress party unit or state government.[22]

Finally, in December 1952, the floodgates of lingualism were opened when Potti Sriramulu, in a gesture of self-sacrifice which aroused the Telegu-speaking peoples of northern Madras, fasted unto death on the issue of a separate state for his people. Shortly after this, the Government of India promised to create a separate Andhra, and the new state came into being in the fall of 1953. As a result of the agitation resulting from the death of Potti Sriramulu, the demand of other areas for linguistic states also became more intense.[23] To this renewed agitation, the center responded with the appointment

[20] Statement in the *Lok Sabha Debates*, xiv, No. 14 (August 22, 1951), 1102.

[21] Nehru, for example, sent a letter to West Bengal PCC President Ghosh "expressing his distress" at the resolution of the PCC demanding reorganization. Nehru stated that, "acrimony should not be spread among Congress leaders," and requested Ghosh to desist from his activities in this regard. At the same time no attempt was made to discipline the state Congress. *The Statesman* (Calcutta), August 26, 1952, p. 5.

[22] The Working Committee, for example, passed in May 1953 a resolution expressing "regretful surprise" at the behavior of the PCC's, on the reorganization issue, and issued a directive barring future PCC resolutions on this issue, but took no disciplinary action against subsequent resolutions of the West Bengal PCC. See *ibid.,* September 1, 1952, p. 5, and May 17, 1953, p. 1.

[23] In West Bengal the actions of Potti Sriramulu prompted two 25-day fasts by Congress workers—Baidyanath Bhowmick and Sikhendhu Bikas Das—both of which were broken at the request of the Chief Minister. See *ibid.*, May 10, 1953, p. 5, and May 22, 1953, p. 1.

of a States Reorganization Commission (SRC): the Working Committee resolved in December 1952 that large-scale inquiries into the question be initiated by the government;[24] a similar resolution was prepared and passed by the Subjects Committee of the Congress party at its Hyderabad Session in early 1953;[25] and finally, in April of 1953, Prime Minister Nehru announced that the States Reorganization Commission would be appointed.[26]

The States Reorganization Commission

The appointment of a States Reorganization Commission was a remarkable device for continuing the policy of the Congress party high command while at the same time representing a middle ground between the alternative paths of coercion and complete surrender to provincial sentiments. The Commission represented a "neutral" body that would listen to all of the demands for reorganization, demands made on the basis of linguistic and cultural factors, as well as those stemming from other considerations. The mere collection of all such proposals (the Commission received more than 150,000 documents from various groups and individuals) by a neutral body of this kind made it possible to lay the basis for negotiation and arbitration, at the same time that it allowed time for demands to solidify around a number of concrete and concise positions.

In the case of West Bengal, the success of the Commission was indeed remarkable. As a result of the mere existence of the Commission, political parties and other interested individuals and groups in West Bengal concentrated on the articulation of precise recommendations which could be placed before the members of the SRC. Groups and parties continued to pass resolutions and in some cases to demonstrate in order to draw attention to their demands, but all (including the leftist

[24] *Ibid.*, December 29, 1952, p. 1.
[25] *Ibid.*, January 18, 1953, p. 1.
[26] *Ibid.*, April 29, 1953, pp. 1, 7.

opposition) agreed that such demonstrations should be conducted in an orderly and peaceful manner, and that the movement for reorganization should be directed at the newly formed Commission.[27] The success of the SRC in mitigating conflict in West Bengal can be seen most clearly from the fact that, during the period when the Commission was hearing evidence, no individual or group in West Bengal either threatened or undertook violent demonstrations on this issue.

Moreover, after the appointment of the Commission in December 1953, the demands of West Bengal came to focus on four specific proposals, each based on a different set of factors, and each demanding different amounts of territory from neighboring states (see Figures 1 and 2). The Memorandum of the state Congress party was the most inclusive, being based on all of the demands that had been made on neighboring states at any time in the past by groups in West Bengal. According to the Memorandum, these claims were advanced on the basis of "historical, linguistic, economic, ethnological, financial, geographical, political, cultural, administrative, and other grounds."[28] The area claimed by the PCC was, as a result of this inclusive demand, extremely large: a total of 21,352 square miles, representing almost three-fourths the total area of West Bengal after 1947, with a population of 8.2 million was claimed from three states (Bihar, Assam, and Orissa).[29] In contrast to the demand of the PCC, the proposals of other organizations in West Bengal were more re-

[27] See for example the speech of Jyoti Basu, leader of the CPI in the West Bengal Legislative Assembly, who argued as late as December 1955 that "the whole of the States Reorganisation Commission's Report must be reviewed," but at the same time pleaded "with everybody present here, with everybody outside, that in these debates and discussions not to rouse evil passions of the people." *West Bengal Legislative Assembly Debates*, XIII (December 9, 1955), 249-50.

[28] Indian National Congress, *Memorandum Submitted to the States Reorganisation Commission* (Calcutta: West Bengal Pradesh Congress Committee, 1955), p. 1.

[29] *Ibid.*, pp. 183-90.

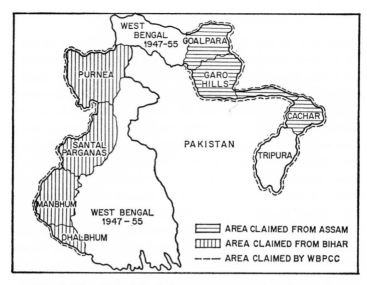

Fig. 1. West Bengal Pradesh Congress Committee Demands
Presented to the States Reorganization Commission

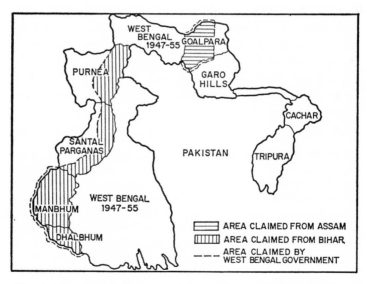

Fig. 2. West Bengal Government Demands Presented to the States
Reorganization Commission

alistic. The state government Memorandum argued that administrative convenience and the promotion of economic development should be the principal factors taken into consideration when reorganizing, and on this basis recommended that portions of four districts in Bihar, and portions of one district in Assam be transferred to West Bengal.[30] In terms of size, the government proposal claimed only slightly more than half of the area claimed by the PCC, comprising 11,840 square miles and containing a population of 5.7 million.[31] A third proposal was drawn up by a coalition of leftist parties (the West Bengal Linguistic States Redistribution Committee) headed by Atul Chandra Gupta, and claimed all of the territory contiguous to West Bengal in which Bengali-speaking people predominated (the amount of territory claimed in this demand was somewhat more than that demanded by the government of West Bengal, but less than that demanded by the PCC, and varied according to the statistics used and the definition of a "Bengali-speaking area").[32] Finally, the Jan Sangh party recommended that no territory be ceded, but rather that the states of Bihar, West Bengal, Orissa, and Assam be combined with the centrally administered states of Manipur and Tripura to form one state, to be called *Purbanchal* (Eastern Region) *Pradesh*.[33]

It goes without saying that the States Reorganisation Commission was faced with an almost insurmountable task. In addition to the numerous proposals advanced by different interests in West Bengal, other proposals were advanced by other interests in the states bordering West Bengal (see Fig-

[30] Although the government Memorandum was never published, it did appear in some detail in *The Statesman* (Calcutta), February 13, 1955, pp. 1, 9.

[31] India (Republic), *Report of the States Reorganisation Commission, 1955* (Delhi: Manager of Publications, 1955), p. 181.

[32] *Memorandum Submitted by the West Bengal Linguistic States Redistribution Committee* (Calcutta: n.p., 1955), pp. 35-47.

[33] *The Statesman* (Calcutta), February 13, 1955, p. 9.

ure 3). In the words of the Commission, "the redrawing of these boundaries has been one of the most difficult problems with which this Commission has been faced."[34] But despite the magnitude of its task, and the possible difficulties that were almost certain to be encountered regardless of the solution proposed, the States Reorganization Commission Report was remarkably successful. Its success stemmed not from its ability to satisfy any of the interests involved, but rather from the fact that it proposed a solution not wholly unacceptable to anyone, and yet demanding minimal concessions from each (see Figure 4).

To begin with, the Commission rejected all of those demands which, in its own words, had arisen out of the "sterile and unfortunate controversies which have claimed a great deal of the time and energy of the leaders of Bengal and Bihar."[35] It rejected the claims of the West Bengal PCC to the extensive areas demanded from Bihar and Assam at the same time that it rejected the claims of Bihar and Assam in West Bengal. Because the extravagant claims of all three state party units had been rejected, and because very few members of the PCC's in each state had ever supposed that their respective states would be conceded such large sections of neighboring states, this recommendation of the Commission was accepted everywhere without major controversy. Some Congressmen even admitted at a later date that they had made extravagant demands to publicize local interests, and that they were happy enough to gain a hearing from the SRC without having their demands accepted.[36]

While it was possible for the Commission to thus eliminate the majority of the proposals which it had been asked to consider, there still remained a very significant area of conflict and dissatisfaction. As the Commission pointed out, this

[34] *Report of the States Reorganisation Commission*, p. 182.
[35] *Ibid.*
[36] Based on interviews conducted in 1963 and 1964.

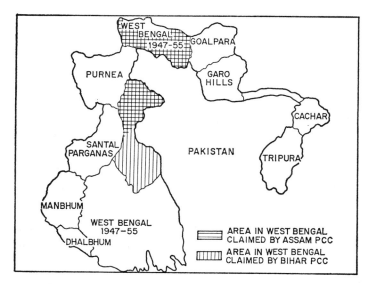

Fig. 3. Demands of Assam and Bihar PCC's to the States
Reorganization Commission

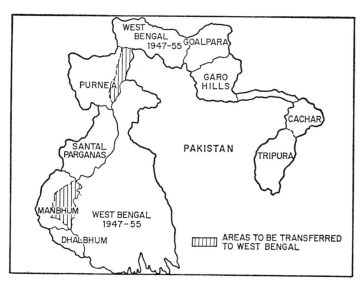

Fig. 4. Recommendations of the States Reorganization Commission
Concerning West Bengal

arose principally from the partition of Bengal that had accompanied Independence:

> Partition has created many problems for West Bengal. Apart from the influx of refugees from Pakistan, which may now be estimated at about three and a half millions, the entire communications system of Bengal has been disrupted since 1947. The northern districts of the Presidency divisions have become less easily accessible from Calcutta; and West Bengal is now the only Part A State which is geographically not a compact and integrated unit.[37]

The Commission also noted that partition had aroused in West Bengal the feeling that the state had "been treated unjustly," and concluded that "there is no denying the fact that the present distribution of territories between Bihar and West Bengal is such as to give rise to some real administrative difficulties from the point of view of West Bengal."[38] The Commission thus recommended that two separate areas of Bihar be transferred to West Bengal:

1. First the SRC Report recommended that a portion of Kishanganj subdivision and the Gopalpur revenue *thana* of Purnea be transferred to West Bengal in order to give the state a land corridor between its unconnected northern and southern districts and allow West Bengal to "acquire control of the Indo-Pakistan border in this region along its entire length."[39]

2. Second, the Commission recommended that Purulia subdivision of Manbhum district be transferred from Bihar to West Bengal. In this case the Commission members argued:

> The transfer of Purulia can be justified on the ground that it will facilitate the implementation of a flood control-*cum*-irrigation project which has recently been taken up in West Bengal. . . . If flood control and irrigation in the Burdwan division are to be efficiently carried out in future

[37] *SRC Report*, p. 172.   [38] *Ibid.*, p. 175.   [39] *Ibid.*, p. 176.

it will be desirable to transfer to West Bengal a major portion of the catchment area because this will facilitate soil conservation measures and also provide perhaps a more appropriate dam site.[40]

Although the Report of the States Reorganization Commission recommended the transfer of territory from Bihar to West Bengal against the wishes of the Bihar government, it was at the same time carefully considered and it did demand concessions from both states. In the words of the Commission members, they had recommended the transfer of ". . . two bits of territory which have been mentioned in every claim during the last seven years; and even in these two cases, they are confined to areas, the transfer of which can be regarded as absolutely essential [to West Bengal]."[41] Indeed, the Commission had also refused to concede the demands to two-thirds of the territory claimed by West Bengal in Bihar, on the grounds that these territories were fully integrated into the industrial and administrative structure of the latter state. The areas that were to be transferred were predominantly rural areas in which Bengali-speaking people formed a majority, and which were useful to West Bengal only as (a) a land corridor in the case of the northern (Purnea) area; and (b) as a catchment area for flood control in the case of the southern (Purulia) area. As the SRC pointed out, "the administrative structure and economy of the existing State [Bihar] are unlikely to be affected materially by our proposals."[42] The SRC recommendation was thus a partial concession to West Bengal, in that it granted only a portion of the area claimed by the state government; but it was at the same time a partial concession to Bihar, since it left Bihar's industrial and administrative structure intact.

The success of the States Reorganization Commission in laying a sound basis for arbitration by the center in the negotiations of the Bihar-West Bengal boundary conflict is indi-

[40] *Ibid.*, p. 179.   [41] *Ibid.*, p. 181.   [42] *Ibid.*, p. 171.

cated by the reception that was given the report by both sides. With the release of the report in October 1955, the West Bengal Government reported that it was not entirely satisfied, but that the recommendations of the SRC were "on the whole not disappointing."[43] At a meeting of Chief Ministers held somewhat later, it was also reported that the Chief Minister of Bihar had accepted the concession of territory involving portions of Purnea, and was willing to grant the remaining concessions pending either a referendum of the population concerned or other minor concessions from West Bengal.[44] In a similar vein, state PCC Chief Atulya Ghosh indicated that he had not given up entirely his demand for more territory, but expressed "general approval" with the SRC recommendations,[45] and the Bihar PCC indicated its willingness to relinquish the territory recommended in the report pending a referendum.[46] The possibility of conflict still existed, and a number of outstanding issues (the question of the necessity for a referendum for example) remained, but the demands of each state had now been diminished and oriented toward specific points of dispute.

Indeed, for three months after the publication of the SRC Report, tempers in both West Bengal and Bihar were calm; agitation was almost nonexistent (and certainly peaceful when it did occur); and it appeared that the long-standing border dispute between the two states might be settled quickly and on the basis of negotiation alone. The possibility of arriving at a peaceful and amicable solution seemed to be even greater after a "phased" discussion of the SRC Report was initiated by the central government. According to the plans of the Home Ministry, the discussion of the Commission's recommendations would take place in four stages, and opportunity would be available at each stage for state Chief Min-

[43] Reported in *The Statesman* (Calcutta), October 7, 1955, p. 1.

[44] *Ibid.*, January 7, 1956, p. 1.

[45] *Ibid.*, November 8, 1955, p. 1.

[46] *Ibid.*, October 20, 1955, p. 7.

isters and other governmental and party personnel to meet and negotiate. Throughout the discussion, a high-powered subcommittee of the Congress WC—composed of Nehru, Pant, Azad, and Dhebar—would act as an arbitrating agency and extend its good offices, and no changes would be made in the SRC recommendations except "those mutually accepted by the groups concerned."[47] Following this plan of action, preliminary discussions by Cabinet members at both the central and state levels were held throughout October (phase one); a meeting of the Working Committee (attended by all state PCC Chiefs) considered the Report in early November (phase two); the Report was discussed further at a meeting of all Chief Ministers held in late November (phase three); and finally the question was taken up for discussion in the *Lok Sabha*, and in state legislatures, in December (phase four).[48] Phased discussion of the Report meant that state leaders had every opportunity to arrive at decisions other than those recommended by the SRC, and the lack of agitation in both Bihar and West Bengal indicated basic acceptance of that procedure.

The Adoption of an "Agitational Approach"

Although it is impossible to determine what would have happened had "phased" discussion resulted in the adoption of a proposal to enact the SRC recommendations regarding West Bengal, it is sufficient to point out that two events interrupted the orderly discussion of late 1955 and led to massive agitation in West Bengal in early 1956. The first event was a statement by Nehru in the *Lok Sabha* on December 21, 1955, and reported in the press as follows: "[Prime Minister Nehru] said that he thought this [West Bengal-Bihar boundary dis-

[47] This was stated by Prime Minister Nehru, and reiterated by Home Minister Pant, President Prasad, and numerous other central party and government leaders. See *ibid.*, November 8, 1955, p. 1.

[48] A discussion of the strategy of the center on states reorganization appears in Vedette (pseud.), " 'Phased' Discussion of S.R.C. Report Proving Useful," *ibid.*, October 16, 1955, p. 10.

pute] the most unimportant problem in the report, and did not see how it mattered very much if a patch of a State were given to another."[49] The second event was the publication in Calcutta newspapers of a rumor that the WC subcommittee had decided to alter the recommendations of the SRC in favor of Bihar. In the words of an editorial in *The Statesman*, it was rumored that: ". . . linguistic statistics (which the Commission showed to be most controversial) may be considered even at Taluk level, and (say more detailed rumors) that West Bengal may even lose the Purnea corridor, on the plea of some scheme for joint administration which seems scarcely operable."[50]

Nehru's statement, and the inability or unwillingness of high-level personnel to immediately deny rumors that the SRC recommendations would be modified, led to immediate charges of "betrayal" by numerous groups within West Bengal, and ultimately forced almost total reconsideration of the entire Bengal-Bihar question. Following the publication of the rumors, an "emergency meeting" of the Executive Council of the West Bengal PCC was called, and a resolution was adopted expressing "deep shock and distress" at the reported decision of the high command.[51] A few days later the leftist West

[49] Quoted *ibid.*, January 13, 1956, p. 6. Nehru's own words, as reported in the *Lok Sabha Debates*, are as follows: "With the greatest respect for our friends in Bihar and Bengal and Orissa, I would say that nothing is more unimportant than their problem. I am really astonished at the amount of heat, about these three or four States, which has been imported. We can consider it and decide it. But what does it matter if a patch of Bihar goes this way and a patch of Bengal or Orissa goes the other way? I cannot get excited about it provided always that they get fair treatment. That is the vital and important point." Quoted in India, *Lok Sabha Debates,* x, No. 25 (December 21, 1955), 3510.

[50] Quoted from an editorial in *The Statesman* (Calcutta), January 13, 1956, p. 6.

[51] *Ibid.*, January 14, 1956, p. 1.

Bengal Linguistic States Redistribution Committee (WBL-SRC) met, and decided to observe a day of protest against the reported decision in the following week.[52] Both Chief Minister Roy and PCC Chief Ghosh immediately traveled to Delhi to obtain more information, and, during this visit, Ghosh made one of his rare speeches in the *Lok Sabha*, a sharp criticism of Nehru's earlier remarks, which exemplified the feelings that those remarks (coupled with the rumors) had evoked:

> The Honorable, the Prime Minister says: "we won't bother about what happens about Bengal or Bihar." I say with due humility that he is going to bother about the condition of Bengal. If 20,000 people come every month to a State, if 2½ lakhs of people come every year to a State, the Prime Minister of India will have to bother his head to solve that problem. Our question is not a Bengal question. If one question is not solved, the unity of India will be hampered. This is not a periodical question.
>
> I do not want to flaunt the sacrifice of Bengal. I do not want to say that Bengal was divided for the emancipation of the teeming millions of India. I will only say, we were a party to that division, because we wanted to free ourselves also. We made that sacrifice for our emancipation. . . .
>
> But, we want a sympathetic treatment from citizens of India. We want a sympathetic treatment from the other states. We want sympathetic treatment from the Government of India. I want to make it clear that I have not come here with a begging bowl. I do not want to evoke the pity and draw the merciful attention of other States. I want to be at par with other States of India. I want that a solution should be found for those persons who, leaving their herths [*sic*] and homes, are coming to Bengal every month, who have no future, for whom there is no silver lining in the

[52] *Ibid.*, January 15, 1956, p. 1.

horizon, those who do not know where they will remain, where they will settle. We have to solve that question.[53]

Although there had been some truth to the rumors that reached West Bengal in mid-January of 1956, it was also clear from subsequent statements made by all of the individuals involved, that the published rumors had been grossly exaggerated. In fact, the modifications of the SRC proposals which the Working Committee had suggested were a result of the long process of negotiation and arbitration that had taken place during the "phased" discussions. Contrary to the rumors, the Working Committee *had* obtained agreement from Bihar to the SRC proposal to transfer the areas in Purnea district to West Bengal without modification. To obtain this concession from Bihar, however, the Working Committee and Chief Minister B. C. Roy had agreed to allow Patamda police station in Purulia, an area of less than 200 square miles, to remain in Bihar despite the SRC recommendation that it be transferred. According to Dr. Roy, this compromise had been suggested by Sir Jehangir Ghandy of Bihar about six weeks prior to the decision of the Working Committee.[54] Bihar had sought retention of this area because it contained a reservoir on the Subarnarekha River (one of Bihar's main water channels) which supplied water to industrial Jamshedpur. Ghandy had suggested that Patamda police station be retained by Bihar in order that the arrangement for managing this reservoir, made by private (Tata) industries with the Bihar government, remain undisturbed. In justifying his agreement with

[53] This speech was also printed by the West Bengal PCC and widely circulated in West Bengal in the following months. See Atulya Ghosh, "Linguistic Affinity Conducive to India's Unity," in *West Bengal Today* (Calcutta: West Bengal Pradesh Congress Committee, 1956), pp. 33-34.

[54] The material presented in this paragraph is based on the reports of a press conference held by Chief Minister Roy four days after the appearance of the rumors. See *The Statesman* (Calcutta), January 17, 1956, p. 1.

this proposal, Roy argued that the intentions of the SRC—to provide a corridor for West Bengal and a catchment area for the Kangsabati project—would be substantially fulfilled despite this small concession. At the same time, he agreed with the principle expressed by Ghandy (that long-standing economic arrangements not be disrupted by reorganization), and also with Ghandy's intention of facilitating a final agreement.

Whatever the intention of Chief Minister Roy, and regardless of who was responsible for the rumor, the events surrounding the Roy-Ghandy argreement disrupted entirely the relatively ordered discussion of the reorganization question as it affected West Bengal and Bihar. Before the rumor could be qualified and the nature of the intentions of the Working Committee made clear, the events of late 1955 and early 1956 had (1) introduced militant agitation into the demands for reorganization in both West Bengal and Bihar; and (2) heightened feelings of distrust on both sides. The leftist LSRC now argued that it had made a mistake in pursuing a peaceful and conciliatory policy, and vowed to adopt an "agitational approach to SRC" in the future.[55] In addition to the day of protest mentioned above, during which a city-wide *hartal* (strike) was observed, the LSRC called for numerous small-scale *hartals*, public meetings, and other demonstrations.[56] These activities had been encouraged by the state Congress Executive Council resolution which made an appeal to

[55] In the words of the Calcutta correspondent for *Thought*, "The feeling is high in the whole of West Bengal that . . . Bengalis are being punished for paying reasonable respect to this appeal for avoiding agitational approach." See "Agitational Approach to SRC in Bengal and Bihar," *Thought* (Delhi Weekly), VIII, No. 3 (January 21, 1956), 5.

[56] In Kharagpur, for example, a meeting was held in late January 1956, under the direction of the West Bengal LSRC demanding the resignation of the local Congress Member of the Legislative Assembly from the Assembly, and also from the municipality. A crowd estimated at 3,000 paraded through Kharagpur and demonstrated in front of the home of the MLA. Based on an interview with K. C. Satpathi, MLA, February 1963.

the people of West Bengal "to take up the issue in all seriousness and make known their feeling to the Central Government. . . ."[57] Subordinate Congress Committees were directed by the state PCC, and local bodies and public institutions were requested, "to hold meetings and pass similar resolutions and forward them to the Prime Minister."[58] In a statement issued by the PCC, it was stated: "The Committee [WBPCC] as a disciplined body has always been against demonstrations because it expected justice from the august bodies that are now in charge of affairs. But the Committee must now protest against this grave and incalculable injustice that is going to be done to West Bengal."[59] In reaction to West Bengal's "agitational approach," interested groups in Bihar also staged demonstrations[60] and reverted to their original demands (either to maintain the status quo with regard to West Bengal-Bihar boundaries or to extend the territories of Bihar into West Bengal).

The introduction of militant agitation into the Bengali-Bihar boundary question was not totally unexpected, but, coming as it did after three years of calm and restrained discussion, it produced shock and anxiety among leaders at both levels of government. Even prior to this time, Congress personnel had been conscious of the physical magnitude of the task of reorganizing, and of the extent to which the resources and energies of the administrative and party structure would be taxed. Leaders at both levels had therefore been anxious to complete the reorganization as early as possible, and to allow considerable time to elapse between reorganization and the

[57] *The Statesman* (Calcutta), January 14, 1956, p. 1.
[58] *Ibid.*   [59] *Ibid.*
[60] The most violent demonstrations in Bihar were those of the Kishenganj Border Struggle Committee which raided markets, attacked sweet shops, and sat in front of trains throughout Bihar in an effort to voice its protest against transfer of the northern (Purnea) area to West Bengal. See *ibid.*, January 19, 1956, p. 1.

elections planned for early 1957.[61] With the introduction of potentially violent and massive agitation at the final stages of decision-making, the situation in Bengal and Bihar understandably prompted a great deal of concern.

In effect what had happened as a result of the events of late 1955 and early 1956 was a process of polarization of attitudes in both states. Whereas a number of individuals and groups had been swayed to a position of compromise and a search for common ground of cooperation during the "phased" discussions of the SRC Report, the focus of almost everyone in both states in late January was on solutions to be brought about either by central government coercion or by the imposition of the views of one state on those of the other. We have already referred to the imperious posture adopted by the West Bengal PCC in response to the rumors of concession, and this posture was also pervasive in Bihar. A number of Bihar Cabinet members, for example, threatened to resign in late January if any territory were transferred to West Bengal, even though these same people had been a party to the negotiations of late 1955.[62] Even the most moderate and temperate of men, those who had previously exercised influence to restrain their respective communities, now spoke in the partisan and unrestrained terms of the most rabid supporters of provincial sentiment.[63]

[61] Vedette (pseud.), "First Signs of Worry Over S.R.C. Report," *ibid.*, October 2, 1955, p. 8.

[62] *Ibid.*, January 19, 1956, p. 1.

[63] For example, Professor Nirmal Chandra Bhattacharyya, a respected leftist leader who had previously argued for great caution in making claims on other states, and who had constantly condemned those who charged "Hindi imperialism," wrote the following letter to a number of Calcutta dailies during the period when rumors first began to circulate: "One of the greatest dangers of federal government is the formation of interest groups seeking to dominate the rest. This danger is a reality in India today. In the Indian Union the dominant group is the Hindi bloc extending right from the border of West Bengal to the

In light of the polarization of attitudes that had taken place and conscious of the necessity for completing reorganization in less than a year, a number of Congressmen began to advocate in mid-January 1956, a change in the previous policy that had been articulated by the center. In the eyes of many observers also, there were now only two alternatives open to the Congress party government, and both demanded a change in policy: (1) that a decision be made by the center regarding each boundary dispute and imposed on unwilling and recalcitrant individuals and groups by force or the threat of force; or (2) that the decision on reorganization be made at the local level, and the chaotic situation that threatened to disrupt entirely the orderly administration of the states be allowed either to spend itself or perhaps shatter the Union. In the words of Nirad C. Chaudhuri, who had seen only these two alternatives from the very beginning: "What will have to be decided bears on the ultimate vision of Indian unity, whether India should remain a unitary State and develop a more homogeneous Indian nationality to preserve the unitary State, or whether the country should become a confederation of sub-nationalities, in which the problem of co-existence of these groups will have to be solved [by the units themselves]."[64] The immediate action that was taken by the government, however, was not one which fell neatly into either of these alternative courses. Instead, the proposal to merge West Bengal and Bihar, promulgated on January 23, 1956 in a joint statement by Chief Ministers B. C. Roy of West Bengal, and Satyanarayan Sinha of Bihar, at once continued the Congress policy of postponing reorganization until cooperation could

---

western border of Rajasthan and East Punjab. West Bengal cannot expect justice in her territorial dispute with Bihar because the latter is a member of the dominant group. Our state is up against a new kind of imperialism." *Ibid.*, January 14, 1956, p. 6.

[64] Nirad C. Chaudhuri, "The SRC Report as a Portent," *ibid.*, December 13, 1955, p. 6.

be effected, allowed the center to again assume the posture of arbitrator, and laid the basis for renewed negotiation and the possibility of compromise. It was in keeping with the experimental attitude that has characterized federation-making in India since 1947.

·III·

States Reorganization: The Response to State Demands

THE DESIRE on the part of the two Chief Ministers who promulgated the merger proposal to avoid either coercion or one-sided concessions was made clear in the joint statement which made it public. The Roy-Sinha statement noted that "neither the report [of the SRC] nor the Government of India's decision[1] has given satisfaction to the people." It accepted these feelings as "natural" and "easy to understand" but went on to say: ". . . we cannot forget the major fact that these two States are part of the Indian Union and are closely allied to each other in many ways. Some of the border areas between the two States have many common features and, from the economic point of view, many projects also concern the two States. Inevitably, there has to be close co-operation between the two for their mutual advantage."[2] In view of the economic benefits to be gained, the administrative problems to be avoided, and the bitterness and conflict to be eliminated, Roy and Sinha proposed that the two states be merged one with the other, and that all parties concerned work to create what they called "an atmosphere of happy voluntary merger." "There is no question in this of either State having to submit to any decision imposed upon it, but rather of their own free will to come to this important decision which, we have no

[1] The decision of the WC in mid-January 1956, is here stated to have been made by government. In effect there was little difference between party and government in this instance since three of the four members of the WC subcommittee, which is reported to have made the decision in most sources, were senior Ministers (one being the Prime Minister).

[2] B. C. Roy and Satyanarayan Sinha, *Joint Statement Proposing the Merger of West Bengal and Bihar* (Calcutta: West Bengal Pradesh Congress Committee, 1956), p. 1.

doubt, will be beneficial to the two States and will lead to a larger life and greater prosperity."[3] While the Chief Ministers noted that "the details of it will have to be carefully worked out," they argued that merger would be "a significant example of the positive approach to the problem of Indian unity," and expressed their confidence that "this approach for the solution of a difficult problem will be welcomed by all right-thinking and far-sighted people not only in our two States but in the country."[4]

Response to the Merger Proposal

The enthusiastic reception given the merger proposal by central government personnel was an indication of the desire on the part of central leaders to continue their previous policy position. When it was proposed by Roy and Sinha at a meeting of the Congress Working Committee, it was reported that "there was jubilation among members of the Committee as the two Chief Ministers put their signatures to the document,"[5] and one member of the WC went so far as to call it "the greatest thing that has happened since Independence."[6] The Working Committee as a body unanimously passed a resolution in which it spoke of the merger proposal as creating "a new wind of integration" and congratulated the two Chief Ministers for their "wisdom and foresight." Dr. H. N. Kunzru of the SRC stated that the move set a "great example" which would "strengthen the foundation of the country's unity and integrate the people as perhaps nothing could have done."[7] The Prime Minister hailed the move as a "great lead" and central government leaders began immediately to speak of the possibility of merging other states.

In view of these expectations, the merger proposal was a

[3] *Ibid.*   [4] *Ibid.*, p. 2.
[5] *The Statesman* (Calcutta), January 24, 1956, p. 5.
[6] *Ibid.*
[7] M. N. Chatterji, "West Bengal-Bihar Merger: The Developments in Bihar," *Indian Affairs Record,* II, No. 2 (March 1956), 4.

notorious failure, for it proved to be unacceptable to both of the states concerned (not to mention other states where merger was even less practical) and was therefore ultimately retracted. But, at the same time, the merger proposal did play an important part in mitigating potential bitterness and conflict over states reorganization in West Bengal and Bihar, and in making possible an eventual decision that was acceptable to both states.

In part the success of the merger proposal was a result of its initial acceptance by both state governments and both state Congress party organizations. In the case of Bihar the state Cabinet voted unanimously to accept "in principle" the merger proposal on the day following its promulgation in the press;[8] the Bihar Congress Legislative party later unanimously indicated similar reserved acceptance;[9] and the bipartisan Assembly voted in favor of accepting the idea of merger by a vote of 157 to 25.[10] In the case of West Bengal, acceptance in principle was voiced by PCC president Ghosh, who called the proposal "a right move at the right time," and by Pradesh Congress secretary Bejoy Singh Nahar, who stated that "Bengal has once again given the lead to India."[11] The West Bengal PCC Executive Council later welcomed "the broad outlook of the Chief Minister" and instructed state Congressmen to "maintain a peaceful atmosphere so as to enable discussion of this issue dispassionately."[12]

To be sure, endorsement by Congressmen in each state was more reserved than that of central government and party personnel, and subject in many instances to qualifications. The Bihar Cabinet, for example, made it clear that it had only accepted the *idea* of merger and not the details that might be introduced, and the Governor of Bihar, R. R. Diwakar, cau-

[8] *The Statesman* (Calcutta), January 26, 1956, p. 1.
[9] Chatterji, *Indian Affairs Record*, ii, No. 2 (March 1956), 5.
[10] *Ibid.*
[11] *The Statesman* (Calcutta), January 25, 1956, p. 1.
[12] *Ibid.*, February 2, 1956, p. 7.

tioned that "careful examination of the problems involved in such a merger is necessary."[13] Some local Congress units in West Bengal did pass unfavorable resolutions[14] and other Congress groups stated specifically those conditions that would make merger appealing.[15] The point is, however, that as a result of the Roy-Sinha agreement both the attention and the activities of party members were directed once again at a possible compromise agreement that envisaged interstate cooperation, and thus moved away from the agitation that had arisen as a result of the events of late 1955 and early 1956.

In addition to the effectiveness of the merger proposal in deflecting the agitation threatened by state Congress party units, it was also instrumental in channeling and dissipating the protest activities of non-Congress groups in both states. First, the merger proposal, unlike other possible solutions, created an issue on which whole communities could not so readily unite one against the other. On the question of territorial transfer, for example, all Bengalis could agree that Bengal should be granted large and major concessions by Bihar, and all Biharis could agree that Bengal should get little or nothing. In contrast, opinion on the merger question was not rigidly solidified on communal or linguistic lines in either state. The result was that cleavages appeared in both states on the basis of interests other than those of community and language, and agitation along strict communal and linguistic lines receded into the background.[16]

[13] Chatterji, *Indian Affairs Record*, II, No. 2 (March 1956), 5.

[14] Congressmen from both the Murshidabad and Nadia districts, for example, met at Berhampore a week after the proposal was promulgated and voted to oppose it. *The Statesman* (Calcutta), February 1, 1956, p. 7.

[15] The West Bengal Parliamentary party, for example, agreed to the merger on two conditions: (1) that there be parity of representation in the state legislature for Bengalis and Biharis; and (2) that both Bengal and Bihar have the right to secede unilaterally from the merged state. *Ibid.*, February 19, 1956, p. 1.

[16] For the divisions that took place within states see Chatterji, *Indian*

Second, the implications of merger were much more dif-
fuse, and the consequences more difficult to assess, than the
question of ceding territory. If territory were transferred from
one state to another, interested parties in both states could
readily charge, on the basis of the amount of territory ceded,
either "injustice" or "imperialism." If the two communities
were merged, however, the problem of grasping the relative
advantage that would accrue to either state would be much
more difficult. In the former case, support for agitation could
be generated on the basis of the clear and unmistakable positions that could be adopted; in the latter instance the issues at
stake were not so clear cut. That this factor worked to limit
the demands of those in protest can be seen from the numerous instances in which individuals and groups "suspended
judgement" on the question of merger until they could find
out more about the details contemplated, and could think out
more closely the possible ramifications of such a proposal.[17]
Because so many individuals and groups agreed to at least
consider the proposal (if not ultimately to accept it), the agitation that had been launched in January of 1956 was not as
massive as it had first appeared it might be, and the unity
among Bengalis that had been effected on the basis of opposition to the Roy-Ghandy agreement broke down.

Third, the merger proposal was an issue toward which it
was difficult to direct protest because it did not envisage the
triumph of either state over the other, but instead sought to
effect permanent cooperation in union. To oppose the cession
of territory on any basis could readily be stated in terms of

---

Affairs Record, II, No. 2 (March 1956), 4-7; and M. N. Chatterji, "West
Bengal-Bihar Merger: The Developments in West Bengal," *ibid.,* II, No.
3 (April 1956), 4-7.

[17] *Ibid.* Leaders of the leftist LSRC acknowledged that the merger
proposal had lessened the intensity of their own agitation because of the
factors mentioned in this paragraph when they charged that the merger
question had "sidetracked" their whole movement. See the LSRC statement in *The Statesman* (Calcutta), January 24, 1956, p. 5.

"opposition to imperialism" or the defense of state interests. Opposition to territorial concessions could therefore generate the passions of linguistic and community conscious individuals and groups in both states. The proposal for continued cooperation between Bengal and Bihar in merger, however, was one on which such feelings could not be so easily aroused. A position opposing merger could easily be interpreted as being the position of an "obstructionist," and adherents of such a position could be said to be against the very possibility of future cooperation. Leaders of the LSRC acknowledged that this factor had limited their ability to bestir agitational activities when they argued that the merger proposal was a government "plot"[18] to deprive them of a good agitational issue at a crucial moment.

Finally, the merger proposal mitigated potential conflict and bitterness over reorganization in West Bengal and Bihar because it provided a concrete issue toward which the most extreme feelings of protest could be directed and eventually spent. Since the proposal channeled the activities of Congressmen and other groups into consideration of the possibility of cooperation, the "agitational approach" that had been adopted in mid-January came to be confined to a small segment of the population in both states, and generally to the most vocal and most dissatisfied of citizens. In fact, militant agitation against government was limited almost entirely to members of the leftist parties in West Bengal, and to two local groups in Bihar. Once these groups had sustained a widespread and militant agitation during the more than three months when merger was being considered, they found it difficult to again rally their supporters to oppose the alternative solution that was finally negotiated. Moreover, since government eventually con-

[18] Based on interviews with leftist leaders in 1963 and 1964. PSP leader P. C. Ghosh, who labeled the merger proposal "a venomous snake under the petals of a rose," felt that the factors mentioned in this paragraph were solely responsible for the ultimate defeat of the LSRC agitation to secure linguistic boundaries.

ceded to the demand to retract the merger proposal, the most militant of those in protest could claim this as at least a partial victory, whatever the alternative effected in place of merger. Because of these factors, the agitation during consideration of the merger was indeed intense and widespread, but it quickly dissipated once the government had conceded on the merger issue. The result was that government was eventually able to promulgate a final territorial settlement that met with little militant opposition.

The effect of this latter factor in controlling militancy can be seen most clearly from an analysis of the activities of the LSRC during and after the period when merger was under consideration. Shortly after the announcement proposing merger the LSRC met in Calcutta and passed a resolution voicing two "imperative" and two "supplementary" demands.[19] The "imperative" demands called for withdrawal of the merger proposal, and withdrawal of the Bill modifying the SRC recommendations, and were designed as the basis for "direct action such as general strikes and satyagrahas." The "supplementary" demands called for implementation of the previous linguistic claims of the LSRC, and the resignation of the Roy Ministry. Nothing was said of the actions that would be taken to present these latter two demands, and ultimately little or no action was taken. Indeed, LSRC members did walk out of the Legislative Assembly during the Governor's speech;[20] lead demonstrations in front of the Assembly;[21] observed an Ultimatum Day on which a state-wide *hartal* took place;[22] and staged numerous smaller demonstrations

[19] *Resolution of the West Bengal Linguistic States Reorganisation Committee* (February 2, 1956), (Calcutta: n.p., 1956). The LSRC was sometimes referred to, both by its leaders and others, as the Linguistic States *Redistribution* Committee and at other times the Linguistic States *Reorganization* Committee.

[20] *West Bengal Legislative Assembly Debates*, Vol. xiv, No. 1 (February 1, 1956).

[21] *The Statesman* (Calcutta), February 2, 1956, p. 1.

[22] *Ibid.*, February 25, 1956, p. 1.

throughout the state.[23] But all of these agitational activities were designed to draw attention to the first two "imperative" demands of the LSRC, and they were so interpreted by leaders of all political parties.

The strategy of the LSRC was to take "direct action" against the two specific decisions of government that had thus far been promulgated: (1) the decision of the WC to modify the SRC recommendations; and (2) the proposal to merge West Bengal and Bihar. It was felt by leaders of the LSRC that they would be able to secure, by the adoption of an "agitational approach," complete concessions from government on their two "imperative" demands, and thus "gather a momentum" for obtaining their "supplementary" demands.[24] However, while this strategy was successful in securing the revocation of both the decision of the Working Committee and the proposed merger, it was ultimately unsuccessful in securing the latter two demands of the LSRC. And the explanation for this again points to the success of the merger proposal in mitigating the effect of militant agitation. For, after almost three months of militancy by the LSRC, feelings of protest resulting from dissatisfaction (feelings that were inevitable in both states and regardless of the solution proposed) were spent. Rather than gather momentum, as the LSRC had planned, the agitation in West Bengal reached its peak intensity during consideration of the merger, and could never reach the same height later on.

Defeat of the Merger Proposal

While the merger proposal was successful in deflecting and eventually dissipating the "agitational approach" that had

[23] The scope and intensity of small-scale agitation in Bengal on the merger issue is demonstrated by the fact that by mid-April, seven weeks after the merger announcement, 7,548 demonstrators had been arrested in the state. *Ibid.*, April 16, 1956, p. 1.

[24] The strategy of the leftists was related in interviews by Makhan Paul, N. C. Bhattacharyya, P. C. Ghosh, and Jyoti Basu.

been threatened in both states in early 1956, it was also evident, from the agitation and discussion which did appear, that the merger would be unacceptable to both states concerned. As has been noted previously, the reaction of political leaders in both states, even among those who had given reserved or qualified endorsement, was not enthusiastic.

In the case of Bihar, the lack of enthusiasm for merger can be traced to several diverse sources. To begin with, Biharis spoke a different language and pursued a different set of customs and traditions from those prevailing in Bengal, and they felt that their separate identity should be protected. Members of the Bihari middle class argued that they would be seriously handicapped against the more highly educated Bengali, and feared that they might not get their fair share of government jobs. Moreover, Bihar was relatively underdeveloped industrially, and overridden by irreconcilable political factions within the Congress party, and many observers argued that this would work to the disadvantage of Bihar in the merger situation.[25] As a reporter for the *Indian Nation* stated, the "crux of the matter" was that: "The handicaps of the past abide and Bihar has a long leeway to make up yet economically, financially and otherwise . . . will Bihar be able to hold her own against the Bengal avalanche? . . . Up till now the exploitation of Bihar's considerable mineral resources has been in the hands of non-Biharis. Will not the process be aggravated by amalgamation and the Biharis left high and dry as ever?"[26] In addition, some groups feared that the merger of the two states would result in a large influx of Bengali refugees into Bihar, with a consequent debilitating effect on the economic and political life of the state.[27] Others—especially the "tribals"

[25] Chatterji, *Indian Affairs Record*, II, No. 2 (March 1956), 6-7.

[26] *Indian Nation* (Patna), January 26, 1956, p. 5.

[27] The States Reorganization Commission had previously considered such fears on the part of Biharis to be "not without justification," and had taken this into account in its recommendations. See *SRC Report*, p. 177.

in central Bihar—feared that they would have less of a chance to influence state administrative personnel within a larger unit. Many intellectuals and politicians argued that the merger would "lead to endless controversy on every conceivable subject between the people of these two states."[28]

In Bengal too the reception of the populace to the merger was not warm. In the proposed merger situation, Biharis would outnumber Bengalis, and it was feared by many that both the state cabinet and the Legislative Assembly would constantly be controlled by the residents of Bihar.[29] Largely as a result of this factor, Bengalis also feared that their own state interests, as well as their cultural and linguistic traditions, might be sacrificed to the interests of those living in the Hindi-speaking areas. This fear was expressed in speculation that the capital of the merged state might be shifted from Calcutta to Patna;[30] that Bengalis might not secure their share of government jobs;[31] and that rapid industrial development in the state might be impaired.[32] There was considerable sentiment akin to that expressed by the opposition parties—that the proposal, once effected, might "strangulate Bengal, its language, and culture."[33]

Acknowledging the lack of enthusiasm that could be immediately generated for the proposed merger, B. C. Roy reported to Nehru within two weeks of the Roy-Sinha agree-

[28] The quotation is from a resolution passed by the Bihar state branch of the Indian Medical Association, quoted in Chatterji, *Indian Affairs Record*, II, No. 2 (March 1956), 6. See also the context in which this quotation appears.

[29] S. N. Sen, "Historical Background to the Merger," *The Statesman* (Calcutta), February 9, 1956, p. 6.

[30] B.U.P. Sinha, "The Cultural Aspect of Merger," *ibid.*, February 9, 1956, p. 6.

[31] "Re-union or Federation?" *Thought* (Delhi Weekly), VIII, No. 5 (February 4, 1956), 2.

[32] Khagendra Nath Sen, "The Economic Implications of Merger," *The Statesman* (Calcutta), February 11, 1956, p. 6.

[33] Chatterji, *Indian Affairs Record*, II, No. 3 (April 1956), 5.

ment: ". . . Feelings for merger are not very strong and positive; popular reaction has been neither unreservedly enthusiastic nor free from hesitation, and this is true of both Bihar and West Bengal. The proposal has changed the tenor of the discussion about States Reorganisation, but the Working Committee should not be confident that it will be accepted."[34] At the same time, the Working Committee had found that merger had been generally unacceptable in other states (except in the case of Andhra where the move to merge Telengana with Andhra gathered momentum after the proposed merger of Bihar and West Bengal).

Faced with a lack of substantial support for the merger proposal in either state, and with pockets of militant opposition to the proposal in both states, central government and party leaders again postponed the decision regarding states reorganization in West Bengal and Bihar. When the first draft of the States Reorganization Bill was made public on March 16, 1956, it thus made no provision for the reorganization of boundaries between these two states, but instead provided for future reorganization with the insertion of the following clause: "In view of the proposal for the union of the two states, now under active consideration, no provision has been made in the draft bill in regard to territorial adjustments between them. A separate Bill will be introduced in due course to implement the decision which may be taken about these States."[35] Shortly after the publication of the first draft bill, the Working Committee met and again agreed that "the states concerned must make up their minds,"[36] and the WC subcommittee reiterated to Chief Minister Roy the position of the center, that "the Central Government did not like to impose any condition or to intervene in the matter."[37]

[34] Letter from B. C. Roy to Prime Minister Nehru, dated January 29, 1956.

[35] *The Statesman* (Calcutta), March 17, 1956, p. 7.

[36] *Ibid.*, March 26, 1956, p. 1.

[37] *Ibid.*, March 28, 1956, p. 1.

The policy of the Working Committee, to allow the state governments to determine the content of a piece of central government legislation, encouraged the pursuit of those conflicts that had developed within the states. In the case of West Bengal, the major areas of conflict that existed were those that grew out of the different positions taken by three sets of political leaders. One approach to the merger proposal was represented by those state government leaders who were engaged in negotiations with the government of Bihar; a second viewpoint on reorganization was that held by the leftist LSRC; and a third that of the state Congress party unit.

The position of the state government was largely determined by the insistence of Chief Minister B. C. Roy that the merger would be beneficial to the states economically, and that this consideration should outweigh all others. In Roy's words:

> It so happens that the richest area in India from the point of view of mineral resources is the area which comprises part of West Bengal, part of Bihar and part of Orissa. If properly developed this area will become the heart of industrial India. Any scheme of development of this area must involve the closest co-operation between West Bengal and Bihar so that both states might benefit fully. There should be no delays in drawing up schemes of development as well as implementing them. Such delays are almost inevitable if the two States function separately or if there is a feeling of rivalry and conflict between the two. In such cases, both will suffer and the areas will not be developed as they should be.[38]

Roy himself was so convinced of the economic advantages of merger that he continued to pursue and defend it long after both the central and state party leadership had despaired of its practicability. At one point he is reported to have said that

[38] Quoted from a statement prepared by B. C. Roy, *ibid.*, February 1, 1956, p. 7.

"he believed in the merger so deeply that he would advocate it even if the whole of West Bengal opposed it, and even at the risk of his being driven out of the State." And, in answer to a suggestion that he might indeed be driven out of the state, he reportedly replied, "I can still practise medicine anywhere I like."[39]

While negotiating with the government of Bihar on the details of the proposed merger, Roy simultaneously sought to make a combined West Bengal-Bihar administrative unit more appealing to the populace of both states. First he suggested that the process of combining be called a "re-union" rather than a "merger," recalling that the two states had once been part of the same British province.[40] He further suggested that the combined state be called "The United States of West Bengal and Bihar," in order that both states maintain their identity in name. At one point he proffered that some of the fears of the residents of the two states could be eliminated by providing for a system of alternating Chief Ministerships; a dual capital (with government offices at Calcutta and the legislature at Patna); two High Courts; and similar proposals.[41] Later, when these suggestions failed to generate interest, Roy suggested the alternative possibility of forming a confederative union of the states, with two separate legislatures and governments that would meet together only on matters of "joint interest."[42]

The position of the WBLSRC was evolved in response to the actions of government, and particularly to the posture of B. C. Roy. As has been mentioned previously, the LSRC had decided at the outset to oppose the merger with an "agitational approach," in an effort to gather momentum for the adoption of its own linguistic demands. However, when difficulty was encountered in sustaining widespread militant pro-

[39] From the report of a press conference *ibid.*, February 27, 1956, p. 1.
[40] *Thought* (Delhi Weekly), VIII, No. 5 (February 4, 1956), 2.
[41] *The Statesman* (Calcutta), February 1, 1956, p. 1.
[42] *Ibid.*, April 17, 1956, p. 1.

test movements against the merger proposal, and when Roy continued to insist on merger despite the lack of enthusiasm for it, the LSRC gradually began to shift tactics. Instead of instigating and leading antimerger demonstrations throughout the state on a large-scale basis, the LSRC in mid-February began to direct its activities only to those areas where Municipal elections were being held.[43] Such activities focused attention in these municipalities on the LSRC demand that the merger be retracted, and simultaneously benefited the leftist opposition in securing seats.[44] In consequence, a number of leftists now began to feel that they could benefit most from the merger agitation, not by "gathering momentum" through militancy on this one issue alone, but rather by building a base of support from which a future electoral majority could be secured.[45]

In consequence of the electoral strategy of the LSRC, the state Congress party unit was placed in a difficult position. The PCC had committed itself to support for the merger proposal, but it was now losing a number of previously held Municipal strongholds as a result of this position. The PCC could hardly fail to back B. C. Roy's adamant position on merger despite Roy's apparently uncompromising attitude, but at the same time, it could ill-afford to see its electoral posi-

[43] Based on interviews conducted in 1963.

[44] Less than two months after the merger had been proposed, the leftist opposition in West Bengal had secured a majority in nine municipalities previously held by the Congress. In at least one of these municipalities (Berhampore), the Congress did not even contest the elections. See *The Statesman* (Calcutta), March 4, 1956, p. 9.

[45] The improvement of the electoral position of the Communist Party of India in West Bengal, as a result of its reorganization position, is frequently given as the reason the pro-Soviet faction of the CPI offered itself as an "alternative government" in West Bengal in the 1957 elections. See N. C. Bhattacharyya, "Leadership Problems in the Communist Party of India: With Special Reference to West Bengal," paper prepared for the International Political Science Association Convention, Bombay, January 1964, pp. 8ff. (Mimeographed)

tion being undermined by this one issue, and at a time when the general elections were approaching. In the face of this apparent dilemma, the PCC decided against a policy of open opposition to the Chief Minister, but at the same time attempted to dissuade him from immediate action on the "re-union" scheme.

The PCC feared most for its position in Calcutta, where it had won the elections for the State Assembly in 1952, and had always dominated the Municipal Corporation. While a majority in other municipalities was not always necessary for the maintenance of a state-wide majority, control of Calcutta Corporation had always been an important link in the Congress state party machine. Because of its importance as a source of patronage for the numerous Calcutta-based rural and urban Congressmen in West Bengal, and because Corporation control was so essential in securing party funds from urban businessmen, it was doubtful that the Congress state-wide majority could continue without control of Calcutta Corporation. Fearing that it might lose the impending Municipal elections in Calcutta, the PCC persuaded the Chief Minister to postpone the elections for seven months, during which time the PCC could work to defeat the merger proposal. In a statement announcing the postponement, the government circular stated: "The Government thinks that with such a vital issue as the proposed merger of West Bengal and Bihar before them, the electorate will not be able to consider fairly and judiciously the issues involved in the Corporation elections."[46]

With the Congress position in Calcutta temporarily secure, the PCC then proceeded to encourage discussion by Congressmen in the localities, both to tap the sentiment of those men who were instrumental in the organization and to alleviate the fears of those opposing merger. Again the PCC secured a promise from the Chief Minister that no action would be

---

[46] *The Statesman* (Calcutta), February 1, 1956, p. 1.

taken in the state Legislative Assembly until Congressmen had had time to consult their constituencies.[47] And, in the constituencies, Congressmen did not attempt to generate support for Roy's unqualified position, but instead took the position that the "re-union" idea was "only a suggestion,"[48] to be adopted or rejected according to the wishes of the electorate. Consistent with this posture, PCC president Ghosh suggested that a forthcoming Parliamentary by-election, which pitted a respected pro-merger Congressman (Asok Sen) against the secretary of the LSRC (Mohit Moitra) in a northwest Calcutta constituency, be considered a test of merger sentiment, and the Congress pledged in this election that "no scheme would be adopted unless accepted by the people."[49]

It was the decisive defeat of Asok Sen in this Calcutta Parliamentary by-election of late April that finally persuaded Chief Minister Roy to withdraw his own support for the merger proposal. Prior to this time Congressmen throughout the state had been conspicuously unable to arouse support for a measure which some did not believe in, and which few fully understood, and the Congress party was consequently having a difficult time controlling factional disputes within its own ranks. But, whereas Roy had previously minimized the possibility that these factors would threaten the Congress electoral position, he now concluded, on the basis of the defeat of a very respected Congressman by such a large majority, that "we cannot ignore this verdict." In view of the importance which the PCC had attached to the election, and the magnitude of the defeat, Roy was convinced that "the people of the city are not willing to accept the union proposal as I visualized."[50]

Negotiating a Final Solution

The withdrawal of the merger proposal by B. C. Roy left the state and central governments in much the same position

[47] *Ibid.*, February 5, 1956, p. 1.   [48] *Ibid.*, March 5, 1956, p. 3.
[49] *Ibid.*, April 28, 1956, p. 1.   [50] *Ibid.*, May 4, 1956, p. 1.

as that which had confronted them in January 1956. The Congress government was still faced with the necessity of coming to a decision on the West Bengal-Bihar border dispute in time to consolidate its position for the ensuing general elections, and there was still potential opposition in both states to each of the possible solutions that could be proposed. At the same time, however, the situation confronting the government had changed in many important respects during the three months when merger was being considered. To begin with, the leftist LSRC had been dissuaded from the pursuit of agitational activities and led to a belief in the efficacy of contesting the issue in electoral skirmishes. The LSRC did continue to denounce the merger proposal, to argue for its own linguistic demands, and it even staged one token *hartal* after the merger proposal had been defeated.[51] But the preoccupation of the LSRC with an "agitational approach" had shifted decidedly, and was ultimately dropped in favor of long-range goals. As PSP leader P. C. Ghosh explained some years later, "We had them [the Congress] on the run! Everyone thought that we would be able to sweep into power in 1957 because of this issue. . . . Why then should we continue with strikes and satyagrahas? That was what we were thinking."[52] Because the leftist opposition in West Bengal had shifted its tactics on the merger issue, the government could be assured of at least a passive acceptance of any reasonable solution, and could discount the possibility of the recurrence of militant agitation as widespread as that of January 1956.

In addition, the state Congress party units in both states were now much more conscious of the elections that were to be held in early 1957, and of the possible consequences that could stem from discontent generated by the boundary dispute. Attention in both state party organizations thus focused on the importance of finding a mutually satisfactory solution quickly,

[51] *Ibid.*, July 1, 1956, p. 1.

[52] Stated in an interview, October 15, 1963.

and was therefore channeled away from the expression of differences that had previously led so quickly to conflict. The Congress Parliamentary party in Bihar, for example, passed a resolution emphasizing the necessity for exploring all possible solutions as quickly as possible, and pleaded for actions that would prevent what it called "a recrudescence of bickering between the two States which had completely subsided as a result of the union proposal."[53] In West Bengal, the secretary of the state PCC, Bejoy Singh Nahar, issued a circular which cautioned restraint on the part of Bengalis, and stated the willingness of the PCC to negotiate. In Nahar's words, ". . . if the result of one by-election is the 'writing on the wall' for West Bengal, then the enemy of the Congress is the same whether in West Bengal or in Bihar, and the danger could be met more effectively by joint, rather than individual, effort."[54]

Because the prospects for militant agitation in Bengal and Bihar had diminished, and because of the necessity for effecting a solution within a short space of time, political leadership in both states feared the possibility of intervention in the dispute by the central government. In an effort to make these fears known to central government leaders, a group of 160 Congressmen from West Bengal met in Calcutta, under the leadership of Amarendra Nath Chattopadhyaya, and drafted a resolution demanding that no decision be made without the support of the state Congress party units. Speaking before this factional Congress group, N. C. Chatterjee, a leading Congress MP, explained the goals of the meeting in terms of the constitutional powers that rested with the center: "What is noticeable is that under our Constitution the President is not under any obligation to act according to the wishes of the majority of the Legislature of the States affected. He can act in opposi-

[53] *The Statesman* (Calcutta), May 6, 1956, p. 9.
[54] Bejoy Singh Nahar, *West Bengal and Bihar in Unity* (Calcutta: West Bengal Pradesh Congress Committee, 1956), p. 11.

tion to their wish."[55] In consideration of this constitutional reality, and with an eye to the political situation prevailing in Bihar and West Bengal in mid-1956, Chatterjee argued that it was necessary to make the views of state Congressmen known lest "Bengal leaders . . . be . . . outmaneuvered by more astute politicians [in the central government]."[56] Fear of central government dominance was also echoed in Bihar by Revenue Minister Sahay, who stated before the state Legislative Assembly that action taken without the consent of the states would make the position of the state government "very difficult and untenable,"[57] and by the Congress Parliamentary party in Bihar, which threatened to resign en masse if central legislation were "forced" upon them.[58]

In response to these anxieties concerning central government interference, voiced in both Bihar and West Bengal, the Union Home Ministry responded with assurances that the "non-interference" policy of the center would continue. Home Minister Pant informed both state governments that final negotiations regarding the West Bengal-Bihar border problem would be taken up only after both state Legislative Assemblies had been allowed sufficient time to submit their own recommendations. He also assured them that the central government bill which gave effect to the legislation that was decided upon would be drafted separately from the general States Reorganization Bill, and that final action would be taken by a Parliamentary committee in which both of the states concerned would have strong representation. Pant further assured both states that the center would be "guided by the wish of the people of the two States," and that the recommendations of the center would most certainly be modified if the two states "came together and found a way out."[59]

In accordance with the policy enunciated by the Home Ministry, the center drafted a Bihar and West Bengal (Trans-

---

[55] *The Statesman* (Calcutta), May 6, 1956, p. 9.
[56] *Ibid.*
[57] *Ibid.*, May 18, 1956, p. 1.
[58] *Ibid.*, July 7, 1956, p. 1.
[59] *Ibid.*, May 19, 1956, p. 5.

fer of Territories) Bill in mid-June and this was immediately sent to both state legislatures for "discussion and modification." This Bill, which was to be finalized in time to take effect on October 1, 1956, contained essentially the same territorial adjustments that had been contemplated by the WC subcommittee in January 1956. The Bill accepted the recommendations of the States Reorganization Commission, with the sole exception that Patamda police station in Barabhum *thana* of Purulia district was left with Bihar. Following the plans of the Home Ministry, the Bill was sent to the state legislatures for "discussion and modification," and then to a Select Committee of the *Lok Sabha* which was heavily represented by MP's from both states.[60]

Although the Bill was accepted by a majority of the West Bengal Legislative Assembly, it was rejected by the state legislature of Bihar, and the final reconciliation of state differences was thus left in the hands of the Parliamentary Select Committee. In Committee a last-ditch compromise was proposed and accepted by a majority of the Committee members, and the Bill was finally reported out of the Committee and passed by the *Lok Sabha* in mid-August.

The compromise that was proposed and accepted in the Select Committee concerned two bits of territory that were to be transferred from Bihar to West Bengal, and was proposed with a view to the future electoral prospects of the Congress party. Within the framework of the compromise, concessions were made to two groups in Bihar that had staged militant protest movements to further their demands. One of these groups, the *Manbhum Lok Sevak Sangha* (MLSS), had been organized to work for the inclusion of the Bengali-speaking areas of Manbhum district in West Bengal. In pursuit of its goal, the MLSS had undertaken a sixteen-day march from Pakbirrah village in Manbhum to Calcutta in West Bengal (a distance of more than 300 miles) as a demonstration of its

<hr>

[60] *Ibid.*, May 7, 1956, p. 1, and July 17, 1956, p. 1.

convictions. During the course of this march the MLSS accumulated more than 965 adherents, who attempted to march down Netaji Subhas Road in Calcutta and into Dalhousie Square. Since assembly of more than five persons is permanently forbidden in the Dalhousie Square area (where government offices are located), the MLSS *satyagrahas* were arrested by the West Bengal Government, and many of them were subsequently sent to jail.[61] A second group that had been especially active in reorganization agitation was the Kishenganj *Sima Sangharsch Samiti* (Border Struggle Committee) which had raided markets, attacked shops, and staged *satyagrahas* by squatting in front of trains, busses, and automobiles throughout Bihar in an effort to publicize its desire to keep Kishenganj in Bihar.[62] Shortly before the Select Committee had met in July 1956, the leader of the Border Struggle Committee, Abu Nayeem Chand, had pledged that a mass *satyagraha* (which would include a no-tax campaign) would again be launched by his organization if Kishenganj were transferred to West Bengal.[63]

The ability of each of these groups to amass large-scale support for its demands was interpreted by Congressmen in both states as an indication of the widespread acceptance of their demands, and the possible implications that this might have for electoral politics was obvious. But, since one group had agitated for inclusion of more territory in West Bengal than had been contemplated by the original bill, and since the demands of the other group called for an extension of the territory that would remain in Bihar, it was possible to make major concessions to both groups while effecting a compromise beneficial to Congress party interests in both states, and still leave the amount of territory to be transferred substantially the same. A compromise formula was therefore evolved which called for the transfer to West Bengal of only a portion of

[61] *Ibid.*, May 7, 1956, p. 8, and May 8, 1956, p. 1.

[62] *Ibid.*, January 19, 1956, p. 1.

[63] *Ibid.*, July 4, 1956, p. 1.

that territory located in Kishenganj subdivision of Purnea district that had been recommended in the transfer envisaged by the SRC and the center's Bill. At the same time, the compromise formula called for the transfer of all of Purulia subdivision in Manbhum district, an area larger than that recommended by the SRC and by the center. As a result of this compromise formula, twenty-five of the forty-eight members of the Select Committee voted in favor of a final Transfer of Territories Bill, and the Bill was thus reported out of Committee and passed by the Lok Sabha.[64]

Despite the numerous compromises that had been effected in securing a boundary revision, or perhaps because of these compromises, no one interest in either state was entirely satisfied with the final solution. Yet, it was reported that "the majority [of the interested parties in both states] seemed reconciled to the view that the bill was the best compromise available." And this was also reflected in the voting on the Bill in both Houses of Parliament. In fact, on the third reading of the Bill in the Lok Sabha, only two MP's (Mohit Moitra of the WBLSRC and S. C. Misra of the PSP-Bihar) opposed the Bill, and in the Rajya Sabha there were also only two dissenting votes (R. P. Sinha of the PSP-Bihar and T. Bodra of the Jharkhand-Bihar).

Conclusions

Despite the constitutional authority of the central government, to redraw state boundaries without the consent of the states concerned, the decisions that were taken on states reorganization in West Bengal were not imposed by a dominating central government. Instead, the center refused on at least

---

[64] Of the twenty-three members who voted against the Bill in the Select Committee, thirteen (all from Bihar) opposed the transfer of some or all of the territories transferred, and eight (all from West Bengal) demanded that more land be transferred to West Bengal. Two members suggested alternative solutions involving other states or central government administration. See *ibid.*, August 12, 1956, p. 1.

three occasions either to impose a solution, or even to persuade the state governments to accept a specific possible solution. The first, and most obvious, opportunity for central government action came in 1948-49 when the Constituent Assembly was considering the question of total reorganization. At this point the states were in the throes of the chaos that accompanied Independence and partition, and the center was attempting a massive revision of the constitutional and administrative framework. In this atmosphere, many observers argued, a readjustment of boundaries could not disrupt the orderly administration of the country any more than it had already been disrupted; and, at the same time, the agitation that could be expected, against any solution that was proposed, would be lessened by the inability of groups to organize effectively during such trying times.

A second likely point at which the center might have brought forth its own solution was that period, following the publication of the SRC Report, when "phased" discussions were taking place. Because the Report of the SRC had been so well-received in both states, it appeared to many observers that the center should have simply endorsed the SRC recommendations, instead of allowing for the possibility of further adjustments, and thus seemingly encouraging conflict. Finally, a third opportune point, when central government interference in fact seemed imminent, was that which followed the defeat of the merger proposal in West Bengal and Bihar. At this juncture, the threat of militant agitation had lessened, and the Congress party organizations of both states were desirous that a solution be effected well in advance of the general elections. It thus seemed likely that the center would be able at this time to bring forth its own solution, and, indeed, there was widespread apprehension among people in both states that this might happen.

At each of these likely points, however, the center refused to change its policy of "non-involvement" or "non-interference" in the Bengal-Bihar boundary dispute, a policy that had been originally adopted in 1948. The anomaly in this situation was that the same government had at once (1) drafted a Constitution granting considerable authority to the center for reorganizing state boundaries; and (2) adopted a policy pledging that this power would not be used. There are a number of reasons that could be advanced to account for the anomalous position of the central government.

To begin with, the inclusion of Article 3 (granting complete authority to the central government to revise boundaries) was adopted by the Constituent Assembly in a spirit of "experimentation," or "trial and error." Those who argued for this provision in the Constituent Assembly debates did not necessarily envisage the creation of a strong central government by the adoption of this provision. Rather, they argued that reorganization must necessarily be postponed in the early years of a new nation's existence, and for this reason it was necessary that the central government have the power to control movements advocating reorganization. In this view, once the central government had sufficient power, it could then experiment with a number of different alternative solutions to the boundary problem until it found one that was at least not wholly unacceptable. This attitude, which is repeated again and again in the Constituent Assembly Debates, and in the JVP Committee Report, is best summarized in the report of the Dar Commission:

India has chosen for herself the destiny of a Federal Republic. In the Constitution, which is now being forged for her, framework may be set up, which would enable her to find her destiny. Provide, if you will, for autonomous provinces and for adult franchise; but also recognize that there will be a period of transition, a period of trial and error, during which India will have to prepare for its destiny and during which the Centre must possess large, overriding powers of control and direction—powers which may be kept in reserve and may be sparingly used and finally abandoned, but which must be available for effective use if and when occasion arises.[65]

In this context, the explanation for the anomalous position of the center on states reorganization stems, at least in part, from the fact that the center did not want immediate reorganization, even though it had the constitutional authority to bring it into being, and even though numerous movements advocating revision of boundaries existed throughout the country. While the constitutional authority of the center was thus meaningless in one respect, since it was never used to effect reorganization by compulsion, it did prove to be extremely valuable to center and states alike. For it permitted the center to postpone reorganization until six years after the adoption of the Constitution; it made possible a policy in which free and open discussion of almost every possible alternative solution could be presented to government; and it allowed the center to act as arbiter of disputes between those in conflict. The center profited by being able to set aside temporarily a most difficult problem that threatened to at least disrupt, if not shatter, the Indian Union; and the states also gained valuable time to consolidate their own positions and to negotiate with neighboring states for mutually acceptable gains.

But the outcome of the states reorganization issue in West Bengal was not simply a result of the intentions of the framers and the central leadership groups concerned. Indeed, the same central leaders who were instrumental in allowing West Bengal and Bihar virtually complete independence in arriving at a solution to the boundary reorganization problem, made decisions on the reorganization question in other states that were imposed on state politicians. In Madhya Pradesh, for example, Prime Minister Nehru himself was responsible for designating Bhopal the capital of the state after reorganization,

[65] Constituent Assembly of India, *Report of the Linguistic Provinces Commission, 1948*, quoted in *Introduction to the Civilization of India: Developing India* (Chicago: University of Chicago Press, 1961), p. 11.

and the central government Home Ministry chose to divide the potentially wealthy Chattisgarh region between Madhya Pradesh and Orissa without consulting indigenous political leadership within the former state.[66]

In the case of the Bengal-Bihar border controversy, neither central nor state political leadership groups could be so certain (at least in the initial stages of discussion) about the sentiments of the voters in the two states, and they were made constantly aware of the possibilities for state politicians to organize the peoples of the state for electoral and agitational purposes. In the one instance where the central Working Committee of the party did vote to accept a solution, which it saw as a compromise between West Bengal and Bihar, the populace of the state quickly began to rally behind state politicians (across the party spectrum) against the decision. Unlike the case of Madhya Pradesh,[67] the highly politicized atmosphere in West Bengal ultimately produced both agitational and electoral reactions to a wide variety of policy positions, and the political leaders of West Bengal effectively demonstrated their ability either to mobilize the population or to make effective use of an already mobilized populace on the states reorganization issue. The mobilization of popular sentiment behind strong and cohesive state party organizations thus accounts for this one instance in which the constitutional authority of the central government was not used.

[66] Ed. D. P. Mishra, *The History of the Freedom Movement in Madhya Pradesh* (Nagpur: Government Press, 1956), pp. 416ff.

[67] The absence of a highly politicized populace in Madhya Pradesh is analyzed in Wayne A. Wilcox, "State Politics in Madhya Pradesh," paper prepared for the Seminar on State Politics, Association for Asian Studies, Massachusetts Institute of Technology, December 1964, pp. 3ff.

IV

The Damodar Valley Corporation: The Creation and Loss of DVC Autonomy

THE Damodar Valley Corporation (DVC) was initially designed to effect a far different pattern of working relationships between the center and the states than that which eventually evolved. In the planning stages, the DVC was to be an autonomous body, free to make its own policy decisions and to draft its own plans and programs, largely on the basis of technical considerations. While it was to be operative in an area that covered parts of two states (West Bengal and Bihar), and while its establishment was to have been dependent on the consent and agreement of the states involved, it was to be made up primarily of technically trained individuals and even administered by engineers; and, once established, neither state nor central government personnel were to be represented on the policy-making board.

Had this kind of organization been in fact created and maintained, a pattern of relationship between the center and states entirely different from that described in the following chapters would have come into being. Decisions concerning the affairs of the Corporation would either have been made on the basis of technical considerations alone, or perhaps a symbiotic relationship would have developed between the Corporation and the particular sets of individuals who live in the Damodar Valley.[1] As the following case study points out, however, most of the powers and functions relegated to the DVC in the initial planning stages were either retained by the central or state

---

[1] The most obvious parallel here, of course, would be to the kinds of relationships between a government corporation and local citizens that developed in the case of the Tennessee Valley Authority, described in Philip Selznick, *TVA and the Grass Roots: A Study in the Sociology of Formal Organization* (Berkeley: University of California Press, 1953).

governments in the final draft of the bill that brought the Corporation into being, or they were regained by the central and state governments in the years following the Corporation's birth. As in the previous case study, state politicians were able to regain a great deal of their independence in policy-making activities concerning the Corporation, despite the fact that the central government had initially passed the legislation creating the Corporation. In this development, party structure and system, as well as the political mobilization of the populace of West Bengal, again played a major role.

The Damodar River flows from western Bihar in a south-easterly direction into West Bengal, where, at a point near Burdwan, it changes its course to a more southerly direction until it joins the Hooghly River 30 miles south of Calcutta and approximately 336 miles from its source. Though it is not among India's largest rivers, it is certainly one of the most unpredictable. It is not a snow-fed stream, like the great rivers of the Gangetic or Indus valleys, but rather a dog-legged, rain-fed channel of constantly changing volume, which has on numerous occasions changed course. In the dry season the volume of water in the channel dwindles almost to a trickle, and at some points to nothing. When there is a monsoon cloudburst, the level of the river has been known to rise five to ten feet in a few hours. In its upper reaches (in Bihar) it is fed by nine other mountain streams and resembles them in character. In its lower reaches (at the point where it enters Burdwan district in West Bengal) it assumes the dignity of a big river and becomes navigable during most of the year. At this point it also takes on the character of a deltaic river, and, instead of receiving feeders, throws out distributaries. It is in the lower reaches of the valley that the river becomes periodically unmanageable, either because it floods or changes course.

Although the Damodar has been the cause of major floods on sixteen occasions since the beginning of the 19th century, it was only the last of these floods that set in motion governmental machinery which led to the establishment of a multipurpose river valley development corporation. The flood of 1943 inundated large portions of the countryside in the lower valley, in some places to a depth of six or seven feet; the Grand Trunk Road (the major road artery linking Calcutta and Delhi) was rendered unusable, railway bridges were washed away, and communications were seriously interrupted for long periods of time. It was estimated that 70 villages and 18,000 homes were destroyed, and at one point even Calcutta was thought to be in danger of being flooded. In a time of war, the Fourteenth Army, stationed in India, was cut off from its headquarters and bases of supplies. The floods contributed to the great Bengal famine of 1943-44 when the breakdown of communication and transport facilities prevented shipments of food to proceed as rapidly as would have been desirable, and when crops that could have been used to alleviate the famine conditions of that year were destroyed.[2]

The floods of 1943 convinced both the British Government and the Indian nationalists of the urgent necessity to undertake some measures that would prevent future floods in the Damodar Valley, and the geographical character of the valley led to the development of a multipurpose regional river valley development scheme. For, while the standard of living in this area is low, the industrial potential of the valley is enormous. It is rich in minerals, containing a large percentage of India's copper reserves, kyanite, iron ore, coal, mica, chromite, fire clay, and china clay. Its location near the great industrial centers of Calcutta and Jamshedpur made it possible to conceive of the valley as a great center for future industrial development, and especially as a center for the supply of hydroelectric power. This meant that a large-scale program, designed initially to prevent floods and to control the course of the river,

[2] Descriptions of the flood of 1943 can be found in Henry Hart, *New India's Rivers* (Bombay: Orient Longmans, 1956), pp. 59ff.; and in *D.V.C. in Prospect and Retrospect* (Calcutta: Damodar Valley Corporation, 1958), pp. 1ff.

could perhaps pay for itself by generating and supplying electrical power to industrial areas. If irrigation facilities were also planned for in the initial stages, the final program could be one that would provide numerous benefits and be self-supporting at the same time. Considerations of this kind led to the expansion of the original Damodar Valley scheme until it was one of the largest of its kind ever planned in any Asian nation.

The Voorduin Plan

The plan for the unified development of the Damodar River (which came to be known as the Voorduin plan)[3] was prepared by the Central Technical Power Board, in cooperation with the Bengal and Bihar governments, in 1945. It envisaged a series of reservoirs providing flood control, a supply of water for irrigation, and a system of hydroelectric and thermal power stations interconnected by transmission lines. It also commented on the possibility of developing a navigable waterway between Calcutta and the coal fields in Bihar as "a subject deserving of future study,"[4] and such other possible projects as malaria control, silt control, sand stowing in the

[3] The plan was prepared under the direction of William L. Voorduin, an American engineer, brought from the TVA to India on a three-year contract. Voorduin was described by Henry C. Hart (who himself was involved in the early stages of the Damodar Valley Project) as "an uncommon engineer. His work in the T.V.A. had given him scope to consider all the uses of a river. As one of the early specialists in engineering planning (the selection as distinguished from the design of reservoirs) he had accustomed himself to decisions involving hydrology, and even economics. He had a tendency to fit apparently unrelated facts together. The War was in its grimmest phase when Mr. Voorduin joined the Central Technical Power Board in Delhi. But in six months the Board, greatly helped by the engineers of Bihar and Bengal, who exchanged data freely with the Board, had its plan ready." See *ibid.*, pp. 66-67.

[4] *Preliminary Memorandum on the Unified Development of the Damodar River (August, 1945)* (Calcutta: Government of India, 1945), p. 2.

coal fields, and a scheme for public water supply to communities in the vicinity.

In the planning stage it was decided to protect the valley against a "design flood," a flood bigger than any that had ever been recorded, but one which was conceivably possible. In the words of the planners: "It is recognized that these design floods are considerably in excess of any which have occurred in the past, and of which reliable records exist, and this is explained by the necessity for taking account of the possibility that a large storm may well be centered squarely over the valley in the future, even if it has not done so in recent years."[5]

To plan for such a flood, the planners estimated that seven dams with storage facilities would be necessary, and that irrigation and power facilities would have to be planned in such a way as to pay for the storage capacity gained. It was thus decided that eight dams should be built (only seven for storage purposes), each containing a hydroelectric generating plant as well as an equally powerful generator driven by steam from coal. The hydroelectric generating plants could turn out 130,000 kilowatts of power during the monsoons; in the dry months, when the capacity of the hydroelectric generators was reduced to about half, the thermal stations could pick up the load with the water wheels operating only at hours of peak demand. In this way the supply of electricity would be steady throughout the year at the same time that floods would be harnessed to produce power and coal would be saved.

The planners also provided for an irrigation barrage at Durgapur, and estimated that it would be possible to irrigate as much as 760,000 acres per year from water caught by the reservoirs. At the same time, the planners were conscious of the fact that irrigation, and the income that could be gained from supplying irrigation benefits, could be secured only with

[5] *Ibid.*, p. 1.

great difficulty. As the Voorduin Memorandum pointed out: "It is clear that, to secure a major part of these irrigation benefits to a large and under-privileged section of the population, will demand a most careful consideration of the land administration and revenue procedure in the districts affected."[6]

In planning the cost of the project at this stage, the formulators of the plan based their estimates on those which had been made for previous schemes, and on 1945 costs for labor and material, and put down a "rough approximation": 55 crores of rupees (one crore equals 10 million rupees). They stated that "the project as a whole could reasonably be regarded as capable of standing on its own feet, and proving an economic success,"[7] but cautioned that this was only possible if the plan were enacted *in toto* and as part of a unified scheme of development, and of course that capital expenditures at the early stages would be high. They suggested that the scheme be pursued immediately under a "single unified administration."[8]

Acceptance of the TVA Idea

Those people—principally engineers and civil servants—who have been concerned with the development of irrigation and flood control measures in India have, of course, been especially aware of the difficulties that arise in effecting legislation that concerns different states, different peoples, and different interest groups along the course of a river. Indian political leaders have also been conscious for a long time of the diversity of India and of the political problems that are created by diversity in a nation of great size. Because of the experiences of those who had preceded them, the members of the National Planning Committee (NPC), appointed in 1938 to devise plans for the future development of India, recognized the difficulty of establishing irrigation projects in a federal system as being among the most serious obstacles that could be expected to stand in the way of its plans. To cope with the

[6] *Ibid.*, p. 2.   [7] *Ibid.*, p. 4.   [8] *Ibid.*, p. 5.

problems that are encountered because of the division of the human community into several jurisdictions, the National Planning Committee therefore suggested a general policy that favored the development of multipurpose regional river valley development schemes. The general approach of the NPC sub-committee on irrigation and river training, for example, was embodied in the following statement: "Our conception of the jurisdiction of existing administrative units must change, and a river should be regarded as one natural economic unit for the benefit of the whole community it can serve, in the full development of which political frontiers must not be allowed to interfere."[9]

The Voorduin Memorandum not only agreed that the development of the river valleys of the subcontinent could best be carried out by an organization which cut across state boundaries, it went on to make suggestions for evolving such an organization (which it prematurely called an Authority) in the Damodar Valley. The Chairman of the Central Technical Power Board, Mr. H. M. Mathews, stated in the Voorduin Memorandum that it was "absolutely essential" that the entire water control and power generation features of the Damodar Valley project "be constructed and operated under a single unified administration." Going further, he suggested that "at least some of the functions which are normally the responsibility of local administrations" should be permanently surrendered to a river valley development Authority. This Authority, he argued, "must be invested with a high degree of autonomy for conducting the undertaking," and he suggested that there even be some safeguards that assured the successful completion of the work "of the Authority should provincial cooperation not be forthcoming."[10]

The drafters of the Voorduin Memorandum clearly had in mind an autonomous governmental agency patterned after the Tennessee Valley Authority in the United States:

[9] NPC Subcommittee Report, p. 47.
[10] Preliminary Memorandum, pp. 5-6.

It is further suggested that the task of continuing the planning, designing, constructing and operating the dams, reservoirs, waterways, power houses and transmission lines be entrusted to an Authority with powers and duties carefully delineated by the three Governments concerned. In this connection a detailed examination of the Tennessee Valley Authority Act may be useful. Many of the provisions of this Act, for instance, those dealing with delegations of authority, co-operation with the various Government agencies and their sub-divisions, manner of reporting, appointment of the directors and personnel, could be made to apply to conditions in India.[11]

For a variety of reasons, the idea of creating an organization patterned after the TVA was one which was acceptable to most Indian planners in 1947. To begin with, many Indian leaders were at that time searching for ways of effecting a society embodying a philosophy of democratic socialism, and the TVA was viewed as a governmental device which stood in that tradition. N. V. Gadgil, the Minister for Works, Mines, and Power, who piloted the Damodar Valley Corporation Act through the Constituent Assembly, thus echoed the sentiments of the vast majority of his colleagues (and drew applause and cheers) when he made statements such as the following:

. . . this enterprise is—let me say for the delectation of my Honourable friend Prof. Shibban Lal Saksena—a State enterprise; and more and more such enterprises are to be undertaken by this Government, because this Government does not believe that its duty to the people ends with the maintenance of law and order. A modern state is something more than a police state; the modern state has come to mean a social service state. How far and to what extent these functions should be carried out is a matter which will have to

[11] *Ibid.*, p. 35.

be considered in the circumstances then existing. But on the major question I think there can be no doubt that the State must guarantee every person a decent standard of life. That also means full employment; and in order to effectuate this policy, if it becomes necessary to socially own the means of production, the State will certainly be justified in doing so.[12]

But the TVA idea, and the creation of an organization patterned after it, was also acceptable to most Indian planners, politicians, and intellectuals because it was a large-scale scheme that promised modernization and technological advance. A Muslim MP from the United Provinces stated for example: ". . . we all realise that this is one of those great schemes that will put this country of ours on a par and in line with those other great countries which are so prosperous in the world today. It is such schemes that have made those countries great."[13] Gadgil himself spoke of "electric light in every village and a radio in every home," and what he called the "multiplier conception":

> In other words, if say public expenditure is undertaken and some purchasing power is, so to say, injected, the result is not merely proportionate to the purchasing power spent but it goes on multiplying. The wheels of industry move, employment grows and the return may be not only three times or four times but it may be much more. In other words, prosperity begets prosperity. It is infectious and in a sense it is invisible. Therefore, when we look upon this scheme from a point of view in which objectively we may not be convinced that it is a paying proposition, or a productive scheme, yet I make bold to say, Sir, that the returns in terms of invisible dividends are so great that any Government charged with the duty of bettering the lot of its people will not shirk from undertaking it.[14]

[12] Constituent Assembly of India, *Debates*, III, No. 2 (December 12, 1947), 1829.

[13] *Ibid.*, 1843.   [14] *Ibid.*, 1830.

But perhaps the major reason why the TVA idea was so overwhelmingly supported was that it offered some kind of a solution to the numerous problems that would arise in a country of diversity when an attempt was made to develop areas crossing state boundaries. Looked at in this way, the DVC, if it were successful, would benefit India, not only in the present situation, and not only in the states of West Bengal and Bihar, but in other states as well, and for many years to come. For the TVA idea, as it was introduced in India, was seen as a device whereby large-scale regional projects could be undertaken, with considerable financial and technical assistance from the central government and with little or no provincial or state involvement. At the same time, given the money, the personnel, and the scope of the projects contemplated, it was almost certain that there would be some measure of success in terms of economic development, as well as the possibilities of evolving a regularized procedure for resolving interstate conflicts. For these reasons, the Damodar Valley Act was held up as a "model" of an administrative pattern that could be used in other areas to develop other river valleys, and there was a great deal of discussion as to other areas that might be developed along similar lines.

Balancing Conflicting State Interests

Although there was general agreement that an autonomous body on the lines of the TVA should be established, there was still the problem of creating the organization, reconciling the various state interests involved, and deciding who should get what benefits from the project and at what costs. From the time of the publication of the Voorduin Memorandum until late 1947, several conferences were held which were attended by representatives of the Bihar, Bengal, and central governments, at which meetings the details were discussed, conflicts resolved, and a final proposal agreed upon.

The most difficult problem that arose at these conferences was that which stemmed from the fact that Bengal would get almost all of the benefits from flood control and most of those from irrigation, while all of the dams would have to be built in Bihar. The low-lying areas of Bengal between Bihar and Calcutta were the areas that had always been subject to the floods of the Damodar in the past, and they were also the areas most in need of irrigation. At the same time, since all of the reservoirs and dams would be built in Bihar, the Biharis would have to bear the hardships of having a large number of farms and villages within their borders submerged under the reservoirs, or otherwise disrupted by DVC construction activities. After a long process of negotiation, this problem was eventually solved, largely on the basis of a formula championed by N. V. Gadgil, and agreed to by all of the governments involved. Essentially it was decided to share the costs of each aspect of the project—flood control, irrigation, and power—according to the incidence of the benefits and the ability to pay. On the basis of this formula, irrigation investment was divided between Bengal and Bihar in exact proportion to the water they would receive for that purpose. Since Bengal would receive by far the greatest share of DVC irrigation benefits, it would also be expected to pay the greatest share of the 13 crores of rupees to be expended on irrigation (the estimates used were in all cases those given in the Voorduin Memorandum). The financial cost of flood control aspects of the project—estimated at 14 crores of rupees in the Voorduin plan—was to be shared by Bengal and the Government of India, with the stipulation that the central contribution would not exceed 7 crores of rupees (half of the estimated cost in the Voorduin Memorandum). All three governments would equally share the power cost, which was estimated at 28 crores of rupees. The costs to the individual governments, based on the estimates of the Voorduin Committee, could be calculated as shown in Table 1.

Because of contributions from the central government, and because of the savings resulting from the construction of multiple-purpose reservoirs, the formula arrived at was one that

TABLE 1

ESTIMATED COST OF DVC SCHEME TO PARTICIPATING GOVERNMENTS
(in crores of rupees)

	Flood Control	Power	Irrigation	Total
State of Bihar	0	9.33	1.3	10.63
State of Bengal	7	9.33	11.7	28.03
Government of India	7	9.33	0	16.33
Totals	14	28.00	13	55.00

SOURCE: Statement by West Bengal Irrigation Minister, *West Bengal Legislative Assembly Debates*, 1 (November 21, 1947), 11.

was acceptable to both Bihar and Bengal. Bengal received all of the flood control benefits, even though it paid only half of the total cost under this head; Bengal also received half of the power benefits while paying only one-third of the total cost; and Bengal received almost all of the irrigation benefits, and at a much cheaper cost (because they were linked to other aspects of the total scheme) than would have been possible had West Bengal undertaken the project alone. At the same time, Bihar gained abundant electricity and some irrigation benefits, both rendered cheaper by the economics of multiple-purpose reservoirs and by central assistance.

The mere fact, however, that the contemplated amount of expenditure was so high, especially in the case of West Bengal, created a second difficulty that had to be resolved before a bill could be drafted. There was always the possibility that in a developing economy, and especially in its first few years of development, a given state might not be able to raise funds in the amounts needed to maintain contribution to such a large-scale project. To meet this difficulty, the center promised voluntarily that it would be willing to assume the responsibility of providing capital for the project in the early years with the intent of relieving the burden of the states. The central government thus would incur expenditures necessary for establishing the DVC and maintaining it during the initial stages. At the same time, however, such capital would be "adjusted between the participating governments" in accordance with the formula described above. This meant in effect, that the center would find all of the money to cover not only its own share of capital expenditures but also the shares of West Bengal and Bihar, with the amounts advanced to the DVC as part of the state shares being debited against the two state governments as loans from the center.[15]

A third problem that arose during the period 1945-47 was that resulting from the existing constitutional provisions of that time, which delegated power over most of the governmental activities involved in the scheme to the states. Water supplies, irrigation, canals, embankments, and water storage were all provincial powers in the Constitution, and electricity was a concurrent power of the center and the provinces. Moreover, each province had previously adopted schemes under these powers—Bihar's grid plan to electrify its mica mines and Bengal's Damodar-Hooghly Flushing and Irrigation Scheme—which conflicted directly with the proposals involved in the Damodar Valley scheme, and which had to be abandoned before the DVC proposals could be enacted. Such conflicts were finally resolved by a compromise, which worked essentially as follows. The two provincial governments surrendered their powers in this instance to the central Parliament, thus making it possible for a central government act to give effect to the scheme. At the same time, it was decided that the government Corporation that was to be created by an act of the central government would guarantee to the provinces "the right to retail distribution of electricity from the scheme and to control irrigation from Damodar waters within their boundaries."[16]

Implicit in the compromises that were effected during the

---

[15] D. S. Ganguly, *Public Corporations in a National Economy* (Calcutta: Bookland Private Ltd., 1963), pp. 224-25.

[16] Hart, p. 74.

1945-47 meetings was the assumption that large-scale involvement by the center in the Damodar Valley project was necessary. It was assumed that a government Corporation would be created by an act of the central parliament, that the center would contribute a major share of the funds for the Corporation (especially in its early years of development) and that the center would have the power to issue instructions and to influence the policy-making aspects of the scheme. At this point, facing the monumental task of reorganization after Independence, and lacking skilled personnel, neither state government was capable of coping with such a large-scale project. Nor was either state government willing to trust the other with large amounts of control over an important measure that affected the whole of the eastern region. For these and other reasons, the contemplated large-scale involvement of the center in a regional development scheme was encouraged and welcomed by both provinces. It should also be pointed out that the people who were most actively involved in the 1945-47 conferences—administrators, technical personnel, and nationalist Congressmen—were those who were most anxious to bring into being an independent India dominated by a strong central government, and pursuing economic development solely on the basis of rational planning procedures. The views of those who participated in the 1945-47 conferences were summarized by N. V. Gadgil when presenting the scheme to the Constituent Assembly:

Today we are all anxious to give ample powers to the Centre so that that power may be used for the conferment of benefits on the people of the provinces. If you study the financial provisions of this scheme, the Central Government is going to share quite a large portion—50 per cent so far as flood finances are concerned, and in other matters also to a considerable extent. It is therefore only meet and proper that the Central Government must have some voice—some power to issue instructions, and to see that the development and execution of this scheme is in consonance with the general policy laid down by it in this connection for the whole country. There should be no lop-sided development; we are all thinking of planning and we are also thinking that the planning should be on a regional basis. . . .[17]

The Principle of Autonomy

But, while the participants of the 1945-47 conferences were willing to surrender policy-making and administrative powers over state subjects to the central government, it soon became evident that many state leaders were not willing to go one step further, and to allow the central government to create a state corporation invested with a great deal of autonomy. Thus, when the original DVC bill, which did envisage a government Corporation with a great measure of autonomy, was placed before the Constituent Assembly in December 1947, it was immediately referred to a Select Committee dominated by state legislators and political leaders, who proceeded to modify the provisions of the bill in many important respects.

In the original bill the DVC was to be created by the central government, and the central government was to have the power to appoint the governing board of the Corporation and the major officers. Aside from this provision, however, the Corporation was to have a high degree of independence in framing its own policies, plans, and programs. The only provision of the original act that impinged in any way on DVC autonomy was that which stated that, "In the discharge of its functions the Corporation is to be guided by such instructions on questions of policy as may be given by the Central Government. As to whether a question is or is not a question of policy, the decision of the Central Government is final."[18]

[17] Constituent Assembly, *Debates*, III, No. 2 (December 12, 1947), 1834-35.

[18] *The Damodar Valley Corporation Act* (first draft), presented to the Constituent Assembly in December 1947 (New Delhi: Government of India, 1947), p. 3.

This provision, along with the power of appointment, did give the central government some control over the Corporation, but it was felt that this control was as minimal as could be expected. N. V. Gadgil, the person most responsible for the original draft of the DVC Act, even referred to the DVC as "a sort of provincial government," and stated:

> The general principles on which this Corporation will have to work are that for all purposes it is going to be an autonomous body, that it will be free—within the framework as contemplated in the provisions of this Bill—to manage the affairs of the Corporation. There is only one limitation—and the House will agree that it is a very good limitation—that in matters of policy the Central Government will have the final voice. That provision was already in the Bill before it went to the Select Committee. . . . I want to assure this House that there is not the slightest intention to create any difficulties in the smooth working of this Corporation.[19]

So anxious were the framers of the original bill to preserve DVC autonomy that they expressly provided that any dispute between the Corporation and any participating government (and this included the central government) was to be referred to an arbitrator to be appointed by the Chief Justice of India. In addition, they provided in the first draft of the bill that all of the finances of the Corporation were to be looked after by an employee whose only responsibility to the center would be the submission of a yearly report in the *Lok Sabha*. Finally, the original draft bill did provide for an "advisory committee," made up of technical experts from the three participating governments, but this committee was to be appointed by the Corporation and was to meet at times set by the Corporation.

The principle of autonomy, which was largely preserved in

[19] Constituent Assembly of India, *Debates*, 1, No. 12 (February 13, 1948), 701-02.

the original bill, was quickly modified by the work of the Select Committee to which the bill was referred when it was first introduced in the Constituent Assembly. The Select Committee, heavily weighted with representatives from the states of West Bengal and Bihar, recommended six major changes each of which could be used to diminish the autonomy of the Corporation in one respect or another. The first three of these changes dealt with financial considerations. First, the Select Committee introduced a clause which provided for a Financial Adviser, to be appointed by, and responsible to, the central government. The introduction of a Financial Adviser controlled by the central government in place of a DVC-controlled treasurer gave the center considerable potential power and control in reviewing and influencing the financial aspects of the Corporation. In addition, the Select Committee provided that the annual budget of the Corporation, as well as an annual report, were to be presented, not only to the central Parliament, but also to the legislatures of the two provinces involved. Third, the Corporation was made subject to central government taxation, providing another avenue by which the central government could have reason to investigate and possibly influence DVC affairs.[20]

A second major area in which the Select Committee chose to interfere was that which concerned central government influence in policy-making. In this respect the Committee introduced clauses into the bill which specified the circumstances under which the central government could remove either the chairman or the two members of the board before the expiration of their five-year terms, thereby making it easier to remove board members and giving the government greater leverage should it seek to influence board matters. Second, a

[20] The changes discussed in this paragraph are those which suggested themselves when comparing the original bill with the bill that was reported out of the Select Committee. Some discussion of the actual working of the Committee is contained in *ibid.*, 701-12; (February 14, 1948), 720-39; (February 16, 1948), 746-84.

clause was inserted into the bill which made the day-to-day regulations promulgated by the DVC (such as employer-employee relations) subject to consultation with the center should the center desire consultation. Third, at the behest of the Select Committee it was decided that the advisory committee was not to be appointed by the DVC, but now was to be appointed by the central government.

While the Damodar Valley Act, as it was passed in final form in 1948, provided for numerous contacts between the participating governments and the Corporation (see Figure 5) and, therefore, for a number of spheres in which the governments could potentially influence DVC affairs, it continued to be viewed as an autonomous body. Gadgil continued to call it "a sort of provincial government," and liken it to the TVA. Commenting on the potential power that had been given to the center in the act, he stated:

> ... it is not the intention of the Central Government at all to interfere with the day to day administration; if that was the intention we could have immediately made the Damodar Valley Corporation as one of the departments. We would have appointed a Minister in charge of the Damodar Valley Corporation. But that is not so. To give autonomy and to keep policy control are not incongruous things and certainly are not conducive to inefficiency.[21]

Indeed, it was argued by members of the DVC as well as by others who were familiar with the affairs of the Corporation, that the DVC Act of 1948 did grant sufficient power to the DVC for it to remain as autonomous as the TVA or any other government corporation. It did have the power to make its own plans, to prepare its own budgets, and to appoint most of its own personnel. Disputes between participating governments were to be arbitrated by a "neutral" institution or person appointed by a "neutral" Chief Justice of India. The only

[21] Ibid., 1, No. 14 (February 16, 1948), 757.

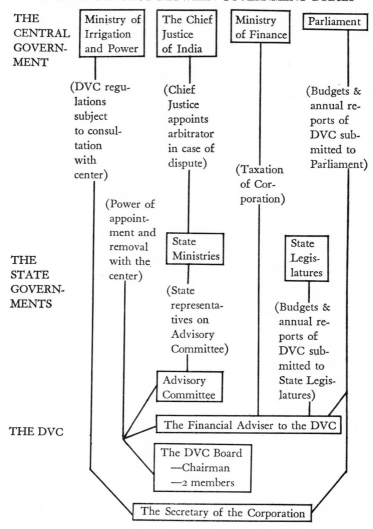

POINTS OF CONTACT BETWEEN GOVERNMENT BODIES

THE CENTRAL GOVERNMENT

Ministry of Irrigation and Power

The Chief Justice of India

Ministry of Finance

Parliament

(DVC regulations subject to consultation with center)

(Chief Justice appoints arbitrator in case of dispute)

(Budgets & annual reports of DVC submitted to Parliament)

(Taxation of Corporation)

(Power of appointment and removal with the center)

THE STATE GOVERNMENTS

State Ministries

State Legislatures

(State representatives on Advisory Committee)

(Budgets & annual reports of DVC submitted to State Legislatures)

Advisory Committee

THE DVC

The Financial Adviser to the DVC

The DVC Board
—Chairman
—2 members

The Secretary of the Corporation

Fig. 5. Damodar Valley Corporation Organization Chart as Envisaged in the DVC Act, 1948

danger of encroachment in DVC affairs that could be antici-
pated at the time the Act was passed, were those that might
come from the central government. But here the DVC had
assurances that the center had no intentions of interfering.

The Loss of DVC Autonomy

The Damodar Valley Corporation Act was passed in March
1948 and the Corporation was formally inaugurated on July 7,
1948. In the early stages of the project it was assumed by all
parties, even by those people who felt that the DVC should
be completely autonomous, that the links between the central
government and the DVC in the beginning would be very
close. Thus, the first administrative staff of the DVC was
drawn almost exclusively from the hydroelectric section of the
Central Technical Power Board, as were the majority of the
first engineers.[22] The Corporation was first administered by an
officer with his headquarters in the Works, Mines, and Power
Ministry in New Delhi, and various central government Ministries were very active in the making of two of the Corporation's early major policy decisions: (1) that the Board of the
DVC would not be made up of technical personnel; and (2)
that the construction activities of the Corporation would be
carried out by firms of consulting engineers and supervised by
the DVC, rather than through DVC departments acting
alone.[23]

Within a year of the creation of the Damodar Valley Corporation, however, there arose a number of conflicts between
the Corporation and the governments participating in the
Damodar Valley project. In one way or another, each of these
conflicts focused on the question of the degree of autonomy
that was to be given to the Corporation. In each case the Cor-

[22] K. P. P. Menon, "The Damodar Valley Project: Harnessing a
Turbulent River," *The Statesman* (Calcutta), February 21, 1953, Sec.
II, p. 2.

[23] Damodar Valley Corporation, *Annual Report, 1948-49* (Calcutta:
Damodar Valley Corporation, 1949), pp. 3-7.

poration contended that it could carry out its projects most
efficiently and most economically if it were given freedom to
set its own policies, to appoint its own personnel, to plan its
own budgets, and so forth. In each case the participating governments argued that government control over the affairs of
the Corporation was necessary.

The first major conflict between the Corporation and the
participating governments stemmed from the difficulties that
arose when trying to find a suitable Chief Engineer for the
Corporation. The Chief Engineer, in the words of the Corporation, was to be a man "who would co-ordinate the engineering activities of the various departments and advise the
Corporation on all technical matters." In terms of the future
development of the project, the Chief Engineer was therefore
an extremely important individual. He would not only be in
charge of implementation of a large portion of the project, he
would also have considerable influence in determining what
aspects of the project would be carried out, what aspects would
be expanded or dropped, and similar questions. Though he
was to be a man with a technical background and (theoret-
ically) with a technical role to play, it was recognized by all
of the parties concerned that his recommendations would play
a large part in shaping future policy. For these reasons, each
of the participating governments, and the DVC as well, considered the appointment of a Chief Engineer to be a matter
of extreme importance.

Here then was an issue which directly involved the question
of DVC autonomy. The Corporation had the power, under the
Damodar Valley Corporation Act of 1948, to appoint its own
Chief Engineer, and the participating governments were immediately sensitive to, and jealous of, this power. If the Corporation were to maintain its autonomy, it would appoint the
engineer by itself, or at least play a major role in the eventual
selection of the engineer. If it allowed the appointment to be
made by the participating governments (either individually

or in concert) it would risk losing control over one of its key officials.

In considering the appointment of a Chief Engineer, a number of factors were considered, including, in addition to the question of competence, questions of salary; whether the engineer would be an Indian or a foreigner; and whether he would be a Bengali or a Bihari, or perhaps an individual from another state. The DVC considered the question of competence to be overriding, and for this reason was inclined to engage a foreign engineer even at a high price.[24] But, in the early years of independent nationhood, many Indians were extremely wary of employing non-Indians in government projects, and the major criticism of foreign personnel took the form of charges that they were more costly than they were worth. In fact, the major complaint against the DVC, even in its first year of operation, was that which revolved around what the Auditor-General of India called "grants of irregular or excessive benefits to employees." In his first report on DVC finance, the Auditor-General devoted a large section to this problem, making such charges as the following: (1) that the Corporation had unnecessarily paid the air passage of the wife of an officer recruited from Canada; (2) that the DVC had made advances to foreign personnel for "hiring houses, purchasing household goods, and even to an employees' association for the purchase of cloth for sale"; and (3) that the DVC had rented luxurious houses in Calcutta for its foreign officers and had provided the finest of hotel accommodations for long periods of time until luxurious permanent accommodations could be found.[25]

[24] In the words of the Corporation report, "The Corporation felt that it must not take any chances on a vital issue like this and must take every possible step to ensure, through the appointment of a high-calibre Chief Engineer, both quality and economy in the execution of a complex project costing tens of crores of rupees." See *ibid.*, p. 5.

[25] Government of India, Auditor-General, *First Audit Report of the*

In this atmosphere, the central government decided to launch a widespread search for an Indian engineer of proven competence, and, in the event this failed, attempt to hire a foreign engineer, but at a salary closely comparable to salaries paid to other engineers in India. After an intensive search, however, it was found that the appointment of an Indian engineer was not possible. Indian engineers were either unwilling to enter into a project that appeared so uncertain in its future development, and under the terms of which they would be subjected to control by a civilian government administration, or they were considered incapable of doing the job.[26] In addition, it was decided at the outset that the Chief Engineer would have to have the approval of all participating governments, and consent from the state Ministries of both West Bengal and Bihar was long in coming.[27]

Finances of the Damodar Valley Corporation, signed by K. C. Chaudhuri, November 26, 1949 (New Delhi: Government of India, 1949), pp. 17ff.

[26] These were the reasons commonly given in Parliament in answer to questions on the matter, and they were verified in interviews with DVC personnel and other engineers. For example, Jaipal Singh, who was on the committee responsible for finding a Chief Engineer for the DVC, answered a southern MP who complained that a large number of DVC personnel were foreigners as follows: "If I can find anybody from Mr. Velayudhan's area who can do the work, I would be willing to pay him thrice as much. I shall be only too glad to do so." Government of India, Parliament, *Lok Sabha Debates*, II, No. 7 (June 20, 1952), 2303-04.

[27] S. K. Patil, Central Government Minister of Irrigation and Power, has explained this aspect of the difficulty in finding Chief Engineers for such projects as the DVC as follows: "Sometimes it is said, why a particular Chief Engineer or Superintending Engineer was not appointed for a year, why not do it here and now. If such a power existed, we will do it in a minute. That is not so . . . I have got to see which State is interested and what is the view of that State and whether they are going to quarrel. I write to one State, no reply. I write to another State, no reply. Then I write to both the States, no reply . . . it is not really proper for me—I am not speaking for myself alone;

As a result of the conflict between the DVC and the participating governments over this issue, no Chief Engineer was appointed until twenty-one months after the passage of the DVC Act. During the course of this delay, a widespread search was launched within India; the Prime Minister was brought in, and he personally contacted in this regard both the Bureau of Reclamation and the TVA (during the course of a visit to the U.S.A. in 1949); the Chairman and the Financial Adviser of the DVC made further attempts to find an engineer when they visited America in early 1950 in connection with the negotiations for a dollar loan from the International Bank.[28] The DVC admitted that it had been seriously "handicapped" by the absence of a Chief Engineer, but argued that the matter was "beyond the Corporation's control."[29] In the final analysis, the Corporation did obtain the kind of Chief Engineer it was seeking,[30] but in the process a precedent was established wherein state and central government representatives were brought into the policy-making process of the Corporation and indeed were eventually allowed to make the final decision.

A second conflict between the Corporation and the participating governments developed over the question of financial relations between the various governmental authorities involved in the project. Specifically, this conflict centered on the

---

my predecessors have been there—to come overnight and say [publicly], this Chief Minister has not replied. As it has very often happened, I can assure you, wherever there is delay, sometimes unpardonable I admit, the delay is not due to any slackness on the part of the Central Government. The delay is due to the fact that between two states, the differences could not be compromised." See *ibid.*, IV, No. 15 (August 1, 1957), 6488-89.

[28] *DVC Annual Report, 1949-50*, pp. 2-3.

[29] *DVC Annual Report, 1948-49*, p. 5.

[30] On December 2, 1950, more than two years after the creation of the DVC, an American (Andrew M. Komora) was hired as Chief Engineer. He had had extensive experience in the TVA as well as six years of experience in hydroelectric development in Peru.

budget grants that were to be made to the DVC each year, on the procedures to be followed by the DVC in effecting transactions involving foreign exchange, and on the manner in which estimates of DVC projects would be made and approved. In each case, the DVC sought a large measure of independence (to frame its own budget, to create its own agency for the purchase of materials from abroad, and to make its own estimates) and in each case the participating government objected and pursued measures to overrule the Corporation. In the year 1950-51, for example, the DVC requested 19 crores of rupees from the central government for its operations during that year, but was only granted a total of 12 and ½ crores. The DVC argued that the irregular supply of funds to the Corporation was responsible for the slow progress of the project,[31] but the Advisory Committee of participating governments continued to insist in all of its meetings that: ". . . the Corporation has so far always been very well supplied with funds . . . it is quite unfair to put the blame [for the slow progress of the project] on the shortage of hard currency or the deepening economic crisis."[32] Similarly, the DVC contended that it could not obtain materials from America either efficiently or economically through the regular purchasing agency of the Government of India, and it thus appointed its own agency for obtaining materials from outside of India. But this procedure was strongly censured by an MP from Bihar (and a member of the Advisory Committee) in the *Lok Sabha*,[33] and a government Ministry immediately launched an investigation.

By far the most serious conflict that arose between the Cor-

[31] The Chairman of the DVC, S. N. Majumdar, even held press conferences of his own in which he tried to make this clear. See, for example, the report of the press conference in *The Statesman* (Calcutta), March 21, 1952, p. 1.

[32] This was quoted from a report of the Advisory Committee by a member of that committee in the *Lok Sabha*; see *Lok Sabha Debates*, VIII, No. 13 (February 21, 1951), 3298.

[33] *Ibid.*, VI, No. 4 (February 8, 1951), 1280.

poration and the participating governments, however, was that which centered on the issue of the estimates to be submitted by the Corporation. It was decided at the first Advisory Committee meeting that was held (on May 9, 1949), that a comprehensive estimate was to be submitted by the Corporation. This estimate would bring up to date the estimates made by the Voorduin Committee and would be broken down individually for each dam and power station. On this matter, however, the Corporation delayed. The DVC argued that it was reluctant to submit detailed estimates of its projects in light of the financial difficulties of the country, primarily those involving the uncertainty of the availability of dollars and the devaluation of the rupee;[34] and also that reliable estimates could not be made before detailed designs of all of the dams were finalized (and this depended on the appointment of a Chief Engineer).[35] The Corporation thus submitted a partial estimate at the meeting of the Advisory Committee in the next year (April 1950), but the Advisory Committee found that "the material supplied by the Damodar Valley Corporation was quite inadequate to come to any decision."[36] At this point "pressure was brought to bear upon them [the DVC],"[37] and a detailed estimate was finally submitted to the Advisory Committee in April 1951.

The revised estimates furnished by the Corporation called for the completion of the project outlined in the Voorduin Memorandum in two stages. The first stage was to involve the building of only four of the eight dams planned by the Voorduin Committee, with other changes being introduced as well. The estimated cost of the first phase program, given by the DVC, was just slightly less than 75 crores of rupees, or

[34] DVC Annual Report, 1948-49, p. 15.

[35] DVC Annual Report, 1950-51, p. 6.

[36] Quoted by a member of the Advisory Committee in the Lok Sabha Debates, VIII, No. 13 (February 21, 1951), 3298.

[37] In the words of B. R. Bhagat, MP from Bihar and member of the Advisory Committee; see ibid.

almost twice that contemplated in the Preliminary Memorandum of the Voorduin Committee.[38] The DVC argued that the revised estimates had doubled primarily because of three factors. (1) A significant extension had been made in the scope of the projected first phase, involving additional power plants, an increase in the scope of the transmission system, and additional irrigation, drainage, and navigational benefits. These additional projects, the DVC estimated, would cost approximately 16 crores of rupees.[39] (2) A second reason for the estimated increase in cost, given by the DVC, was the devaluation of the rupee which the Government of India had effected in September 1949. Devaluation, the Corporation estimated, had been "directly responsible for a net addition of almost 4 crores of rupees to the capital cost of the first phase programme."[40] (3) Finally, the DVC argued, the postwar rise in prices had made necessary a total revision of the costs estimated by Voorduin in 1945. The DVC estimated that wholesale prices in the West had risen by 60 to 80 per cent between 1945 and 1951, and that the wholesale price index in India had risen from 86.3 in 1945 to 456.2 in 1951. Moreover, the DVC argued, the cost of heavy construction work had risen even more than would be indicated by general price indexes.[41]

Although the technical committees appointed by the respective participating governments found that the increase in the estimated cost of the project was justified, the nontechnical political and governmental leaders representing the participating governments remained distrustful of the Corporation and all the more desirous of maintaining governmental control over the DVC. But at the same time they wished to

[38] In the *Preliminary Memorandum*, the cost of what came to be the first phase of the program would have been 37.81 crores. The revised estimates of the DVC, submitted in 1951, called for an expenditure of 74.98 crores for the first phase program. See Damodar Valley Corporation, *The Damodar Valley Project Revised Estimates for First Phase with Economic and Financial Justification* (Calcutta: Damodar Valley Corporation, 1951), pp. 4, 12.

[39] *Ibid.*, pp. 13-14.   [40] *Ibid.*, p. 14.   [41] *Ibid.*, p. 15.

preserve the DVC, primarily out of fear that without it they would not be able to complete the project. During this period, when the working of the Corporation was first being evaluated, sentiments like those expressed by Sri Prakasa, the Minister of Natural Resources and Scientific Research, were common.

I may say that it is not difficult—in fact it is quite easy— to find defects in the whole [DVC] scheme and its working. The problem, however, is to find a practical solution that would be acceptable to all the three participating Governments, and at the same time achieve the object that we have in view, namely, the early completion of the Damodar Valley Project at a cost which the participating Governments can afford.[42]

The Process of Reorganization

From the sentiments expressed by Prakasa and others, it became clear that the participating governments, including the center, had become thoroughly disenchanted with the idea of allowing the DVC to operate as an autonomous regional river valley development corporation. This was also evident from the fact that the device which above all others was originally designed to secure the autonomy of the DVC—the resort to the Chief Justice of India as arbiter of disputes—was never used. At the same time, however, all three participating governments were concerned lest, in taking upon themselves control of DVC affairs, they seriously brought into question any hope for completion of the project. To resolve this dilemma, several investigations were called for at all governmental levels. The Planning Commission undertook in 1951 a study which included within its scope the question of reorganization of the DVC; the question of reorganization was also "thoroughly discussed" at two conferences between the representatives of the West Bengal, Bihar, and central governments; a commit-

[42] *Lok Sabha Debates*, VIII, No. 13 (February 21, 1951), 3300-01.

tee (the Rau Committee) was appointed by the Participating Government Conference of the DVC, and charged with the sole responsibility of investigating all aspects of DVC organization; and the Estimates Committee of the *Lok Sabha* included within its Fifth Report specific suggestions with regard to the DVC question.

From all of these reports there emerged a variety of viewpoints. The Estimates Committee Report recommended that the DVC Board be reconstituted as a "merely functional body," charged "only with implementation," and staffed only with personnel—an administrator, engineer, and financial expert—responsible directly to the central government Ministry of Irrigation and Power.[43] The Rau Committee, however, held this suggestion as "inappropriate," and argued for a "semi-autonomous" corporation with "proper safeguards."[44] The Rau Committee, in effect, wanted to keep the DVC as autonomous as it was originally conceived it would be under the DVC Act of 1948.

A third report did not take a stand one way or another, but suggested that either the government should allow the DVC to be autonomous, or else it should abolish it altogether.

All in all, if an example was needed of how not to treat an autonomous corporation, this instance furnishes it. If government is of the view that it made a mistake in having a corporation and that it would really rather do the work departmentally, it would be best to repeal the Act. If its view is that the present personnel of the corporation is not suitable for the work it has to do, it should replace it. In any case, there is no point in having a corporation and treating it as an administrative department subordinate to the Secre-

[43] Government of India, Parliament, *Lok Sabha, Fifth Report of the Estimates Committee* (New Delhi: Government of India, 1952), Sec. III.

[44] Damodar Valley Corporation, *Damodar Valley Corporation (Rau) Committee of Enquiry Report*, P. S. Rau, Chairman (New Delhi: Government of India, 1953), see especially pp. 1-5.

tariat. If it is desired that the corporation should work, its autonomy must be respected. The flow of funds to it must be rational and not erratic. It must conform to a schedule and not be decided on a hand to mouth basis. Foreign exchange must be allotted to it on an annual basis and it must be left free to decide how to spend it, how much of it to spend and for what purpose. A report on expenditure may of course be called for . . . [but] the engineering decisions arrived at by it after the fullest technical advice should not once again be subjected to examination by government engineers. Annual reports are essential, but the corporation's time should not be wasted in continuously having to defend its existence.[45]

In the face of varying opinions on the future status of the Corporation, the matter was finally decided at a meeting of the participating governments. Reporting on this decision, Sri Prakasa stated: "No change in the financial set-up or in the autonomy of the Corporation is at present contemplated. . . . It was agreed at these conferences that instead of taking recourse to the letter of the law, conventions should be set up with a view to making the desired improvements in the working of the D. V. C."[46] But while the Minister continued to insist that the autonomy of the DVC had been preserved by this decision, it became clear from the "conventions" that were established under this policy that the participating governments were henceforth going to make all important policy decisions.

Indeed, even before the policy was formally articulated a number of conventions, each restricting the sphere of operations of the Corporation, had already been effected. One of these established that: ". . . the Damodar Valley Corporation

[45] Government of India, Planning Commission, *Report on the Efficient Conduct of State Enterprises*, by A. D. Gorwala (New Delhi: Government of India, 1951), pp. 32-33.

[46] *Lok Sabha Debates*, ix, Part i, No. 3 (August 9, 1951), 149.

would send to the Government of India before conclusion any contract or agreement which the Corporation propose to enter into other than contracts or agreements arising as a result of a public call for tenders or quotations."[47] Another established that: ". . . the Damodar Valley Corporation also come to Government in cases of contracts of which the value is not definitely ascertainable at the time of the placing of the contract or the signing of the agreement."[48] These two "conventions" meant in effect that the Corporation could only transact business involving expenditures where a legally iron-clad contract could be written. Contracts involving estimates, or those that made allowances for future revision—and the majority of construction contracts are of this nature—were to be concluded only with the approval of the central government. Since the Financial Adviser, a central government administrator, audited the books of the Corporation and supervised all transactions, there was little chance that the Corporation would be able to violate the convention once it was instituted. Indeed, the participating governments even strengthened the hand of the Financial Adviser in this respect by establishing another convention: ". . . that whenever there is a difference of opinion between the Financial Adviser and the Corporation, the former should refer the matter to the Government of India under intimation to the D. V. C. and ask for a decision."[49]

While these conventions dealt quite effectively with the question of DVC expenditures, the question of estimates still remained. And to assure the control of the participating governments in the matter of estimates it was decided that: ". . . plans prepared by its [the DVC's] Chief Engineer and approved by its consulting engineers . . . are . . . to be further examined by the engineering sections of the three participat-

[47] This was reported by Sri Prakasa, *ibid.*, vi, No. 4 (February 8, 1951), 1277.
[48] *Ibid.*
[49] *Ibid.*, ix, Part i, No. 3 (August 9, 1951), 149.

ing governments."[50] Thus, before work on either of the first two dams that were constructed could be undertaken, the DVC was asked "to prepare a detailed estimate within two months and obtain the approval of the participating Governments. . . . The Corporation [was] also asked to keep the participating Governments informed of any increase in the cost of estimates from time to time and to send a monthly statement showing the cost accounts to the technical representatives of the participating Governments."[51]

The fact that the DVC was never going to become an autonomous government Corporation was thus certainly evident in the early years of the project. But this fact became even more obvious as the Corporation proceeded with its work: members of the DVC board became, by custom, representatives of the participating governments (one from West Bengal and one from Bihar) and thus susceptible to state pressures; vacancies on the board remained open for long periods of time without being filled; and the act was eventually amended (in 1958) to make the members of the board only "part-time" members and the Chairman only a "part-time" Chairman, thus formally acknowledging the lessened spheres of their activities. To the present day all major decisions have been made after conferences between the participating governments, and the provision that the Chief Justice be called in as arbiter of disputes has never been used.

The failure of the DVC to gain the large measure of autonomy that was originally intended for it can be accounted for in several ways. To begin with, the expenditures of the state governments on the DVC project represented a significant portion of the total budget expenditures of these states, and almost the sum total of their expenditures on power develop-

[50] The consequences of this "convention" in practice is pointed out by A. D. Gorwala in his *Report on the Efficient Conduct of State Enterprises*, p. 32.

[51] Reported by C. D. Deshmukh, Minister of Finance, in the *Lok Sabha Debates*, I, Part 1 (June 20, 1952), 1106.

ment, irrigation, and flood control. Because of this factor, each of the states shared an interest in gaining control of the policy-making apparatus of the Corporation, both to assure policies that were to the advantage of each of the states and to keep the costs of the Corporation's projects as low as possible. Because of these shared interests, neither state was willing to surrender the power to make policy decisions, either to a neutral autonomous body (the DVC) or to a neutral arbiter (the Chief Justice) so long as the states themselves felt that they could influence the decisions and gain their own ends. And the actions of leadership within the central government made it possible for the states to play a large part in the decision-making process. When conflicts did arise, central leaders were willing to listen to the viewpoints of each state (or to appoint a commission with representatives from all three participating governments to do the same), and were even willing to act as arbiter of state-DVC disputes in an effort to reach joint decisions arrived at by joint consultation. Thus, when the appointment of a Chief Engineer led to conflict between the state governments and the DVC, central leaders assumed the burden of finding a Chief Engineer acceptable to all three governments, even at great costs (resulting from the delay) to the progress of the DVC scheme and to the autonomy of the Corporation. When conflicts arose over budgetary grants, foreign exchange, and estimates, the center again acted only as a party to the "conventions" that were established, and indeed worked for decisions reached outside of the DVC structure and acceptable to the three participating governments.

Because the central government was willing to act only as arbiter between the states of West Bengal and Bihar on the one hand, and the DVC on the other, and because the two states both had an immediate interest in proceeding slowly with the project (because of costs), it became possible to arrive at the "conventions" that were ultimately established. At the same time, the adoption of the "conventions" reflected the negation of whatever degree of autonomy the Corporation was designed to possess. The upshot of all of this was that the autonomous government corporation was rejected as a useful device in the solving of conflicts and the reaching of joint decisions in the development of large-scale river valley projects, while the process of conflict resolution simultaneously took place at another level. The following chapter traces the relationships between governments that did develop within the sphere of endeavor that had been assigned to the DVC.

V

The Damodar Valley Corporation: Center-State Relations and the DVC

Power Generation in the Damodar Valley

PRIOR to the establishment of the DVC scheme, India already possessed a fairly elaborate network of thermal power stations in, and contiguous to, the Damodar Valley. Beginning in 1897, private companies had created large networks of power transmission systems in an effort to supply the majority of the jute mills, cotton mills, engineering workshops, and the numerous small industrial concerns that had grown up in and around Calcutta. In addition, there were other concerns, also privately owned and operated, which supplied electric power to the iron and steel industry, and to the collieries located in the vicinity of the valley. Largely owing to the operations of war, however, these facilities had been severely strained. Constant overloading and the inability to replace parts during wartime had led to the deterioration of equipment, making maintenance difficult and major overhaul necessary. As the Voorduin Memorandum noted, "the existing installations of generating capacity (all thermal) in the valley are inefficient and largely obsolete, with a resultant high average cost of generation."[1]

To rectify this situation, the *Preliminary Memorandum* proposed a combination of eight hydroelectric plants (with a total generating capacity of 200 megawatts) and supplementary thermal electric plants (with a total generating capacity of an additional 150 megawatts). The Voorduin Committee argued that: "Only in this way could the whole of the hydro-electric energy be satisfactorily utilized and the over-all costs become quite economical."[2] As was noted earlier, the Voorduin Com-

---

[1] *Preliminary Memorandum*, p. 2.   [2] *Ibid.*

mittee recommendations were only partially adopted by the Advisory Committee of the DVC in its first phase program. And the DVC continued to insist that only after completion of all of the projects planned for in the Voorduin Memorandum would it be possible to replace all obsolete equipment and to meet all of the rising demands for power in the valley.

But the state governments contended that the demand for electric power would not be able to keep up with supply, and pointed for evidence to the fact that in the early years of power generation by the DVC, there was a surplus of power that was not being used. To convince the states that the demand for power would be forthcoming, the Central Technical Power Board did undertake a "power market survey" in the DVC region. The conclusions drawn from this survey were (1) that "there is almost a power famine in the Valley," and (2) that "the existing market is capable of rapid expansion."[3] But the states remained adamant. At a meeting of the Advisory Committee in April 1951, which met to review the report of the Central Technical Power Board, the states concluded that "the growth of the load will be slower than the forecast made."[4]

In part, the position of the state governments was determined by the fact that they were at the time attempting to diminish the scope of the original Damodar Valley scheme. Wary of the ever-increasing costs that were to be incurred by the Corporation, and conscious of the fact that they would be responsible for supplying most of the funds, the states balked whenever expansion of the scheme was discussed. It was for these reasons that the original Voorduin recommendation to build eight dams was altered, and that it was decided to pursue the project in two stages (with four dams being built in each stage). At the same time, the states attempted to diminish the scope (and the cost) of even the first stage, by

[3] *The Damodar Valley Project Revised Estimates,* p. 86.
[4] "Demands for Electric Power from the DVC System," *The Statesman* (Calcutta), February 21, 1953, Sec. II, p. 10.

eliminating some of the hydroelectric aspects of certain projects.[5] In addition to the desire to save money, certain state leaders were also convinced that the demand for electric power would not rise as fast as the DVC and the Central Technical Power Board had estimated. In fact, West Bengal refused even to grant licenses for expansion of private power companies, arguing that the DVC supply of power would be more than would be needed by the state in the immediate future.[6]

As a result of their firm conviction that the DVC would be able to meet the power demands of almost all of the eastern region, neither Bihar or West Bengal undertook large-scale power projects on their own until more than a decade after Independence. The West Bengal State Electricity Board (SEB) concerned itself with the distribution of DVC power to the coal field areas of Pandaveswar and the districts of Burdwan, Bankura, and Midnapore. But it did not build any major power plants of its own, and it allowed the DVC and the private companies already existing to monopolize the power market. In 1955, the Chief Minister of West Bengal in fact admitted that of a total of 39 crores of rupees allocated to power during the first two five-year plans, more than 30 crores had been spent through the DVC, and the bulk of the rest was only planned expenditure.[7] The state of Bihar, which did not have the advantage of large private generating units within its borders before Independence, was even more dependent on DVC power. Even as late as 1962, almost 90 per cent of its total power supply was furnished by the DVC.[8]

During the early years of the DVC experience with power generation the states thus attempted only to influence DVC policy in an effort to obtain power on their own terms from

[5] *The Statesman* (Calcutta), October 28, 1953, p. 1.

[6] *Ibid.*, January 10, 1952, p. 1. See also the statement by West Bengal Chief Minister B. C. Roy in the *West Bengal Legislative Assembly Debates*, xii, No. 4 (September 30, 1955), 151.

[7] *Ibid.*, 150.

[8] *The Statesman* (Calcutta), July 19, 1962, p. 1.

the DVC grid. But they did not look upon the DVC as a competitor in the power field. To maintain control over the distribution of DVC power, the conference of participating governments first ruled that the DVC would be allowed to distribute power only in bulk quantities and only with approval from the states of the proposed plan of distribution.[9] This meant that the DVC could not retail power directly to the consumer, but could only generate it through facilities owned by one of the states, or by a private power company. Each contract for distribution of power required approval of the states.

Under the terms of this arrangement it was decided by the states that the DVC would supply power to Calcutta in West Bengal, and to the cities of Patna and Gaya in Bihar as well. This decision was made at the same time that it was decided that the original plans of the Voorduin Committee would be cut back by the deletion of the hydroelectric plant from the Konar dam,[10] and only shortly before it was decided to electrify the Burdwan-Howrah railway from the DVC grid.[11] Although the interstate conference acknowledged that this action might entail the necessity for future expansion of some of the DVC power plants, it did not at the time sanction such expansion. What this decision meant was that, in effect, the DVC had been asked to supply far more power than was planned for in the original scheme at the same time that the scope of the original scheme, with regard to power generation, was diminished. The upshot of all of this was, as the central government and the DVC had predicted, an eventual shortage of power in the eastern region; a shortage that first became noticeable in 1958 and which has lasted until the present day.

Even before the power shortage, however, the policy of the West Bengal Government with regard to the generation of electric power was in the process of change. In early 1957, West Bengal undertook the construction of two small (30

[9] *Ibid.*, August 7, 1952, p. 8. [10] *Ibid.*, October 28, 1953, p. 1.
[11] *Ibid.*, January 19, 1954, p. 1.

megawatts each) thermal power plants at Durgapur, which would be expected to supply the new industrial connurbation growing up in that region.[12] At the same time, the state began to make elaborate studies of further large-scale projects that could possibly be undertaken by the state during the third five-year plan.

The reason for this change in policy on the part of West Bengal stemmed primarily from two sources. First, it became obvious that the power shortage that had been predicted—some estimates ranged as high as 750 megawatts in West Bengal by the end of the third plan[13]—was now almost a certainty. By 1957 the DVC was operating to capacity, and in fact even overloading during peak hours, while demands for electrical power were growing. By December of 1958, a central government Minister, Ajit Prasad Jain, labeled the situation in the valley a "power crisis,"[14] and the DVC offered to "immediately undertake further expansion schemes" should it be granted the necessary approval of the participating governments. Power users in the valley, and in Calcutta, immediately began to pressure both the state and central governments for expansion of the DVC project.

The state of West Bengal at this point continued to balk at the proposals to undertake new power development schemes within the framework of the DVC, but now began immediately to press for its own large-scale entry into the power field. Perhaps the primary reason for this change of policy was the realization, on the part of the state government, that power development had begun to be a sound financial proposition. For, during the first nine years of the life of the DVC, power generation had returned no dividends to the Corporation and, indeed, in the early years had even caused great deficits. But

[12] Manoranjan Datta, "Power Development in India," *ibid.*, April 30, 1957, Sec. II, p. 8.

[13] This was the estimate of the DVC board; see *ibid.*, February 19, 1960, p. 4.

[14] *Ibid.*, December 10, 1958, p. 1.

by 1957-58, the Corporation had shown a clear profit from the power aspects of its activities,[15] with the promise of more to come in the future. The West Bengal Government, in need of funds and desirous of maintaining control over the consumers of electricity within its own borders, quickly decided to enter the power field on its own.

The state government was also interested in extending power facilities to other areas of the state—principally to the north and east—in which the DVC could not be logically expected to go. By initiating its own power program, which envisaged its own power grid, the possibility of extending power to these areas was greater than it would have been had the states' expenditures on power been closely linked to the DVC grid. It was argued, for example, that the extension of power to all areas of the state would be an incentive for the future industrialization of these regions. As one state government spokesman stated, the policy of West Bengal was: ". . . to encourage capital to invest in the rural areas, where labour can be easily obtained . . . with cheap power available anywhere in the state, the industrialist will readily realize the advantages."[16]

Beginning with the third five-year plan, then, the state of West Bengal became a competitor of the DVC in the power field. To effect a policy of large-scale power development it was decided by the State Electricity Board to divide the state of West Bengal into four "power regions": (1) the Durgapur-Calcutta industrial belt; (2) the Asansol-Burdwan area and the coal belt; (3) Malda and West Dinajpur in the eastern part of the state; and (4) Bagrakot-Siliguri in the northern part of the state. According to the plans of the West Bengal State Electricity Board the second of these regions, the Asansol-Burdwan area and the coal belt, could be supplied by power

[15] *DVC Annual Report, 1957-58*, pp. 1-2.

[16] Quoted in Manoranjan Datta, "Electricity in the Development of Small-Scale Industries," *The Statesman* (Calcutta), February 14, 1959, p. 16.

from the DVC grid, and the DVC would eventually be restricted to supplying electricity only in this area (except for loads that had already been promised outside of it).[17] Under the State Electricity Board, West Bengal would then undertake a number of its own projects during the third five-year plan. These would include a 20 megawatt thermal unit at Malda (in region three above); a 20 megawatt unit at Jaldhaka and another 20 megawatt unit at Bagrakot (in region four above); and five large-scale projects in the Durgapur-Calcutta industrial belt (region one); expansion of the Durgapur state unit by 275 megawatts; the building of another new 175 megawatt unit at Durgapur; a 300 megawatt unit at Bandel; a 15 megawatt unit at Gouripur and a 100 megawatt unit at Azimganj south of Calcutta.[18]

Once West Bengal decided to enter the power field on its own, it became necessary for the state government to relieve itself of its obligations to the DVC. This it immediately proceeded to do. At a meeting with the central government Minister of Power and Irrigation, Chief Minister B. C. Roy stated that he had "made it clear to the Center and the DVC that the West Bengal Government would not be agreeable to share the cost of any new thermal power stations either in the Damodar Valley region or outside as it [West Bengal] has itself undertaken an ambitious power development program."[19] During the next year, the West Bengal Government vetoed every proposal that was made to extend the operations of the DVC in West Bengal, as well as those which envisaged the building of the four dams planned for in the second stage of DVC development. In addition, it was proposed by the two state governments, and accepted by the interstate conference, that the DVC transmission lines and power stations outside the valley itself be taken over by the states.[20] Once this was done,

---

[17] "Controversies over Bengal's Power Needs," *ibid.*, May 4, 1962, p. 6.

[18] *Ibid.*, July 26, 1961, p. 1.   [19] *Ibid.*, October 14, 1961, p. 1.

[20] *Ibid.*, October 27, 1962, p. 12.

it became quite clear that the DVC could only undertake new projects within the Damodar Valley itself, and then only if such projects were undertaken without the financial support of the West Bengal Government. As the state Chief Minister stated, once the transmission lines and power stations outside of the valley were transferred to the state governments, "the DVC will then be left with enough power to feed the valley, [and] there is hardly any scope for acceptance of the Corporation's scheme."[21]

Although central leadership groups tried for a time to preserve the DVC and to extend its sphere of operation in West Bengal, they finally relented (in January 1963) and granted the demands of West Bengal. At a meeting between the participating governments it was decided that the states would from that time onward be responsible for all power requirements in their respective areas outside the valley. Moreover, while the DVC would no longer generate power outside of the region presently supplied by it, the states would be allowed to set up their own generating units in the Damodar Valley if state leaders found this necessary. A number of central leaders still wanted a single integrated grid to cover the eastern region—including West Bengal, Bihar, Eastern Uttar Pradesh, and northern Orissa—but, again, it was decided at a meeting of the participating governments that this could best be done by a "regional coordination committee" rather than through an organization such as the DVC.[22]

The effect of this decision was to grant all of the demands which the state of West Bengal had made, and to pave the way for a large-scale program of power development on the part of the state. Soon after this decision was announced, approval for a large-scale power program in West Bengal's third five-year plan was forthcoming, including plans for a state multipurpose river development project on the Ajoy River, and a 1,000 megawatt power plant in the Durgapur-Cal-

[21] Quoted *ibid*.   [22] *Ibid.*, January 30, 1963, p. 9.

cutta region.[23] By the time the fourth five-year plan was under consideration, West Bengal had planned to spend 160 crores (of a total plan outlay of 617 total crores), or 26 per cent of its total plan outlay, on power generation.[24]

Another result of these activities was severe disappointment with the Damodar Valley Corporation on the part of almost everyone concerned. T. T. Krishnamachari stated that in the DVC "politics has taken precedence over technique," and appealed to Hafiz Mohammad Ibrahim, Union Irrigation Minister, to repeal the Damodar Valley Act or to introduce in it "drastic amendments."[25] The state governments agreed. Prafulla Sen, Chief Minister of West Bengal after B. C. Roy's death, stated that the DVC "creates more problems than it solves,"[26] and argued for complete reorganization. A Congress party MP from West Bengal stated in Parliament that "hopes over the DVC have turned illusory and it should now be scrapped. The power and irrigation schemes should be handed over to the different states, or they should all be taken over by the Centre."[27] Soon after these statements it was reported that: "Both in West Bengal and Bihar, the feeling has gained in strength that a reasonable solution of the present deadlock in the DVC lies in its re-constitution into a regional power authority which will be responsible only for generation and distribution of electricity."[28] Although the DVC still exists and is charged with projects that may not be completed until the end of the fourth five-year plan (the Chandrapura project in Bihar), it is significant that no new DVC projects have been sanctioned since these statements were made. Moreover, it has been decided that the second stage of the Damodar Valley project is to be dropped, and that the Corporation is hence-

---

[23] *Ibid.*, February 11, 1963, p. 7.   [24] *Ibid.*, December 8, 1964, p. 1.

[25] *Ibid.*, February 5, 1963, p. 1.

[26] Statement made in a personal interview; this is also the position taken by Chief Minister Sen at a press conference in early 1963, see *The Statesman* (Calcutta), March 28, 1963, p. 1.

[27] *Ibid.*, March 27, 1963, p. 7.   [28] *Ibid.*, March 28, 1963, p. 1.

forth to be charged only with production and transmission of power from its existing facilities.[29]

The field of power generation in the Damodar Valley provides an instance in which the state governments were able to pursue their own plans, based on their own assessments of their own needs, almost at will. When the states wanted to use DVC power to meet most of the power needs within each state, they were able to gain control over the policy-making apparatus of the Corporation and to channel power into almost all areas of the two states. When they wanted to diminish the scope of the power projects within the valley they were able to alter the initial plans of the Corporation and in fact to eliminate completely the entire second stage of the project. When Bihar wanted to use the DVC to build a number of large thermal power plants at Chandrapura, the DVC was almost immediately charged with construction of the Chandrapura project; and at the same time when the West Bengal government decided to enter the power field on its own, it was able to curtail almost entirely the power development activities of the DVC in the state of West Bengal.

Even more important, a study of the decisions that were made with regard to power generation in the valley reveals a distinct lack of willingness on the part of central government leaders either to pursue conflict with the states or to interfere in state planning activities. At least on two accounts, the policies adopted by the states, and accepted by the center, ran counter to the interests of national planning and policy-making bodies. First, the decision by the states to diminish the scope of the *hydroelectric* projects of the Damodar Valley scheme, and to simultaneously undertake or promote *thermal* power projects, ran directly counter to the policies of both the Planning Commission and the Ministry of Power and Irrigation. Both of these bodies have insisted in all of their statements and publications on power development that the

[29] *Ibid.*, March 14, 1964, p. 1.

preservation of high-grade reserves of coal, and the development of hydroelectric as opposed to thermal power, were crucial to the future development of India. Despite the obvious conflict between state and central government policy involved in the decisions that were taken in regard to power development, however, neither the Planning Commission or any central government body was willing to oppose the policies of the states. Second, the decision by the West Bengal Government to create its own power grid in West Bengal ran counter to that policy of the central government wherein the electricity grids in the eastern region were to be combined and standardized under a regional authority. In fact, at least one central government Minister argued that the creation of separate state grids, equal in size to that of the DVC, would end all possibilities of ever effecting a uniform policy for power generation in the eastern region.[30] But even this Minister began to work merely for the "regional coordination committee" that had been suggested by the states, rather than attempt to persuade the states to conform to nationally established policies.

A number of factors account for this lack of willingness on the part of the central government to interfere in state planning and policy-making activities. Before proceeding to an analysis of such factors, however, it is essential to understand more clearly the position of the central government by focusing on the irrigation aspects of the DVC scheme, with regard to which the center did attempt to dissuade the state of West Bengal from pursuing a specific policy.

Irrigation and the DVC

In the DVC Act of 1948, it was clear that the Corporation was to have control over the irrigation facilities provided by its network of storage reservoirs, subject only to a provision that the states be called in for consultation when levying

[30] *Ibid.*, January 30, 1963, p. 9.

rates, and that the water from DVC irrigation facilities be distributed through state-constructed irrigation distributary channels. In the words of the Act: ". . . the Corporation may, after consultation with the Provincial Government concerned, determine and levy rates for the bulk supply of water to that Government for irrigation."[31] The Corporation's responsibility was to supply water in bulk to the West Bengal Government; the state government was merely to act as the relay agent in the distribution of the water and was to be brought into consultation with the Corporation for the levying of rates. Under the terms of this arrangement, the DVC and the state government met in 1951 and agreed to set a betterment levy[32] of 8 rupees per acre on land irrigated by the DVC system. This figure, it was estimated, would bring in up to 18 crores of rupees annually when all of the projects were completed, and make it possible eventually to pay the costs of the irrigation benefits provided by the scheme, and perhaps even to secure a profit.[33] The betterment levy of 8 rupees per acre was to be enacted immediately and levied on the cultivators as soon as irrigation water was provided. The proceeds that were collected by the state government from this levy were then to be given either to the DVC, as West Bengal's contribution to the Corporation, or to the central government, to pay off that portion of West Bengal's debt to the center that had accumulated in setting up the project.[34]

Although the government of West Bengal did agree to charge a betterment levy for irrigation water furnished by the

[31] *The Damodar Valley Corporation Act* (Act xiv, 1948), Section 14.

[32] In the following discussion, the distinction between a "betterment levy" and an "irrigation cess" is implicit. A "betterment levy" is a one-time charge, based on the increase to the capital value of benefited land. An "irrigation cess" is an annual fee paid to secure the right to use irrigation water during the year.

[33] U. K. Ghosal, "Economics of the DVC," *The Statesman* (Calcutta), December 5, 1959, p. 7.

[34] *DVC Annual Report, 1954-55*, p. 3.

DVC, it soon became evident that, because of the opposition of the cultivators, a great deal of difficulty would be encountered in collection. In the planning stages it had been argued that the cultivators in this region would eventually be able to grow two and possibly three crops on land that presently supported only one crop, and that improved crops would result from the additional irrigation benefits being provided. But this argument was based on the assumption that the cultivator could be convinced that crop rotation was both desirable and possible, and that he would be capable of using the water in such a way as to increase crop production. It was assumed, for example, that the cultivator could be expected to know what benefits would accrue to him should he contract for a regular supply of DVC irrigation water; that he could be convinced of the necessity for joining with other cultivators along the same irrigation channel to contract for irrigation water. It was also assumed that he would know such technical matters as the water requirements of two or three different kinds of crops, both as regards timing and quantity; the methods of applying water to different crops; the necessary kind of equipment, seeds, and fertilizers to be used when double and triple-cropping; and other crop rotation techniques. It soon became obvious that these had been hopeful assumptions. When the betterment levy and the annual irrigation fees were introduced, the cultivator saw these as oppressive measures. In his eyes, he would be expected to pay a number of irrigation fees for water he would need only in an occasional year when the rains failed. When rainfall was plentiful, he would not require irrigation benefits and therefore saw no need to pay the fee.[35] In the words of one observer who sampled five villages in the valley in 1956, the cultivators ". . . know nothing of the changes in cropping, in relations between cultivator and landowner, between adjoining owners, or the whole train of

[35] S. R. Vasudev, "The Reluctant Ryot: Why He Objects to Using Irrigation Water in His Fields," *The Statesman* (Calcutta), April 21, 1958, p. 6.

agricultural adjustments which intensive irrigation requires."[36]

As a result, the cultivators refused to contract for the irrigation benefits provided by the DVC system under the terms contemplated by the planners. Instead, they proceeded to take the water surreptitiously. By breaching or obstructing the bunds in the DVC channels, or by building their own channels from the DVC system to their villages, the cultivators were able to make the water flow where they wanted it to, and thus get water free (or at the expense only of their own labor) and under conditions which were acceptable to them. Rather than use the water for double and triple-cropping, or according to other plans intended by the creators of the Damodar Valley Corporation, they came to use the water only for the same purposes as they had used their own crude irrigation and water-storage devices. Thus, when the rains failed, the DVC irrigation channels were tapped; when the rains were plentiful, the DVC irrigation channels were unused.

The reaction of both the West Bengal Government and the Congress party of Bengal was to take the side of the cultivators. Thus, when the state government did agree to press for the imposition of the water rates, it did so only in the most cumbersome and time-consuming manner. Rather than pass legislation effecting a uniform rate for each acre, it was decided to draw up contracts with each individual cultivator and potential user of the irrigation water provided by the DVC system. The result was, of course, that by the time all negotiations with cultivators could be finalized and adequate machinery set up for the collection of the rates, a number of years had passed and the precedent for nonpayment of irrigation rates was well-established.[37] Such precedents were reinforced by the support which members of all political parties gave to the cultivators in the valley. In a visit to the villages in the valley in 1955-56, for example, Hart found that ". . . po-

[36] Henry C. Hart, *Administrative Aspects of River Valley Development* (New York: Asia Publishing House, 1961), p. 11.

[37] *DVC Annual Report, 1955-56*, p. 7.

litical workers had already been to one village suggesting to the potential irrigators that DVC water rates would be exorbitant and that by concerting not to use the water they could compel a reduction of the rates."[38] The Chairman of the Burdwan District Congress Committee later reported in an interview:

> Of course we were not going to stand by and see the people of Burdwan paying these fantastic rates—that is why we had fought against the British for so many years. This is a social service state and we were going to see to it that the people of Burdwan received irrigation from the government . . . after all, that is the only way food production will ever be increased and our country will escape from its miserable condition.[39]

By 1957 then, resistance to the use of DVC water had stiffened. The opposition parties in West Bengal insisted that water from irrigation projects was lying idle because the betterment levy was too high, and they were using this as a campaign issue in the districts during the election. As a result, many Congressmen in these districts also took the position of the cultivators and argued for a repeal of all betterment levies.[40] Even those newspapers which generally supported the central government and the DVC in their conflicts with the state government began to take exception to the imposition of a betterment levy.[41]

To consider the opposition to the betterment levy present in West Bengal, a series of conferences were held at which

[38] Hart, *Administrative Aspects of River Valley Development*, p. 12.
[39] Personal interview, March 1963.
[40] *Ibid.*
[41] *The Statesman*, for example, in an editorial titled, "Real Purpose of D.V.C.," stated: "a betterment levy has been imposed at the Central Government's insistence. The theoretician in the Planning Commission justifies this on impeccable arguments; the practical administrator gapes at this incredible measure." See *The Statesman* (Calcutta), August 2, 1957, p. 6.

the West Bengal Government placed its position before the DVC and the participating governments. As a result of these conferences, a compromise between West Bengal and the other parties in the DVC project was effected. To assist the West Bengal Government in its attempt to cope with the opposition, it was decided that water from the DVC system would be supplied free to those people living in a 150,000 acre area, most of which was located in Burdwan district. This was to be undertaken as an "experimental measure,"[42] the assumption being that this would commit the cultivators to planned use of the water and allow them to become better acquainted with the benefits to be gained from planned use of irrigation facilities. Once the cultivator was made aware of the benefits he could derive from the project, the betterment levy would be introduced. The other part of the compromise was that the West Bengal Government would pass legislation enabling the state government to collect annual irrigation fees, in which legislation a maximum rate for such fees would be mentioned. The central government hoped in this way to secure the betterment levy (the charge based on the increase to the capital value of the benefited land) and to commit the state government, at least in principle, to the position of imposing an annual irrigation fee (cess).[43]

The bill enabling the state government to levy this cess, the West Bengal Irrigation (Imposition of Water Rate for Damodar Valley Corporation Water) Bill of 1958, was drafted by July of the following year. This bill made it compulsory that owners or occupiers of land in the DVC area pay a fee for water furnished by the DVC. While it did not state what that rate would be, it was drafted in such a way as to set a ceiling (12.50 rupees per acre for *kharif* [autumn] crops and 15

[42] *Ibid.*, August 15, 1957, p. 7.

[43] This was the impression of the state Minister of Irrigation during this time. It was his impression that this was a compromise measure, and it is on his authority that it is called a compromise measure here. Interview (April 1963).

rupees per acre for *rabi* [spring] crops) on the amount the state could assess. The central government had hoped that by mentioning a ceiling, and by allowing for discretion on the part of the state government in the assessment of rates, opposition to the bill would be mitigated.[44] But despite these measures, opposition to the bill was intense and came from all quarters of the state. The Communist and leftist parties threatened that, if the bill were passed, "a movement would be started throughout the state to prevent the government from implementing the provisions of the measure which ignored farmer's interests."[45] A Congressman from Katwa constituency in the DVC area drew applause in the Legislative Assembly when he described the bill as a "punitive measure which would annoy farmers and affect food production." The measure, he warned, would "create a stir in Burdwan district."[46] Opposition to the bill was so strong that there were as many as twenty-six divisions on a single clause,[47] and, while the bill eventually passed by a vote of 119 to 59, the vote on the bill found all of the opposition members of the Legislative Assembly either opposed or not voting, and thirty-three of the Congress members (mostly from the DVC area) not voting or absent.[48]

State government leaders argued that they had proposed the bill because of pressures that stemmed from the central government.[49] West Bengal was at this time attempting to proceed with other irrigation projects—principally the Kangsabati Irrigation project and Farakka Barrage—but these schemes were not being sanctioned by the center, and the center had stopped the flow of central loans and grants that

[44] *Ibid.*

[45] *West Bengal Legislative Assembly Debates*, xx, No. 4 (August 1, 1958), 1621.

[46] *Ibid.* (July 21, 1958), 1503-04.

[47] *Ibid.* (July 30, 1958), 1551-52.

[48] *Ibid.* (August 1, 1958), 1625.

[49] Based on interviews; see also references below.

were necessary to maintain construction progress.[50] A number of Union Ministers took the position that the center could not continue to supply the state of West Bengal with irrigation funds unless the irrigation facilities constructed would be utilized, and proceeds collected from the projects.[51]

But while the state agreed to pass the bill enabling it to charge an irrigation cess, its subsequent actions in large part negated any possible effect this might have had on the situation in the valley. The Chief Minister assured the Congress MLA's from the DVC area that he would meet with them before fixing the final rate;[52] the state did little in the way of collecting the revenue in the first few years after the fee was fixed, and, in many instances, did nothing to prevent cultivators from taking water from the DVC channels without payment.[53] Finally, the state Congress party refused to discipline its own members who took the side of the cultivators and worked against collection of the cess. In fact, shortly after the passage of the 1958 bill, fourteen MLA's from Burdwan (including eight Congressmen) held a joint press conference in which they admitted that farmers had raised cross-bunds to obstruct the regular flow of DVC irrigation water, and that cultivators had siphoned large amounts of water off illegally. Despite the policy of their government, however, they

[50] *The Statesman* (Calcutta), March 7, 1958, p. 9.

[51] See the statement by A. P. Jain, Union Food Minister, *ibid.*, January 21, 1958, p. 1; by M. S. Sivaruman, advisor to the Planning Commission, *ibid.*, March 7, 1958, p. 9; and the report of a communiqué issued by the Planning Commission, *ibid.*, September 12, 1958, p. 1.

[52] *Ibid.*, July 24, 1958, p. 1.

[53] The state government collected no revenue during the first year after the passage of the 1958 Act. Nor did the state take any kind of punitive action against interference by cultivators in the irrigation facilities. The state government argued that ". . . it would not be proper to take police action against interference with canals because of abnormal drought conditions. When adequate supplies [of water are] available, people in their own interests will remove the obstacles." Reported *ibid.*, July 31, 1958, p. 1.

argued that this was necessary lest farmers lose crops for lack of water.[54]

Conscious of the political situation in the districts, the West Bengal Government now turned its attention to criticism of the DVC, and began to press for the transfer of the irrigation system from the Corporation to the Irrigation Ministry of the state itself. The state government refused to collect any of the cesses levied under the enabling legislation that had been passed until the Corporation would agree to pay the state for the expenses involved in collection. And the amount which the state government considered its due was considerably higher than that which the other participating governments and the DVC were willing to grant. The state government wanted to deduct 50 per cent of the proceeds from the cess as payment of its own cost in (1) maintaining the channels; (2) enforcing laws that would prohibit cultivators from using the water illegally; and (3) for collecting the fees.[55] Members of the DVC Board, and of the central government Ministry of Irrigation and Power, contended that these demands were "absurd" and "irresponsible" and therefore refused to accede to the demands.[56] The result of this conflict was a stalemate that lasted for more than five years, during which time irrigation facilities were used only in a haphazard manner while negotiations between the parties concerned took place.

Throughout this period (1959-64) the tactics of the West Bengal Government were clearly obstructionist. Not only were the cultivators allowed to build their own irrigation channels to tap DVC water illegally, but, in addition, the West Bengal Government refused to construct its own village and field channels in conformance with DVC plans. Moreover, part of the DVC system could not be put into operation until the West Bengal Howrah Drainage project was completed, and in mid-1959 the West Bengal Government announced that

[54] *Ibid.*, August 5, 1958, p. 1.   [55] *Ibid.*, April 22, 1959, p. 5.

[56] Related by a member of the DVC Board during this time, in an interview, January 24, 1964.

it was going to postpone this project "indefinitely."[57] Finally, the state government in 1960 began to make unreasonable demands: it proposed that the DVC undertake all capital expenditure on irrigation in the valley in the future, but at the same time transfer complete control over DVC irrigation facilities to the state Irrigation Ministry.[58] It refused to pay any of its dues to the Corporation, or to guarantee that the state would use any of the irrigation facilities provided by the DVC.[59]

Faced with such tactics on the part of the state government, the reaction of the center was to postpone a decision on the matter while a number of investigations were launched and a variety of persuasive tactics were attempted. In 1959, the National Council of Applied Economic Research (NCAER) was charged with investigating the question of water rates and reported its opinion that charges ranging between 20 to 50 per cent should be levied on the net additional benefit accruing to cultivators from the irrigation facilities.[60] Later in the year a two-man commission (composed of two retired engineers) was appointed by the Central Water and Power Commission and eventually suggested the gradual introduction of a betterment levy similar to that recommended by the NCAER.[61] The Public Accounts Committee of the *Lok Sabha* later investigated the situation (in 1961) and also arrived at conclusions similar to those of the other committees.[62]

In each instance for which evidence is available, the conclusions reached by central government bodies charged with the task of investigating the situation with regard to irrigation in the Damodar Valley were such as to go against the position of the West Bengal Government. In each instance the central government administrator or engineer argued that

---

[57] *The Statesman* (Calcutta), May 21, 1959, p. 7.

[58] *Ibid.*, June 21, 1960, p. 12.   [59] *Ibid.*, April 9, 1961, p. 9.

[60] *Ibid.*, February 16, 1959, p. 1.   [61] *Ibid.*, May 20, 1959, p. 1.

[62] India (Republic), Parliament, Public Accounts Committee, *Report* (New Delhi: Government of India, 1962), pp. 27-28.

the facilities of the Corporation should be utilized, that illegal use of the water should be prevented by state law enforcement agencies, that betterment levies and an annual irrigation fee should be enacted and collected, and that the proceeds from these levies should be used to reduce the debt of West Bengal to the center and to the DVC. The Central Ministry of Irrigation, acting on these recommendations, attempted for five years to persuade the West Bengal Government to conform to what had become central government policy. Perhaps the major attempt at persuasion by the center came in 1961, when the Planning Commission agreed to the construction of two West Bengal irrigation projects—the Ganga Barrage project and the Bhagirathi-Hooghly Flusing scheme—on condition that West Bengal make a renewed effort to collect irrigation cesses.[63] At this time, it was stated that the center would refuse to release funds to cover the capital costs of any of West Bengal's irrigation schemes, unless the state agreed to take off and pay for a stated amount of water each year for irrigation purposes.[64]

In response to persuasion by the central government, the West Bengal Government did begin regular collection of the irrigation cess. At the same time, however, it continued to refuse to make its payments to the DVC, and refused to guarantee that it would take off a certain amount of water each year.[65] Unwilling to attempt to coerce the state further, the center finally relented in late 1963, and agreed to transfer the irrigation barrage at Durgapur and all other irrigation facilities of the DVC in West Bengal to the state government.[66]

[63] Based on personal interview with West Bengal Irrigation Minister Ajoy Mukherjee, conducted in April 1963. See also the report in *The Statesman* (Calcutta), April 5, 1961, p. 1.

[64] *Ibid.*, April 9, 1961, p. 9.

[65] *West Bengal Legislative Assembly Debates*, March 11, 1963.

[66] Statement by K. L. Rao, Union Minister of Irrigation and Power, in *Lok Sabha* on February 20, 1964. Reported in *The Statesman* (Calcutta), February 21, 1964, p. 12.

It was agreed that West Bengal would assume control of the DVC irrigation and barrage system beginning April 1, 1964,[67] and that all of the DVC technical personnel concerned with irrigation would from that date become employees of the West Bengal Government.[68]

The evolution of a policy for the construction, maintenance, and distribution of DVC irrigation facilities provides an example of a situation in which the proposed plans and programs of the central and state governments came into direct conflict. The West Bengal Government found a great deal of resistance within its borders to the proposed DVC plans for the distribution of irrigation benefits. And West Bengal—by working against the collection of the irrigation cess, by allowing cultivators to sabotage the irrigation channels and bunds, and by refusing to contribute its share to the Corporation or to pay its debt to the center—clearly took a position in support of the conception of state interests that was present in the minds of most Bengalis. At the same time, a number of central agencies did attempt to evolve a nationally standardized policy that conflicted in many respects with the declared policy of the government of West Bengal: they favored the imposition of a betterment levy and an irrigation cess, they argued for strict law-enforcement measures in response to violations, and they attempted to pressure the state government into paying its dues to the Corporation.

At least in this case, however, the actions of the central government were not such as to assure state compliance with federal policy. To be sure, attempts were made to compromise with the state—when the center agreed to the free distribution of DVC water in return for the enactment of state enabling legislation. Fairly effective persuasive techniques—the withholding of central funds for other projects pending conformance by the state to the policies of the center—were also tried. But it is significant that, while the state government was will-

<hr />

[67] *Ibid.*, March 1, 1964, p. 5.   [68] *Ibid.*, March 4, 1964, p. 7.

ing to become a party to a compromise with the center and to make minor concessions in the face of massive persuasion, it was, in the final analysis, allowed to pursue its own conception of its own interests and to veto or negate most of the center's planned programs. As a result, central leaders were able to secure the passage of state legislation effecting an irrigation cess, and to gain some concessions from the state in enforcing this legislation. But, the state of West Bengal was allowed to neglect entirely its irrigation dues to the DVC and eventually to even gain control over all DVC irrigation facilities. Control over policy matters involving the levy of an irrigation cess and the enforcement of regulations governing such collection is now entirely in state hands.

Flood Control in the Damodar Valley

Thus far an attempt has been made to trace the relationships that evolved between the central government and the state of West Bengal in effecting a policy for power development and the distribution of irrigation facilities in the Damodar Valley. But the discussion has thus far said little of the primary purposes for which the DVC was created: (1) the control of floods in the valley, and (2) the quest for cooperation between the states of Bihar and West Bengal in this endeavor. In the following section, therefore, an attempt will be made to assess the ability of the participating governments to cope with these two problems. How successful was the Corporation in preventing floods? How successful was the Corporation device in effecting cooperation between two states on a multipurpose project? What was the relationship between the two state governments, and how did the center react to instances of interstate cooperation and conflict?

As was mentioned earlier, the Voorduin Committee had planned initially for the construction of seven dams with storage reservoirs, the intention being to protect the valley against a flood bigger than any that had ever been recorded, but one which might conceivably occur. However, at a meeting of the

Advisory Committee in 1951, when both state governments wanted to cut costs and proceed slowly, the scope of the original plan was diminished. At this meeting it was decided that the project would be pursued in two stages: only four dams and reservoirs would be built in the first stage, and full flood control protection would have to wait until the completion of the second stage of the project. It was emphasized at this meeting that the second stage of the project would be taken up as soon as financing permitted.[69]

Soon after this decision was announced, the Corporation began to argue for the consideration of plans to complete the project. The arguments of the Corporation were based on at least seven technical considerations.[70]

1. With only four dams and storage reservoirs, flood protection in the valley was only relative. To assure complete protection from floods would necessitate the building of the three additional dams contemplated in the original Voorduin Memorandum.

2. Industrial needs for water were growing, particularly in the area where the three additional reservoirs were to be built. The Aiyar Dam, for example, would provide water for the future development of the Bokaro industrial connurbation (in Bihar) and it was doubtful that the large Bokaro steel plant, contemplated by the Bihar Government and the Planning Commission, would even be feasible without an adequate supply of water.

3. As industry continued to require more and more water,

[69] This is clear from the report of the meeting furnished in the *DVC Annual Report, 1950-51*, p. 4; see also the *Rau Committee Report, 1952*, pp. 2-3.

[70] While these arguments appear, either in part or together, in numerous sources, they are most consciously developed in the *DVC Annual Reports*, and in the following articles: R. Maclagan Gorrie, "The Technique of Flood Control," *The Statesman* (Calcutta), October 9, 1953, p. 6; and "Harnessing the Damodar," *ibid.*, September 2, 1959, p. 6. Both of these articles were written by DVC executive officers.

the Corporation would be faced with a water shortage. It would then be forced to either (1) provide less water for irrigation and navigational purposes or (2) restrict the use of DVC water by industry. Building three additional reservoirs would prevent any such shortage of water.

4. The building of three additional dams with reservoirs would also make it possible, not only to build more hydro-electric power plants at dam sites, but also to release more water in the upper reaches of the river, thus increasing the flow of water in the river and making possible more power plants further down.

5. An increase in storage capacity in the upper reaches of the river would also make possible periodic flushing of the river channels in the lower valley, thus alleviating to some extent the increasing problem caused by silting of the channels in the lower portions of West Bengal.

6. The building of reservoirs near the Ramgarh coal fields (where the three additional reservoirs were contemplated) would be beneficial both to the coal fields and to the people in the lower valley since the sand trapped in these reservoirs could be used by a coal industry in need of sand, and since the drawing off of sand in the upper reaches would also alleviate silting further down.

7. Finally, the building of the three additional dams shortly after the completion of the first stage would make possible the employment of the staff in charge of building the first stage projects, thus eliminating staffing costs and preventing unemployment.

While the DVC could justify its demands for consideration of the second stage on sound technical arguments, neither state government was willing to sanction a second stage proposal during the first decade of the life of the DVC. To begin with, neither of the states was willing, during this time, to sanction such a large-scale expenditure when costs were already so high. And, for a number of additional reasons, the project did not appeal to West Bengal. West Bengal would receive flood control protection, which brought in no state revenues, and, furthermore, it would be required to pay half the cost for this protection. Faced with large deficits, the state government was necessarily forced to consider the possibility of undertaking revenue-producing projects rather than those for flood control protection. In addition, even though the three additional dams and reservoirs would be designed to provide flood protection for West Bengal, they would necessarily be built in Bihar, and the West Bengal Government feared that, with water storage and power facilities within her borders, Bihar would have an advantage in attracting industry. It was consideration of these two factors that led West Bengal to a posture of permanent opposition to the second stage of the DVC project.[71]

Because of the benefits that would accrue to Bihar, with the completion of the entire project, it was inevitable that the Bihar Government would eventually press for consideration of the second stage. In early 1959, when the first stage was nearing completion, the Bihar Government thus raised for the first time the question of extension: consideration of the three dams with storage reservoirs (Aiyar, Bermo, and Belpahari) and the hydroelectric station without a reservoir at Bokaro. Both Bihar and the DVC were in favor of immediately undertaking these projects, all of which had been contemplated in the Voorduin Memorandum.[72]

The reaction of the West Bengal Government was immediate and clear. Returning from the meeting of participating governments at which Bihar had proposed the second stage, Chief Minister B. C. Roy stated at a press conference that "West Bengal cannot agree to Aiyar Dam at this time." Roy argued that the water from the projects built in the second

[71] Based on interviews with state government officials; see also *The Statesman* (Calcutta), September 2, 1959, p. 6, for a discussion of official views.

[72] *DVC Annual Report, 1959-60*, p. 8; see also *The Statesman*, April 4, 1959, p. 10.

stage would be used for industries in Bihar and would thus diminish the supply of irrigation water for West Bengal. In fact, he argued that this was already happening and that "another dam would worsen the situation."[73] Confronted with a direct clash between the two states participating in the DVC project, the Minister of Irrigation and Power, acting for the central government, refused to take either side. He stated that he would "play the role of observer," and that "if Bihar and West Bengal can agree, then this Ministry will consent to that decision."[74]

Almost before the leaders of the West Bengal and Bihar state governments could meet to negotiate a solution, however, the unexpected happened. Beginning in late September of 1959, the level of the water began to rise, both in the Damodar River and in the DVC reservoirs, and the rains continued to be heavy in the area of the valley for almost one month. By October 4, 1959, a large portion of the state of West Bengal was under floods greater than any that had occurred in 100 years. According to central and state government estimates, an area of 10,983 square miles (one-third of West Bengal) was affected: eight districts were flooded for twelve days, and an area 50 miles long and 3 to 4 miles wide was under water for three weeks.[75] Almost one and a half million acres of paddy land, and 472,000 tons of rice, were submerged during this time. Flood relief was given to 2.3 million persons during and after the flood, and this was acknowledged by everyone concerned to be inadequate. It was estimated that a quarter of a million homes collapsed, and that more than 100 people (and 5,000 cattle) were killed. Communication lines and bridges were washed out, epidemics of disease were rampant, and people lived in trees. The whole of the Durgapur steel plant site was

[73] *Ibid.*, April 8, 1959, p. 7.

[74] *Ibid.*, September 2, 1959, p. 6.

[75] Figures taken from the *DVC Annual Report, 1959-60*; the *West Bengal Legislative Assembly Debates*, October 6, 1959; and the *Bihar Legislative Assembly Debates*, April 29, 1960.

submerged: the newly built channel for the supply of water to the plant was washed out, and the DVC power plant at Durgapur and a supplementary regulator were rendered useless. The estimated loss to the state was 100 crores of rupees, far more than the amount that would have been required to complete the second stage of the DVC project.

In reaction to such massive flood damage, a number of Indian leaders began to argue for the immediate commencement of the second stage projects. Three central government engineers were appointed by Prime Minister Nehru to undertake an investigation, and they quickly called for the construction of additional storage reservoirs on the Damodar and the expansion of those presently existing.[76] The Chief Engineer of the Corporation launched his own investigation and began to reappraise the Voorduin Committee recommendations, both to bring them up to date and possibly to find areas where they could be improved and expanded.[77] The Bihar Legislative Assembly passed a resolution calling for the completion of the project; and the only member of the Union cabinet from West Bengal (Law Minister Asok Sen) stated that he was going to use his "utmost influence personally" to see that the additional four dams were built.[78]

But, in the face of this pressure for the completion of the second stage of the project under the DVC, West Bengal's leading politicians effectively delayed. Snehengsu K. Acharyya, a leading Communist MLA, charged that the floods occurred because "persons who had no knowledge of West Bengal," had been placed in positions of authority in the DVC.[79] The Communist Party thus took the position that the floods were "man-made," and due to defective planning, unscientific and

[76] *The Statesman* (Calcutta), October 31, 1959, p. 11.

[77] B. Parthasarathy, "Appraisal of DVC Projects," *ibid.*, December 5, 1959, p. 8. Parthasarathy was at the time the Chief Engineer of the Corporation.

[78] Quoted *ibid.*, October 8, 1959, p. 7.

[79] *West Bengal Legislative Assembly Debates*, October 6, 1959.

unplanned release of water, and a neglect of drainage and afforestation measures on the part of the Corporation.[80] State Congress leaders neither agreed or disagreed with the Communist position, but used the charges of the Communists as justification for a state investigation of the circumstances surrounding the flood.[81]

The state Flood Inquiry Commission, not surprisingly, returned a report which attributed the floods to DVC negligence,[82] a finding directly contradicting the reports of two central government investigatory commissions.[83] Without going into all of the technical details, it is possible to state that the publication of the report by a state inquiry commission firmly established the position of the state government: West Bengal would not agree to the extension of the Damodar Val-

[80] Quoted from a news conference with Jyoti Basu, leader of the West Bengal Communist Party in the Legislative Assembly, *The Statesman* (Calcutta), October 13, 1959, p. 1.

[81] *Ibid.*, December 25, 1959, p. 11.

[82] The state Flood Inquiry Commission concluded that the flood had been caused by (1) lack of adequate soil cover; (2) the deterioration of drainage channels; and (3) the high tide levels of the Hooghly and Rupnarain. To prevent future floods, the state Commission argued that the DVC irrigation facilities should be transferred to state control to prevent further deterioration of the channels resulting from a lack of coordinated efforts by the DVC and the state; drainage channels in West Bengal should be improved by the construction of the Ganga Barrage and other state projects; and the amount of water used by the DVC for power generation should be diminished. The effect of these measures, of course, would be to cancel the second stage of the DVC project. See West Bengal, Ministry of Irrigation, Flood Inquiry Commission, *Report on the Damodar Valley Flood of 1959*, Sardar Mansingh, Chairman (Calcutta: West Bengal Government Press, 1960), pp. 43-46.

[83] One commission appointed at the center was made up of three engineers and reported directly to the Prime Minister; the other was the commission appointed by the Ministry of Irrigation and Power and chaired by S. D. Khungar. Both of these commissions recommended immediate commencement of the second stage of the project. See *The Statesman* (Calcutta), January 3, 1960, p. 1.

ley project. The position of the state government was also clear from the fact that the West Bengal representative on the Commission appointed by the Irrigation and Power Ministry to investigate the flood (the Khungar Commission) refused to sign the report on the ground that it was against the interests of his own state.

As a result of West Bengal's insistence that the additional four dams in the DVC network were not necessary for flood control, and despite the occurrence of the massive floods of 1959, the conflict between West Bengal and Bihar remain unresolved. Finally, a few months after the floods and at the time of the publication of the Khungar Commission Report, the central government found a solution acceptable to both states. The Minister of Irrigation and Power announced that: ". . . to enable the state governments to plan in advance for flood control, the Centre had decided to transfer flood control to the state sector from the Third Plan period."[84] This decision meant that West Bengal had again been allowed to veto central government proposals for extension of the DVC scheme. But, even more interesting in the present context is the fact that, in the conflict between Bihar and West Bengal, the center had stalled for time in making a decision and had eventually gone against all of the advice given by its personnel in an attempt to bring about a decision satisfactory to both of the state governments involved. For, while transferring flood control to the state sector for the "third-plan" period, and thereby granting the demands of West Bengal, the center had at the same time agreed to join with Bihar in supporting the large-scale DVC thermal power project at Chandrapura, thereby meeting the major demands of Bihar. Because of this arrangement, West Bengal was eventually able to sever almost all of its future connections with the DVC, while at the same

[84] *Ibid.*, December 30, 1959, p. 1; see also India (Republic), Ministry of Irrigation and Power, *Report of the Inquiry into the Damodar Valley Floods of 1959*, S. D. Khungar, Chairman (New Delhi: Government of India Press, 1960), p. 4.

time Bihar was assured that the DVC would provide the electricity benefits demanded by state leaders in Bihar.

Summary and Conclusions

Center-state relations in the present case study were similar in many respects to the relations described in the case of states reorganization. The central government again was involved in all of the negotiations that took place when attempting to allocate those benefits that would derive from the DVC project, and the power to make final decisions in all cases was vested in an agency of the center. But in every instance in which a major decision was reached, the decision itself consisted of concessions by the central government to state conceptions of state interests. This is most clear with regard to the irrigation benefits that were to be distributed by the DVC program. Here central government leadership groups agreed on a number of approved goals: (1) to work for the collection of the irrigation fees in an attempt to maintain the revenue position of the Corporation and provide for economy of operation and construction; (2) to prevent interference by cultivators in the planned operation of the irrigation channels; and (3) to promote community development and other projects that would teach cultivators the possible benefits that could accrue to them from double and triple-cropping and planned use of irrigation facilities. In the final analysis, however, these approved goals were set aside because they would have necessitated central coercion, and decisions were made on the basis of the choice that had been made by the cultivators and other state groups (with the support of the state party government).

Similarly with other aspects of the DVC project. The state government in fact drafted its own plans for power development, for the distribution of irrigation benefits, and for flood control schemes, and many of these were contradictory to those evolved by the DVC and supported by agencies of the central government. In the conflicts that resulted, the state did make some concessions to the center (and to Bihar), but it refused to implement all of them, and central lenders were reluctant to attempt to coerce the state into abandonment of independent courses of action. Rather than being forced to submit to centrally planned programs and policies, state leaders either pursued obstructionist tactics, or, in the words of Chief Minister B. C. Roy, tried to acquire "a little more strength to our elbow"[85]—by rallying state interests involved, by making extreme demands, and by other tactics.

In this case, too, the role of the state Congress party, and of the populace in a highly politicized state, was crucial in the determination of policy decisions. Indeed, the actions of the West Bengal Government in matters related to the development of DVC policies were for the most part a mere response to the wishes of state Congress party supporters and constituents. Thus, the state party worked against an enlarged DVC project in the initial stages of development when expansion would have entailed an extremely large expenditure in one area of the state (the Damodar Valley) to the neglect of other districts. Instead, the party sought to develop alternative power projects throughout the state in response to the demands of statewide potential users. With regard to other aspects of the DVC scheme, the state party assisted those cultivators in the valley who took water surreptitiously from DVC channels, even in those instances where such action interfered with the normal functioning of the entire DVC project; and the state party government eventually refused either to pay its dues to the Corporation or to cooperate in the planned expansion of the DVC project when it became clear that such expansion would entail either the unpopular collection of irrigation fees or the diversion of state revenues from other popular projects.

In those instances where central government leadership did try to persuade the state through the use of central powers— for example, when central funds were withheld from other West Bengal projects pending conformance by the state to pre-

[85] *West Bengal Legislative Assembly Debates,* III, No. 2 (March 9, 1951), 258-59.

vious agreements with the DVC—the state Congress party was effectively able to rally the populace in its own defense. Because the state party could so readily adopt the slogans and tactics of the leftist parties in the countryside, and because it could refuse to discipline dissident Congressmen who supported the cultivators in the Legislative Assembly (or who assisted in the building of illegal irrigation channels), the state party unit was able in fact to acquire the kind of "strength to the elbow" which B. C. Roy regarded as being necessary for the continuance of independent state action. Thus, despite the constitutional and legislative powers of the central government in this case, central party and governmental leaders frequently felt themselves completely lacking in effective political power,[86] with the result that they felt compelled to make substantial concessions to the wishes of state leaders.

[86] In the words of S. K. Patil, who was Minister of Irrigation and Power in the central cabinet when he made this statement: "If you tell me that if the Chief Minister of a particular place does not act in a correct manner, [and that] I must have a whip hand and do something about it, that is impossible. . . . They won't tolerate it for a day. . . . All we can do is, use our good offices, extend our good offices, smile a little more when they come and meet us and so on. That is all. We can't do more than that, or better than that. . . . Beyond that, we cannot go, we have no power."

· V I ·

Land Reform: The Absence of Consensus

MOST aspects of agricultural policy, and in particular those concerning land reform measures, are enumerated in the Indian Constitution among the legislative fields reserved to the states. The relationship between landlord and tenant, matters concerning the transfer and alienation of agricultural land, the collection of rents, land improvement and agricultural loans, colonization, water supplies and irrigation, agricultural education and research, duties in respect of succession to agricultural land, and taxation of lands, buildings, and agricultural income—all of these are specifically mentioned in the Constitution as falling within the purview of state legislation and administration.[1] In fact, if the central government has any real authority in the field of land reform, it stems only from the general fiscal powers of the center and from the strategic position of central leadership regarding amendments to the Constitution. The center can give or withdraw financial assistance to the states for the implementation of land reform schemes and for payment of compensation, and can thus conceivably promote or hinder state land reform programs.[2] Central leaders can also introduce constitutional amendments in the *Lok Sabha* and use the prestige and influence of their own offices to work for passage (three amendments to the Indian Constitution—the First, Fourth, and Seventeenth—are concerned with land reform matters).[3] But both of these are,

[1] Konrad Bekker, "Land Reform Legislation in India," *The Middle East Journal*, v, No. 3 (Summer 1951), 323.

[2] A. N. Vij, "Financial Aspects of the Abolition of Zamindari," *Reserve Bank of India Bulletin* (Bombay), IV (June 1950), 389.

[3] For a detailed review of the first fourteen amendments, and the process of amendment, see M. Ramaswamy, "The Indian Constitutional Amendments," *Indian Yearbook of International Affairs*, Vol. XII (1963), ed. T. S. Rama Tao (Madras: The Indian Study Group of International Law, University of Madras, 1963), pp. 161-91.

of course, limited constitutional powers, and neither of them can be used in all conceivable situations.

While land reform is a state subject it is, however, also one on which the Congress party had developed a clear, fairly detailed, and almost irrevocable policy even before Independence.[4] Congress (and especially some Congress leaders) became committed to a program of agrarian reform under Gandhi's leadership, and the nature of this program was elaborated in the Congress Resolution on Fundamental Rights at Karachi in 1930, at the Congress Kisan Conference held at Allahabad in 1935, and at numerous other party meetings, large and small. As Brecher has pointed out, the pledge of agrarian reform was in no small way responsible for the victory of the Congress party in the 1937 Provincial elections, and for the creation of a party capable of arousing mass interest and participation. These facts were recognized by a number of Indian leaders who came to power in an Independent India in 1947.[5] The desire on the part of these men to undertake a program of nationwide land reform was indicated by Prime Minister Nehru in his numerous pronouncements on the subject immediately following Independence, of which the following is representative:

> One of the main causes of social instability in many parts of the world, more especially in Asia, is agrarian discontent due to the continuance of systems of land tenure which are completely out of place in the modern world. In a country of [sic] which agriculture is still the principal industry, land reform is essential not only for the well-being and contentment of the individual, but also for the stability of society.[6]

[4] The background of Congress land reform policy is traced in Susanne Hoeber Rudolph, *Some Aspects of Congress Land Reform Policy* (Cambridge: Center for International Studies, Massachusetts Institute of Technology, 1957), pp. 1-17.

[5] Michael Brecher, *Nehru: A Political Biography* (London: Oxford University Press, 1959), p. 229.

[6] Quoted from a speech made in Washington, D.C., October 13, 1949.

Committed to agrarian reform, but lacking the constitutional power to carry it through, Nehru and other Union leaders found themselves in a highly frustrating position in the emerging post-Independence federal system. On the one hand, they could advocate constitutional changes that permitted greater scope to Union activities in this field, or they could work in disregard of constitutional arrangements. But neither of these were very realistic alternatives. On the other hand, if they allowed constituent units free rein in those instances where they pursued policies and programs divergent from those elaborated at the all-India level, the possibilities for instituting effective reform rapidly diminished.

In large part, of course, the question of what some central leaders wanted to do about land reform is academic, for neither central or state political leadership was agreed on reform strategy. In the absence of such a strategy, land reform policy, at least in West Bengal, was left to the pushes and pulls of political forces within the state. Lacking constitutional power, and lacking the support of influential colleagues, men like Prime Minister Nehru were relatively powerless in their attempts to persuade powerful state political leaders to adopt their personal predilections on the land reform question. State political leaders, in turn, were forced to experiment, research, and negotiate within their own states until such time that they themselves could be relatively certain about the nature of the wide variety of divergent viewpoints that obtained on the land question.

Constitution-Making and the Lack of Consensus

One of the first situations in which India's national leadership exhibited their differences on land reform was that which arose when drafting the Constitution of the Republic. Here it

See *The Washington Post*, October 14, 1949, p. 3. See also Nehru's Independence day speech of August 15, 1947, in which he placed a high priority on radical agrarian reforms, Brecher, p. 358.

was to be decided whether the center or the states would have power over matters that would affect reform, and this would in turn determine the basic policy orientations of both Union and state governments for the future. In this instance, the framers chose to set themselves against the alternative of coercing the states: they refused to amend the Constitution in favor of central dominance[7] or to adopt policies that envisaged Union activity outside a constitutional framework, and they refused to enact precise and unambiguous constitutional definitions on all matters concerning property rights.

The decision by the Constituent Assembly to grant to the states far-reaching constitutional authority in the field of land reform was the result of several factors, but was made with little consideration of other alternatives. The Indian Dominion was being governed between August 1947 and January 1950, by the Government of India Act, 1935, under the terms of which matters related to land tenure were relegated to the Provincial Legislative List.[8] Since several provinces (Assam,

---

[7] As mentioned above, the Constitution was later amended three times in the *Lok Sabha*, but in none of the three cases was central dominance over state legislatures intended. The First Amendment (1951) placed certain land reform laws above challenge by the Courts; the Fourth Amendment (1955) "made a wider range of laws immune from such [judicial] challenge and declared that they shall not be deemed to be void on the ground that they are inconsistent with, or take away or abridge any of the Fundamental Rights conferred [elsewhere in the Constitution]." See Alexandrowicz, *Constitutional Development in India*, p. 93. The Seventeenth Amendment redefined the word "Estate" as used in the Constitution, in order that the existing constitutional provisions would explicitly apply to the *ryotwari* areas in the south and west, as well as to the northern *zamindari* areas. For a review of the First and Fourth amendments, see Trimbak Krishna Tope, *The Constitution of India* (Bombay: Popular Prakashan, 1963), p. 518. The Seventeenth Amendment is reviewed in *The Statesman* (Calcutta), May 28, 1964, p. 1, and June 21, 1964, p. 6. The issues that led to amendment are discussed in Alexandrowicz, pp. 80-94.

[8] For an analysis of the provisions dealing with land tenure in the 1935 Constitution, see Arthur Berriedale Keith, *A Constitutional His-*

Bihar, Bombay, Madras, Punjab, and the U.P.), and some Part B and Part C states had already passed land reform laws in 1947, 1948, and 1949 (under the 1935 Act),[9] a change in constitutional provisions would have called into question the authority of these laws and created only chaos and confusion in these states. Moreover, subjects relating to land tenure had been delegated to provincial lists in 1935 in consideration of the confusing diversity of land tenure systems throughout India on the grounds that central government legislation in the face of this diversity would have been extremely confusing and time-consuming, if not impossible, to carry out. No matter how desirous some members of the new government were to reform the agrarian structure, the reasoning of the drafters of the 1935 Act was still relevant; it would only have complicated matters far more than was conceivably tolerable in 1947-50 if subjects pertaining to land tenure were placed under central authority. Finally, of course, it is also likely that the center would have encountered considerable opposition from the states if it had attempted to transfer land matters from the provincial to the central lists, but, in lieu of other considerations, this question did not arise.

Instead of seeking a change in the structure of constitutional authority, the Constituent Assembly thus accepted the provisions of the 1935 Act regarding the allocation of power to the states, and proceeded to construct constitutional provisions that would determine in broad outline the contemplated pattern of reform. Here the framers committed themselves to a policy of *reform through law*, a policy defended by Nehru himself before the Constituent Assembly:

There are some honourable Members here who, at the

---

tory of India, 1600-1935 (London: Methuen and Co., 1936), pp. 254-55, 371.

[9] A list of those laws passed by state legislatures prior to 1950 appears in M. L. Dantwala, "Land Reforms in India," *International Labour Review*, LXVI (July-December 1952), 442-43.

very outset, were owners of land, owners of zamindaries. Naturally they feel that their interests might be affected by this land legislation. But I think that the way this land legislation is being dealt with today . . . is a better way and a juster way, from their point of view, than any other way that is going to come later. That way may not be any process of legislation. The land question may be settled differently.[10]

Like the delegation of powers over land reform to the states, the adoption of a policy advocating reform through legislative action was also adopted largely out of necessity, rather than being a deliberate or calculated choice of the center. The Union government was committed to a rule of law, and it was inconceivable that it would have attempted to effect land reform by administrative fiat or by other nonconstitutional means.[11]

While the delegation of authority to the states and the adoption of a policy embedded in a rule of law were both decisions that presented central leadership groups little or no alternative, there were at least two other opportunities where some observers saw a possibility for the constitution-makers to influence future land reform programs. First, the Constituent Assembly was faced with the task of striking some kind of balance between (1) "the freedom to acquire, hold and dispose of property (one of the seven fundamental freedoms to be guaranteed in the Constitution)," and (2) the restrictions which the state would impose on this freedom in the interest of future land reform measures. By influencing the wording of the Constitution, the framers could conceivably have played a part in tilting the balance either in favor of an individual's

[10] India (Dominion), *Constituent Assembly Debates*, IX, No. 31 (September 10, 1949), 1195.

[11] The decision to pursue land reform by legislative action is discussed in Richard Morse, "Land Tenure and Indian Society," *Far Eastern Survey*, XIX, No. 22 (December 1950), 237ff.

right to property, thereby lessening the scope for governmental reform, or, alternatively, weighting the Constitution in favor of restrictions on the right to property, thereby facilitating the possibility of governmental reform. Moreover, the decision of the framers in this instance could then have been either strengthened or weakened by a second decision, that which concerned the extent to which the courts would be allowed to interfere in agrarian reform matters. If the courts were allowed considerable freedom to review state land reform laws and the constitutional provisions pertaining to property rights, the progress or implementation of land reform programs would invariably be slowed down by litigation. The alternative before the Constituent Assembly was thus to limit the freedom of the courts, and thereby facilitate the implementation of any state laws that were passed.

Here, the lack of any kind of agreement on a policy on land reform at this time made it all but inevitable that the framers would not take an unqualified or affirmative stand on either of these crucial issues. With regard to property rights, the constitution-makers did guarantee in Article 19, the right of citizens "to acquire, hold and dispose of property," but they then made this right subject to "reasonable restrictions . . . in the interest of the general public."[12] In Article 31 they laid down the basic principle that "no person should be deprived of property save by authority of law," but they then empowered the state to acquire property "for public purposes and provide for compensation."[13] In light of the phraseology of these two articles, the weight of the Constitution rested neither with protection of private property nor with the power of the state to interfere with property rights. In fact, attempts to weight the Constitution, in favor of either one or the other of these alternatives, were defeated in the Constituent Assembly as a result of decisions effected by the high command. For example, when Prime Minister Nehru sought to insert in

[12] Alexandrowicz, p. 53.   [13] Ibid., p. 81.

Article 31 a clause that would have empowered the state to acquire property without compensation (thus putting the weight of the Constitution behind state interference in property rights), he was dissuaded by the threat of an open contest on ideological grounds by both Vallabhai Patel and Govind Ballabh Pant.[14] Similarly, when some Congressmen tried to insert the words "just" or "adequate" before the word "compensation" in Article 31 (thus putting the weight of the Constitution squarely behind private property rights), their motion was defeated by the interference of Nehru and some members of his Cabinet.[15]

The result was that the final draft of the Constitution turned out to be remarkably vague on questions concerning the power of the state to interfere in property rights. Moreover, the view that was finally adopted by the Constituent Assembly was consciously ambiguous, having first been outlined by Sir Alladi Krishnaswami Ayer in a detailed explanation submitted to the Assembly on the behalf of government. Sir Alladi recognized the rights of individuals to hold, acquire and dispose of property, but he also stated that: "Our ancestors never regarded the institution of property as an end in itself. Property exists for Dharma. . . . Dharma is the law of social well-being . . . capitalism is alien to the root idea of our civilization."[16] On the basis of this reasoning, Sir Alladi argued that the adequacy or fairness of compensation "must be viewed in the light of two supreme considerations, i.e., the protection of private property and the welfare of the community which postulates social and economic reform."[17] Since it was decided that the state should aim at *both* the protection of private property *and* an equitable distribution of wealth, the wording of the Constitution was necessarily left sufficiently vague and ambiguous to allow for future choice between the two alternatives. On the one hand there was no absolute con-

[14] This was explained some years later by Dr. Ambedkar in the Rajya Sabha *Debates,* ix, No. 19 (March 19, 1955), 2451.

[15] Alexandrowicz, p. 82.   [16] Quoted *ibid.*   [17] *Ibid.*

stitutional guarantee of private property, although there was some guarantee nonetheless; and, on the other, room was left open for reform, but no clear lead was given to the states regarding the nature of that reform.

Similarly, with regard to judicial review of land reform legislation, the Constitution allowed for ambiguous interpretation. A clause was inserted prohibiting judicial action regarding clause 2 of Article 31 (that the state could acquire property for public purposes and must provide for some compensation), but it did not prohibit judicial review of other aspects of the Constitution relating to property rights. The Constitution thus discouraged court cases that could delay land reform programs, but with regard only to the *principle* of state acquisition and the question of the legitimacy of compensation. It was still possible, as the following pages will indicate, for individuals to delay land reform in the states by contesting other sections of the Constitution in the courts.[18]

The inability of central government leaders to agree, and their consequent desire to remain uncommitted to any one approach on the question of reform was a reflection of the wide area of disagreement within the Congress party at this time. For, while the Congress had developed a fairly detailed program for land reform in the course of the nationalist movement, not all sections of the party were in agreement with that program after Independence was achieved. The differences between Nehru, Patel, and Pant over the question of property rights has already been alluded to, and these differences were shared by the party rank-and-file. In fact, when the party appointed an Economic Program Committee, with Prime Minister Nehru as Chairman, the recommendations of the committee which pertained to land reform failed to gain complete acceptance at the Annual Session of the Congress which met

[18] Nehru himself acknowledged that his government had not sought to eliminate entirely the possibility of judicial review in his speech summarizing the planned effects of the *Constitution*. See *Constituent Assembly Debates*, IX, No. 31 (September 19, 1949), 1196.

at Jaipur in December 1948.[19] Similarly, the Report of the Congress Agrarian Reforms Committee (1948), which received either written or oral evidence from almost 600 Congressmen scattered across the subcontinent, was never formally approved by the party hierarchy, and the party was never formally committed to its recommendations.[20]

As a result of party disunity, the constitutional provisions enacted in 1949 did not envisage large-scale central government interference in matters concerning land reform. Nor did they give a clear and unambiguous lead to the states on questions concerning the nature of reform and the speed with which laws should be enacted. If any specific policy was intended by the constitution-makers it was one that envisaged state control over land reform measures, adopted by "evolutionary methods," and allowing for a lengthy period of trial and error.[21]

Faced with the enormous diversity and complexity of land patterns that exist in India, and with a tradition vesting authority in this sphere to regional governments, most Congressmen felt that there was little or no alternative to such a policy, unless it would be one pursued outside of a democratic framework and a rule of law. And, it was in this light that a policy of "evolutionary methods" was defended. In the words of M. L. Dantwala, a member of the Congress Agrarian Reforms Committee,

There is no doubt whatever that, judged as an attempt at democratic and peaceful change and the improvement of the socio-economic conditions within agriculture, what is being undertaken in India has few parallels in history. . . . The only relevant question is . . . whether this is the most that

[19] H. D. Malaviya, *Land Reforms in India* (New Delhi: All-India Congress Committee, 1954), p. 81.

[20] *Ibid.*, p. 83.

[21] M. L. Dantwala, "India's Progress in Agrarian Reforms," *Far Eastern Survey*, XIX, No. 22 (December 1950), 243.

can be done. Would a quicker pace or a more radical content necessitate abandonment of the democratic process and, if so, should it be abandoned? No unequivocal answer to these questions will be expected here and now. It is enough if they are constantly present before men of intelligence and goodwill.[22]

In a similar vein, Prime Minister Nehru told the Constituent Assembly:

The House has to keep in mind the transitional and the revolutionary aspects of the problem, because, when you think of the land question in India today, you are thinking of something which is dynamic, moving, changing and revolutionary. These may well change the face of India either way; whether you deal with it or do not deal with it, it is not a static thing. It is something which is not entirely, absolutely within the control of law and Parliaments . . . if law and Parliaments do not fit themselves into the changing picture, they cannot control the situation completely. . . . If you look at the situation (in this way) nothing is more important and vital than a gradual reform.[23]

Party Involvement and Party Disunity

While the Constituent Assembly was unable to give a clear constitutional lead to the states in 1947-49, party policy-makers did not immediately abandon the hope of influencing in significant ways state land reform programs. Indeed, shortly after the attainment of Independence, acting Congress President Rajendra Prasad convened a "Conference of the Revenue Ministers of the States" at New Delhi to discuss the possibilities of achieving some degree of national uniformity and enactment of significant reforms, and this conference did pro-

[22] M. L. Dantwala, "Land Reforms in India," *International Labour Review*, LXVI (July-December 1952), 442.
[23] *Constituent Assembly Debates*, IX, No. 31 (September 10, 1949), 1195.

duce a small area of consensus. In the words of a Congress historian,

> The general consensus of opinion at the Conference was that the system of intermediaries having come into existence in the different States at different times, and there being a great divergence in the conditions, background, etc., of the landlord system from State to State, they should be free to deal with the question of abolition of the system in accordance with their peculiar circumstances. It was, however, felt that a great deal of uniformity was possible in the post-abolition land reforms.[24]

The work of this conference pointed to the minimal areas of agreement among Congressmen in 1947: first, a belief that uniformity in land reform policy was possible despite the diversity of the land tenure systems prevailing in different provinces; and second, that both abolition of the old system and uniformity in the reformed system were desirable. The obvious difficulty at this point was that which arose when attempting to state the uniform pattern of development that land reform would take. And, in order to overcome this difficulty, the conference unanimously agreed to the formation of a Congress Agrarian Reforms Committee, empowered to act as both a "fact-finding and policy-making" body.[25]

The work of the Congress Agrarian Reforms Committee (ARC) was a major attempt by the party leadership to define a far-reaching, but nationally standardized, agrarian reform policy: the ARC Report was comprehensive in scope, based on systematically gathered evidence of party feeling throughout India, and concerned primarily with the search for patterns of uniformity. The reasons for its comprehensive character, its meticulous attention to detail, and its concern for standardization, is indicated in the Report itself: "The Committee

[24] Malaviya, *Land Reforms in India*, pp. 81-82.

[25] Indian National Congress, *Report of the Agrarian Reforms Committee* (New Delhi: All-India Congress Committee, 1949), p. 4.

would request the Indian National Congress to look upon its set of recommendations not as isolated pieces but as a single integrated pattern. One can neither appreciate nor implement them in parts. Some of them are, no doubt, of a fundamental character. But fundamental problems can never be tackled by patch work reforms."[26] In the eyes of the Committee, then, it had chosen to cover the entire range of agrarian matters, from those concerning the abolition of intermediaries to those dealing with agricultural marketing and crop insurance, in order to achieve effective (or "fundamental") land reform legislation.

Regarding "land reform" proper,[27] the ARC Report was an attempt to build on previous Congress agrarian programs while coming to grips with the differences of opinion prevailing within the party after Independence. The Report argued that "the existing pattern of agrarian economy is so complex and the problems which it has to face are so variegated that no single uniform method of land utilisation can meet the requirements of the situation."[28] What the Report therefore recommended was a policy that allowed for the possibility of numerous types of land tenure systems, all guided by a set of

[26] *Ibid.*, p. 13.

[27] In this case study, "land reform" will be distinguished from "agrarian reform" on the basis of a distinction made by Frank J. Moore in his discussion of S. Thirumalai, *Post-War Agricultural Problems and Policies in India* (New York: Institute of Pacific Relations, 1954): "Thirumalai defines land reform as '. . . the reform measures relating to land tenure, ownership, tenancy and other aspects closely and directly related to them such as the status of agricultural labor, i.e., the measures affecting the relations among persons having some interest in land.' The term agrarian reform '. . . connotes all measures that are necessary to raise agricultural efficiency.' These measures include land reform, but refer more specifically to changes directly affecting techniques of production, such as the development of irrigation, technology, rural credit facilities and methods of farm management." See Frank J. Moore, "Land Reform and Social Justice in India," *Far Eastern Survey*, xxiv, No. 8 (August 1955), 127.

[28] *Report of the Agrarian Reforms Committee*, p. 8.

basic principles (in the Committee's words, "variety in form
. . . unity in idea"). These principles were stated as follows:

(i)   The agrarian economy should provide an opportunity
      for the development of the farmer's personality.
(ii) There should be no scope for exploitation of one class
      by another.
(iii) There should be maximum efficiency of production.
(iv) The scheme of reforms should be within the realm
      of practicability.[29]

Attempting to remain consistent with these principles, the
Committee recommended four major policy positions: (1)
that subletting of land should be prohibited by law (except in
the case of widows, minors, and other disabled persons); (2)
that the state should guarantee permanent, transferable, and
heritable rights of cultivation to the cultivators; (3) that ceilings should be imposed by the state on the amount of land
that could be held by any one person; and (4) that the state
should encourage both cooperative and collective farming for
cultivators with uneconomic holdings.

For a variety of reasons, the ARC Report was not received
with enthusiasm. The most frequently stated criticisms of the
Report stemmed from two factors. First, the Committee, in its
declaration of principles, argued that its recommendations
would produce social justice and effect an increase in agricultural production as well, but many individuals were conscious
of the possibility that these two things might not be com-
patible. In the eyes of West Bengal Development Commissioner S. K. Dey, for example, they were clearly at odds one
with the other:

> What are we really after? Is it a more equitable distribu-
> tion of property in arable land and its income? Or, is it the
> maximum extraction of value from the production factor
> which this land represents? The unstated assumption in

[29] *Ibid.*

most discussions of the subject is that these two aims are identical. This is not necessarily true. In our current circumstances, this is patently untrue. Equity in distribution can have material significance only when there is substance to distribute. Our over-riding need is effecting an increase in that substance.[30]

It was on the basis of sentiments like these that a conference of state Agricultural Ministers rejected the ARC Report shortly after it was submitted to the party, on the ground that "no ceiling should be put to land holding if that would lower production."[31] Similarly, partisans either of social justice or of increased agricultural production also took sides on other recommendations of the ARC, with the result that its report was the object of opprobrium for both parties to numerous disputes.[32]

But the ARC Report was also unacceptable to many Congressmen because it advocated far-reaching changes in the administrative structure that was to deal with land reform matters, and these recommendations were unacceptable to many state governments. In the words of the Report, the Committee "strongly believes . . . that the present system of administration pertaining to the various aspects of land use and management is very faulty."[33] It therefore sought to create a "functional," or "single and integrated machinery," in place of the decentralized "political approach to land administration."[34] At the apex of this machinery there was to be a statu-

[30] S. K. Dey, "The Perspective of Land Reform," *The Statesman* (Calcutta), August 5, 1952, p. 11.

[31] S. K. Basu and S. K. Bhattacharya, *Land Reform in West Bengal: A Study of Implementation* (Calcutta: Oxford University Press, 1963), p. 8.

[32] For other conflicts of this nature, see Moore, "Land Reform and Social Justice in India," *Far Eastern Survey,* xxiv, No. 8 (August 1955), 124-28.

[33] *Report of the Agrarian Reforms Committee,* p. 11.

[34] *Ibid.*

tory Central Land Commission "whose primary duty would be to evolve an all-India scheme for crop-planning and allocate scarce resources according to priorities."[35] Subordinate to the Central Land Commission would be a number of Provincial Land Commissions, as well as a "Rural Economic Civil Service," to execute the Commissions' recommendations. In the summary of its report the ARC concluded that "Agrarian Reforms Commissioners with necessary powers should be immediately appointed both at the Central and Provincial levels."[36]

Because a Central Land Commission, vested with sweeping powers over the administration of land reform measures, would have infringed on the constitutional authority of the states in this sphere, it was rejected by state leaders[37] and by the Congress party as well. Recognizing the difficulties inherent in the recommendations of the ARC Report, the party's Working Committee refused to place the report before the Annual Congress Session or the AICC,[38] the two Congress organs most representative of party feeling, and instead appointed an Economic Planning Subcommittee, with Govind Ballabh Pant as Chairman, to draw up an alternative program on agriculture and agrarian reforms.[39] While the recommendations of the ARC were not entirely disregarded in future party pronouncements, its Report was never officially approved by the Congress party.

The Memorandum that was prepared by the WC Economic Planning Subcommittee was less massive in scope than the Report of the ARC, but it was more consciously drafted with a sympathetic eye to individual state differences and problems. It suggested that land reform be pursued in stages, the first stage aiming at the abolition of intermediaries in the land tenure system, and the other stages being pursued according to

[35] *Ibid.*   [36] *Ibid.*, p. 13.
[37] See, for example, the speech by B. C. Roy in *West Bengal Legislative Assembly Debates*, I, No. 2 (March 6, 1950), 43-45.
[38] Malaviya, *Land Reforms in India*, p. 83.
[39] *Ibid.*, p. 89.

the progress made by individual constituent units. This Memorandum was then submitted to a Conference of Chief Ministers and PCC presidents, convened by the Congress president in April 1950.[40] On the basis of this Memorandum, and the comments made by the state leaders at the April Conference, a resolution on "Agriculture and Agrarian Reforms" was then drafted and placed before the Annual Congress Session. This resolution indicated the minimal consensus that could be obtained by the party hierarchy at this time: it called only for the abolition of "zamindari and *malguzari* systems by paying compensation, if necessary," and for state laws providing for fixity of tenure to the tiller.[41] It remained vague on the more controversial issues that had arisen between political leaders, both at the central and state levels: the amount of compensation to be paid, the mode in which it would be paid (in kind, in cash, or in bonds), the question of ceilings on land holdings, and the nature of tenancy rights. It also said nothing of the role of the center, and allowed almost complete freedom for individual state differences.[42]

As a result of the experiences of the Congress party, first with the Report of the Agrarian Reforms Committee and then with the WC Economic Planning Subcommittee, it became evident by 1950 that no uniform land policy could be effected on the basis of a broad party consensus. Yielding to the implications of this reality, the central organs of the party began to sidestep the land reform question by speaking of a "phased program," which envisaged reform in stages, and by settling on a policy of "evolutionary methods" that allowed for future experiment at the state level.

Divisions within West Bengal

At the state level, West Bengal was perhaps in a better position than most states to undertake land reform legislation, if only because of the large volume of information and experi-

[40] *Ibid.*   [41] *Ibid.*, p. 90.   [42] *Ibid.*, pp. 89-90.

ence that had been gained by previous reform efforts. After the Permanent Settlement of 1793, attempts had been made by the provincial administration and legislature—in 1859, 1885, 1928, 1930, 1938-39, and 1940—either to enact new legislation or to amend prior administrative acts in an effort to achieve generally desired reforms. In addition, the Bengal Rent Commission of 1880 and the Bengal Land Revenue (Floud) Commission of 1940 had both undertaken elaborate surveys of the agrarian structure, and both had made detailed recommendations for proposed change.

But the experience of previous policy-makers had indicated a number of difficulties inherent in attempts to reform the structure of the agrarian society of Bengal, from both the point of view of social justice and that of production efficiency, and many recommendations (frequently contradictory) had been made in the past. From this great body of literature, the two principal recommendations of the 1940 Floud Commission occupied the attention of both government and observers of the state's economy after Independence. The first of these proposals called for the abolition of the Permanent Settlement system entirely. In the words of the Floud Commission: ". . . the Permanent Settlement and the zamindari system should be replaced by a raiyatwari system, under which the Government will be brought into direct relations with the actual cultivators by the acquisition of all the superior interests in agricultural land."[43] In this view, the government would become the "sole landlord" in West Bengal, with all cultivators paying their rent directly to the state. Absentee landlords would be divested of their lands by government, unless they were willing to cultivate them personally, and the numerous intermediaries between the cultivator and the state would also be eliminated. With the state as "sole landlord," the Floud Commission argued, "Government . . . would be in a very much stronger position . . . to initiate schemes for the consolidation of holdings, the

[43] *Report of the Land Revenue Commission*, Bengal, I, 41.

restoration of economic holdings, the provision of grazing land, and the prevention of transfers of land to non-agriculturists."[44]

The second major proposal made by the Floud Commission was one designed to eliminate the sharecropping (*barga*) system so prevalent in West Bengal. Under this system, the *bargadar* (sharecropper) had provided all of the implements, seed, fertilizers, bullocks, and other paraphernalia necessary for harvests, as well as all of the necessary labor. In return he received a share of the proceeds of the crop (usually one-half), with the rest going to the *zamindar* and other intermediaries with superior rights. In this system, the most that the *bargadar* could usually attain was a surplus that allowed him to feed and clothe his family, but his dependence—on a good price for his crops, on the vagaries of the weather, and on the good will of the landlord—made his position extremely insecure. The Floud Commission had sought the elimination of the *barga* system by recommending that *bargadars* be regarded as tenants, with definite rights to the property they worked,[45] and that their rents be reduced from one-half of the produce to one-third.[46]

In the recommendations of the Floud Commission report, then, absentee landlords and intermediaries would be eliminated by state acquisition of *zamindari* estates; working peasants would gain security of tenure by being placed directly under the state (the "sole landlord"); and a large number of cultivating laborers (the *bargadars*) would be raised to the legal status of working peasants. The result would be a fairly uniform agrarian structure, with most peasants holding land directly under the state and secure in their rights of tenure.

While the state government expressed a "general acceptance" of the recommendations of the Floud Commission, it preferred to proceed slowly with legislation. It was repeatedly emphasized by state government Ministers that, while they

---

[44] *Ibid.*   [45] *Ibid.*, 73.   [46] *Ibid.*, 69.

had accepted the principle of *zamindari* abolition, three "difficulties" stood in the way of immediate enactment.[47] The first of these difficulties was one that had plagued reform measures in the past, and which occupied the attention of policy-makers in other states in the post-Independence years. This involved the legal questions associated with reform: questions concerning the wording of the planned legislation, its constitutional legitimacy, and its likely fate in the courts of law. Referring to this aspect of the land problem, B. C. Roy argued in 1950 that his government had not submitted a bill to the legislature because: ". . . the matter is in the hands of the lawyers. They are investigating into this matter for the purpose of getting proper legislation done."[48]

The second difficulty facing the West Bengal Government was financial in nature, revolving for the most part around the question of paying compensation to those *zamindars* and other intermediaries that would be dispossessed by the impending legislation. Since the state had the power to determine the amount of compensation that would be paid to those landlords that were dispossessed, and since the state would also have to pay such compensation from its own treasury, this was a question requiring the most careful consideration.

In light of the likely financial burden of compensation, there were proposals for the abolition of *zamindari* without compensation, but these were quickly rejected by the government in light of other considerations. As Land Revenue Minister Bimal Chandra Sinha pointed out in 1950:

> When speaking of the abolition of rent-receiving interests without compensation, we should bear in mind that we are taking away the assets of not only the big landlords but also the vast multitude of the middle-class people. Therefore

---

[47] These are set forth explicitly by state Land Revenue Minister Bimal Chandra Sinha in the *West Bengal Legislative Assembly Debates*, I, No. 2 (March 6, 1950), 45.

[48] *Ibid.*, 44.

it is not easy nor is it desirable to rush to hasty conclusions in the matter, because it is not only a legal and financial question, but is also a question of economic adjustment.[49]

This points to the third difficulty mentioned by Sinha, that the state government was extremely wary of adversely affecting significant sections of the state population. As Rosen has recently pointed out, some few large intermediaries in India in the immediate post-Independence years were absentee landlords, men who had often been pro-British or pro-prince (or at least anti-Congress), and considered by almost everyone concerned as people who performed no economic function.[50] From the beginning, there was no question about the need to do away with this group of intermediaries, since abolition here would produce no political or economic tensions in the state. On other reform measures, however, there was a distinct lack of agreement among the other larger segments of the population as to the desirability of specific reforms: "Those who were the intermediaries would obviously suffer directly by the loss of their rights, although the amount of the loss would vary with the importance of these rights. Those who had rented land to tenants were not in favor of reducing rent; those who hired farm labor were not in favor of directly raising the wages of their laborers."[51] The position of the West Bengal Government, in the face of a divided and relatively unmobilized populace on the land reform issue, was also complicated by the fact that, before Independence and immediately following, it had depended on property holders for party support. As Morris-Jones has pointed out, the Congress organization created by Gandhi had, between the two World Wars, established "a large and firm following among the middle and lower classes of the medium and smaller district

[49] *Ibid.*, 45.
[50] George Rosen, *Democracy and Economic Change in India* (Berkeley: University of California Press, 1966), p. 142.
[51] *Ibid.*

towns,"[52] and, in West Bengal, a large portion of this middle class depended on its property interests for social position.[53] Since the party had never contested an election that was not restricted to property holders, it had no clear idea as to the consequences that might flow from radical agrarian reform in an electoral system based on universal adult franchise. One alternative open to the party government was thus to risk the alienation of its past supporters through radical reforms, in the hope that a larger base of support could be gained by appealing to the cultivators who would benefit by such reform. The other alternative, and the one that was finally adopted in West Bengal, envisaged the framing of land reform measures in a manner favorable to previous Congress supporters, in the hope that the cultivating peasants would not revolt or defect *en masse* to the opposition. The reasons for the adoption of this latter policy and the role of center-state relations in the evolution of this policy are the subjects of the next chapter.

[52] Morris-Jones, *Government and Politics of India*, p. 30.

[53] Myron Weiner, "Notes on Political Development in West Bengal," in *Political Change in South Asia* (Calcutta: Firma K. L. Mukhopadhyay, 1963), p. 323.

Center-State Relations and the Development of a Land Reform Policy for West Bengal

CONFRONTED in the early years of Independence with a divided, but unmobilized population on the land reform issue, the West Bengal Government contented itself until 1953 with temporary measures, designed to test the possible consequences of various reforms. One of these was undertaken in 1948, and concerned the preparation of elaborate records of land rights, analysis of numerous village records, and the collection of countless pieces of evidence from a variety of individuals in one area (the Sundarbans) in the southern part of the state. In the words of the Chief Minister, the intention of the state government was to:

> ... take up the area of Sundarbans, either the whole of it or a large part of it, and see whether it is possible to give to the tiller of the soil the full proprietorship of the land and, if so, on what conditions. And secondly, whether we can pass any such legislation that the tiller of the soil does not become again a miniature landlord; and if that experiment proves successful we have got to pass it on to the neighbouring areas.[1]

A second measure was the Bargadars Act of 1950, which, on the ground that it was a temporary measure, stated specifically that it did not provide for anything in the way of a landlord-tenant relationship between the "owners" and the *bargadars*. What the act did do was to provide for government *Bhag-Chas* Conciliation Boards, empowered to effect settlements in cases of disputes between *bargadars* and landlords; and to har-

---

[1] *West Bengal Legislative Assembly Debates*, 1, No. 2 (March 6, 1950), 44.

vest or thresh crops when disputes prevented this being done.[2]

The Response to Early Postponement

The effect of these measures was to postpone any kind of far-reaching land reform legislation, pending the resolution of the "difficulties" felt by the state government and the outcome of its experiment in the Sundarbans area. To those who argued for an immediate government bill, or at least some promise of swift action, the government replied in the manner of Mohini Mohan Barman, Minister of Land Revenue in 1948:

> Wait for a few years. We have already drawn up our scheme, the financial implications of which is under examination. . . . Our preliminary work has already been started in the Sundarbans area where we are reviewing the record of rights. . . . I assure this House that although we are faced with many urgent problems arising out of the partition of the province we are determined to put through our scheme of abolition of the zamindary system at an early date. We are going to introduce the Bill as soon as possible.[3]

Despite the assurances of state government personnel that far-reaching reform would be forthcoming, postponement of land reform was severely criticized, both by the political opposition within the state and by some central government and party leaders. Within West Bengal, the most severe criticism of postponement was made by members of the Marxist-left and Communist parties. These parties were united in advocating immediate reforms, designed to eliminate all *zamindars* and other intermediaries (with either no compensation, or only token payment), and to redistribute land among the tillers. Postponement of reforms was interpreted by the leftists as an

[2] The Act is analyzed in Govindlal D. Patel, *The Indian Land Problem and Legislation* (Bombay: N. M. Tripathi, 1954), pp. 289ff.; see also Thorner, *The Agrarian Prospect in India*, p. 33.

[3] *West Bengal Legislative Assembly Debates*, II, No. 2 (March 15, 1948), 133.

indication that the Congress party of West Bengal was contemplating little or no reform, and as a sign that the Congress had "sold out" to the landholders in the state. In the words of the leader of the CPI legislative party: "The Chief necessity today, as has been recognised by the Congress (at the center), by everybody in fact in the country, is the abolition of the zamindary system . . . but we find that there is no such attempt worth the name which is being made for the abolition of the zamindary system, probably because the gentlemen sitting opposite have started representing this very class. . . ."[4] In an attempt to force the quick enactment of far-reaching legislation, the CPI had in fact launched a revolutionary movement designed to overthrow the newly independent government immediately after Independence, as a result of which many leftists were jailed, and the CPI was banned until 1951. After 1951, the All-India Kisan Sibha (AIKS), the Communist peasant front organization, had continued to organize tenants and *bargadars* against landlords, hoping to foment a class struggle which would sweep them into positions of power and influence in the countryside.[5] While these tactics were on the whole unsuccessful, the leftist leaders continued to threaten the government with agitation in an attempt to secure more immediate reforms. Bibhuti Ghosh, a prominent leader of the Marxist Forward Bloc, for example, told the Legislative Assembly in 1952 that: "If the hunger of the people is not satisfied, discontent will grow and time will come when this will burst into activities which the Government might consider illegal. The Government should realize that it will not always be possible for it to suppress these activities by repressive measures."[6]

Criticism of postponement also came from a number of central government leaders. These men were concerned, not only

[4] From a speech by Jyoti Basu, *ibid.*, II, No. 1 (February 20, 1948), 86.

[5] Gene D. Overstreet and Marshall Windmiller, *Communism in India* (Berkeley: University of California Press, 1959), pp. 277-79.

[6] Quoted in *The Statesman* (Calcutta), July 24, 1952, p. 5.

with the slow pace of land legislation in West Bengal, but also with the possibility that future reforms might not be consistent with—in fact, might not even approach—the recommendations of the Planning Commission and the Agrarian Reforms Committee. The most vocal individuals in this respect were some members of the Congress Working Committee, most members of the Planning Commission, and the Prime Minister, Jawaharlal Nehru.

But both the Working Committee and the Planning Commission were handicapped in the attempt to influence state legislation, not only because of the limited constitutional authority of the center, but also because of the lack of agreement within their own organizations. One section of the Working Committee, for example, had proposed that the Congress party All-India Congress Committee be allowed to appoint a representative for each state to act as a liaison officer between the AICC and the state PCC's and state legislatures. His main function, according to this proposal, would be to "keep in touch with members of the state legislatures and their activities, and to convey to them the sentiment of the Congress High Command."[7] But this proposal was ultimately rejected by the Working Committee itself, as a result of the lack of agreement clearly evident at a later WC meeting. As one member of the WC related to the press, at the end of this twelve-hour session on land reform, "they could not have chosen a topic more in dispute."[8] Because of its inability to effect agreement, the WC finally concluded that land policy would be left entirely to the discretion of the states, and the only recommendation it could agree on was the relatively mild statement

[7] *Ibid.*, June 2, 1952, p. 1.

[8] *Ibid.*, June 30, 1952, p. 1. Also discussed at this meeting was the controversial issue related to the question of whether there should be ceilings on *future* holdings only, or ceilings on present holdings as well. A review of the issues involved in the debate on ceilings appears in Rudolph, *Some Aspects of Congress Land Reform Policy*, pp. 46-68.

that "zamindari abolition should include abolition of inter-mediaries."[9]

The Role of the Planning Commission

As Professor Morris-Jones has pointed out, the role of the Planning Commission (PC) in the determination of Indian policy is both an important and controversial matter, a subject on which numerous contradictory analyses have been set forth.

Of the two extreme accounts . . . one insists that the PC has acquired such power as to make nonsense of ministerial responsibility, the ordinary machinery of government and even the democratic Constitution. The other view presents the PC as a helpless victim of frustrating resistance from the established administration and of distorting pressures from politicians, the adviser no one listens to.[10]

On the question of center-state relations, the Planning Commission has also been alternatively viewed, either as "victim of federalism, or as its killer."[11]

Whatever the role of the Planning Commission in the Indian political system generally, it is clear that its involvement in the formulation of land policy, at least in West Bengal, has been relatively passive. To be sure, the PC is not mentioned in the Constitution; it was, nevertheless, actively involved in the formulation of plans concerning land reform that could have affected West Bengal. But it is equally obvious that the PC has proceeded in cooperation with other Union agencies concerned with the land problem, and that it has not attempted to work outside of the constitutional framework. Thus, while the PC sought to influence West Bengal in a number of important respects and, while it did succeed in persuading some

[9] *The Statesman* (Calcutta), August 11, 1952, p. 1.
[10] Morris-Jones, *Government and Politics of India*, p. 139.
[11] *Ibid.*, p. 141.

individuals and groups at both levels of government to adopt its own policy positions, it was not instrumental in the evolution of West Bengal's land reform acts.

From its inception, the PC clearly sought to pursue a policy that would result in some uniformity of state land reform programs. The First Five-Year Plan which it drafted, spoke in terms of "broad principles and directions of policy," and of the desirability, "between different states," of "a broad, common approach in land reform programmes."[12] At the same time, however, the PC made clear its intention to devise a long-range plan for reform with allowance for individual state differences.

> While broad principles and directions of policy can be indicated, it is necessary to remember that the form and manner of their application and the adaptations to which they are subject will differ widely in different parts of the country. In the main, land policy has to be worked out in terms of local needs and conditions. The texture of relationships concerning land, conditions of economic life, the social composition of rural communities and the pattern of occupational distribution differ widely, so that no generalisation can have more than a limited value.[13]

Consistent with this position, the First Five-Year Plan laid down a number of the "broad principles" advocated by the PC, but then put them in the form of "suggestions," to be enacted in "stages" by "land legislation . . . under the jurisdiction of the States . . . with due regard to local needs and conditions."[14] These "broad principles," which were subsequently set forth by the PC in its successive plans, were similar in many respects to the recommendations that had previously been adopted by the Congress party, and they were consistent

[12] Government of India, Planning Commission, *The First Five-Year Plan* (New Delhi: Planning Commission, 1952), p. 185.

[13] *Ibid.*, pp. 184-85.

[14] Government of India, Planning Commission, *The New India: Progress Through Democracy* (New York: Macmillan, 1958), p. 186.

with the work of the Indian constitution-makers. The PC reiterated the position that land policy should be pursued in terms of both social justice *and* an increase in agricultural efficiency and production.[15] It also reaffirmed the necessity for using "evolutionary methods" consistent with the Constitution, and pursued in stages acceptable to constituent units.[16] Within this context, the First Five-Year Plan defined the first stage of agrarian reform, which was to be pursued in all states, as encompassing those two aspects of legislation on which there was substantial party agreement:

1. Abolishing, in zamindari areas, the intermediaries between the State and tillers;
2. Tenancy reform, to reduce rents and give tenants an opportunity to acquire permanent rights over the land by payment of fixed compensation, subject to the landlord's right to resume a certain area for his personal cultivation.[17]

However, while both of the PC's "first stage" policies had been previously adopted by various party organs, there was now a significant change in the manner with which they were presented. First, while previous agricultural policy statements (notably the Report of the Agrarian Reforms Committee) had been framed by Congress Committees for adoption as official party policy, the recommendations of the PC were promulgated merely as "suggestions . . . to be further examined with reference to conditions in the principal States in which *Zamindari* has been or is expected to be abolished."[18] Second, unlike the position of the PC, previous agrarian policy positions taken by the party had generally assigned a large role to the central government, with little consideration for the possibility of state recalcitrance. The ARC *Report*, for example, had called for the immediate appointment of Central Land Commissioners, vested "with necessary powers," and "charged with the task of quickening up the pace of the agrarian reforms in

[15] *First Five-Year Plan*, p. 184.   [16] *Ibid.*, p. 185.
[17] *The New India*, p. 186.   [18] *First Five-Year Plan*, p. 186.

the Provinces."[19] In contrast, the First Five-Year Plan proposed only "that the State concerned should give high priority" to their suggestions, and that questions of policy should be worked out by "close cooperation and consultation between the Central and State Governments."[20]

Like the ARC *Report* and other previous party pronouncements, the Planning Commission also committed itself to policies that were the subject of a great many disputes—fixed ceilings on land holdings, consolidation of small holdings, and the development of cooperative village management and cooperative farming—but here too the approach of the PC was more guarded and cautious than that of the ARC. On the question of ceilings, for example, the PC set itself only "in favour of *the principle* that there should be an upper limit on the amount of land that an individual may hold,"[21] and argued again for intergovernmental cooperation:

> In actual land reform operations . . . there must be considerable flexibility in approach and, considerations of theory apart, it becomes necessary to adopt those criteria which will serve best against the background of tenures and revenue arrangements peculiar to a State. . . . The limit which may be appropriate has to be determined by each State in the light of its own circumstances but, broadly speaking, following the recommendations of the Congress Agrarian Reforms Committee.[22]

Similarly, the First Five-Year Plan set forth a number of sug-

[19] *Report of the Congress Agrarian Reforms Committee*, p. 13.

[20] *First Five-Year Plan*, p. 185. Numerous other examples are available. On the question of rents, for instance, the ARC *Report* (p. 8) stated that "there will be provision for determination by Land Tribunals of reasonable rent as well as for the commutation of rents in kind into cash." In contrast, the *First Five-Year Plan* (p. 193) held that "the determination of rent has to be regarded essentially as a question for consideration in the light of local conditions."

[21] *Ibid.*, p. 188 (italics mine).

[22] *Ibid.*, p. 189.

gestions regarding consolidation of holdings and the establishment of cooperatives, but finally concluded that "there has to be a great deal of trial and experiment before patterns of organisation which will best promote the interests of the rural population can be evolved."[23] Because the establishment of ceilings on holdings and the creation of village cooperatives were both policies that were likely to lead to conflict, the PC allowed considerable room for individual state differences on these matters, and it relegated them both to later stages of planned development.

Finally, the PC, like the ARC *Report*, suggested the need for a central government organization to coordinate land reform policy. But, unlike the ARC recommendation for a commission vested with administrative powers, the PC's proposal for a Union organization was one that did not threaten the constitutional authority of the states. In fact, the central land reforms organization proposed by the PC was not to be granted any specific powers at all, but rather would be charged with research tasks only, on the basis of which it would make suggestions. In the words of the First Five-Year Plan, the proposed Central Land Reforms Organization would ". . . pool knowledge and experience gained in the States . . . suggest lines for further investigation . . . and . . . maintain a continuous record of information concerning progress in the implementation of land reform programmes adopted by the States."[24] Unlike the Agrarian Reforms Committee, the PC thus visualized the evolution of a broadly uniform policy on land reform, developed through intergovernmental cooperation. In pursuit of this objective, the PC would formulate plans which it would offer to the states in the form of suggestions; it would define stages that could be pursued and inform individual states as to their positions regarding each stage; it would act as a watchdog on factors shaping events, keep a running account of what had been accomplished and

[23] *Ibid.*, p. 197.   [24] *Ibid.*, pp. 197-98.

what remained to be done, recommend adjustments, and perhaps think up new ideas. But, in the words of a PC publication, "the major burden of reform" would remain "on the State administrations and State legislatures."[25]

In fact, only in the areas of research activities and the investment of funds in experimental programs did the First Five-Year Plan envisage significant involvement by Union personnel. With regard to research, the Plan called for the previously mentioned central land reforms organization to collect data and evaluate experience on a wide scale. In addition, the PC recommended that "during 1953 all States in India should cooperate in undertaking a census of land holding and cultivation."[26] Not only were research activities within the constitutional purview of the Union government, they were also a high priority item in a field as complicated and diverse as Indian land matters, especially for those seeking to establish uniformity of policy. For these reasons, the PC was quick to seize on research activities as an area in which it could make a significant contribution to future land reform legislation. From the point of view of the Commission, the collection of data was not only necessary for the purposes of actually implementing reforms once they were passed by state legislatures (a fact pointed out in the Plan), but such data would also be helpful to Union personnel when attempting to influence state legislatures.

That the Planning Commission could have planned for itself anything but a passive role in matters of land reform in West Bengal, however, is unlikely, given the large areas of disagreement within the central government and within the Commission itself. Indeed, even the minimal kinds of recommendations which the PC made were not accepted by all central party and governmental leaders, or by all of the members of the Commission.[27] For example, while the PC did

[25] *The New India*, p. 186.   [26] *First Five-Year Plan*, p. 187.
[27] The most significant conflict between central government personnel

finally obtain agreement on its recommendations for the establishment of a Central Committee for Land Reforms, and while a committee was consequently brought into being (on May 1, 1953),[28] the Committee did not begin functioning until more than a year later (October 1954), and then it only "directed that the existing legislative provisions in various states should be examined."[29] In terms of its effectiveness for influencing land reform policy in West Bengal, it was obviously established far too late, and vested with inadequate authority for the task at hand. And its inability to even *recommend* policy positions that might give some lead to the states was again a result of the disagreement among its members on a number of crucial issues.[30]

The Role of the Prime Minister

Perhaps the major attempt by central government personnel to influence West Bengal's land reform policy was one

---

was that which developed between the PC and the Ministry of Agriculture over the question of ceilings. For an account of this conflict see *The Statesman* (Calcutta), October 23, 1953, p. 1.

[28] The Central Committee for Land Reforms was initially made up of the Chairman and Members of the Planning Commission, the Minister of Home Affairs, the Minister of Food and Agriculture, and the Minister of Agriculture. It has continued to consist of PC members and Ministers.

[29] Government of India, Planning Commission, *Five-Year Plan Progress Report, 1954-55* (Delhi: Manager of Publications, 1956), p. 87.

[30] Within the Committee, for example, the PC members generally held that ceilings on landholdings should be imposed because of "high considerations of policy," while the Minister of Agriculture argued that "ceilings, usually justified on grounds of social justice, had also to be considered from the point-of-view of their effect on agricultural production," and therefore rejected them. Similarly, the PC argued that compensation could not be paid from increased revenues, and was therefore in favor of little compensatory payment to landlords; the Minister of Agriculture argued that land revenues would be sufficient to afford liberal compensation. See *The Statesman* (Calcutta), October 23, 1959, p. 1.

undertaken personally by Prime Minister Nehru, and without the complete support of his fellow party and government leaders. Nehru later admitted that he had "nursed a grievance" against the West Bengal Government for proceeding so slowly with land reform legislation,[31] and he had therefore sought to speed up the process of land legislation in June 1952, by stating his "grievance" in a letter to Chief Minister B. C. Roy. Dr. Roy was a personal friend of the Prime Minister, as well as his personal physician, and was obviously an influential man in the politics of West Bengal as well. Apparently Nehru felt that, because of his friendship with Roy, he would be able to make clear his own policy position, while taking into account both the difficulties being encountered by the state government and the problems that stemmed from the state's unique agrarian structure. Moreover, by appealing to a personal friend he would not be overstepping the bounds of his constitutional authority, and, if he could win Roy to his views, he would still be effective in dissuading the course adopted by the West Bengal Government.

But Nehru's "multi-point proposal," modeled essentially on the recommendations of the PC's First Five-Year Plan, was ultimately unacceptable even to Chief Minister Roy, and it was rejected by the state government shortly after it had been received in Nehru's personal letter. In a statement issued to the press, the West Bengal cabinet stated that it was "fully in accord with Mr. Nehru on the need for accelerating the execution of the Congress's programme of land reform," but it went on to "doubt . . . the scope of application of Mr. Nehru's proposal in West Bengal."[32] The note pointed out the abnormally high concentration of population in the state, the problems that confronted the state government as a result of partition, and the scarcity of cultivable land in the state's rural areas. Because of these factors, the note argued, Nehru's proposal was "impracticable," both in its insistence on rapid en-

[31] *Ibid.*, December 15, 1953, p. 7.   [32] *Ibid.*, June 29, 1952, p. 1.

actment of far-reaching reform measures, and with respect to some of the specific measures mentioned.

Because of the inability of Union leaders to agree on a set of concrete recommendations, and because of the success of the state government in resisting attempts at persuasion on the part of central personnel, the state government was allowed to pursue its own conception of its own interests with regard to land legislation. This is not to say that the work of the Planning Commission, or even of the ARC, was disregarded entirely by those who drafted the West Bengal land reform bills, but rather that state leaders could be almost unrestrained in choosing or rejecting those policies that had been set forth, and could frame state legislation with an eye solely to relevant factors obtaining in the state. That the legislation, which was finally forthcoming in May 1953, was drafted in this light will be pointed out in the next section.

The Pattern of State Land Reform Legislation

Postponement of the land reform legislation until 1953 permitted the state government sufficient time to explore the possibilities inherent in a number of alternative strategies. To begin with, it allowed the state government time to launch its experimental research programs in the Sundarbans, the area in which the Communist and leftist parties had been most active in their attempts to arouse peasant discontent. By gathering a large quantity of relevant data, and by close detailed observation of contemplated reform measures in this leftist stronghold, the party government clearly enhanced its ability to assess the consequences of both a "class struggle" approach and other alternatives. Regardless of whether the leftists were successful or not, the Congress government was, as a result of this experience, in a position (even before the first general elections) to enact legislation that would promise it desired support.[33]

[33] That the Congress party government *consciously* sought to focus its research and experimental activities in the Sundarbans because of the leftist activities, was suggested by Siddharta Ray, a prominent Congress-

Moreover, the party did not confine itself merely to the experiments and research activities of the government in the Sundarbans in its efforts to gauge the nature of public feeling on the land question. The PCC simultaneously appointed a Labor and Peasants Subcommittee to inquire into the question of reform, and this committee, in 1951, sent out a questionnaire to approximately one-eighth of the local Congress party units throughout the state. This questionnaire, which was answered by 310 *thana*, subdivision, and district committees of the Congress party, provided an opportunity for local units to indicate their desired patterns of reform, and it made possible a statewide assessment of party feeling at the local level.

The replies that were received from local party units on the PCC questionnaire may or may not have been indicative of the real schisms that existed within the party on the land reform issue, but state party leaders did accept them as an accurate measure of party feeling. These figures indicated that there was a significant segment of the party (more than one-sixth of the committees represented in this sample) that did advocate radical reforms, including abolition of all intermediaries without compensation.[34] This segment of the party was generally in favor of giving intermediaries some kind of token "rehabilitation allowance," in the form of a flat cash payment, but opposed to any kind of payment designed to compensate landholders for property taken by the state.[35] On the other

---

man involved in some of the earlier decisions on land reform policy (Mr. Ray has since quit the Congress and is now an independent). Based on interviews conducted in 1964.

[34] Responses to the questionnaire are reprinted in *The Statesman* (Calcutta), July 19, 1952, p. 10.

[35] West Bengal's first Chief Minister P. C. Ghosh, for example, was one of the Congress leaders who first suggested that a rehabilitation allowance be given to dispossessed *zamindars* instead of compensation. See *West Bengal Legislative Assembly Debates*, I, No. 1 (1950), 296. Ghosh later quit the Congress party as a result of this and other issues on which he differed with the Roy government.

hand, there were two party units in which at least a majority of the members had voted against any reform whatsoever. Party members of this opinion argued that reform could only be time-consuming and ineffective; they sought to enhance agricultural output and effect social justice through education and the improvement of technical skills rather than through a reform affecting social relationships.[36]

Despite this schism within the state party, however, there was a wide area of consensus, which was indicated in the replies to the PCC questionnaire. Most party units, in fact, could agree that they wanted abolition of intermediaries between the cultivator and the state, but with some concessions made to the dispossessed in the form of compensatory payments. A large number of local units (91 in this sample) voted to enact the recommendations of the Floud Commission, allowing for payment of 10 to 15 times the amount of annual profits as compensation; 161 units sought to pay compensation computed on other bases, but in no case less than 5 times the amount of annual gross produce from the land.[37]

In other respects as well the party had secured evidence, before it introduced legislation, which indicated the desirability of moderate reform measures. Not only had the leftists failed miserably in their attempts to turn the peasants against the landlords in the state, even many Congressmen had been unable to recruit party support on the basis of a "class" appeal.[38] If it had not been clear previously, it became increasingly obvious after the 1952 general elections that rural political sup-

[36] For a detailed statement of this position, see the speech of Sir Bijoy Prasad Singh Roy, vice-president of the British Indian Association, as published in *The Statesman* (Calcutta), May 7, 1953, p. 8.

[37] *Ibid.*, July 19, 1952, p. 10.

[38] This was pointed out by a rural Congress worker, Kalipada Chatterjee, who had attempted until 1952 to organize his own constituency on a "class" basis—in this case to organize *bargadars* and cultivating laborers on the basis of their mutual interests in securing land—and who abandoned this strategy after its lack of success in the 1952 elections. Based on interviews in 1963 and 1964.

port could be generated most effectively, not by appealing to groups on the basis of economic class interests, but rather by working through influential local citizens, including local landholders.[39]

It was shortly after the 1952 elections then that the state government began to make concrete policy statements on the land question, and these clearly indicated that the previous promise of far-reaching reform would be altered. In a most detailed analysis of the land problem, for example, state Development Commission Chairman S. K. Dey talked about the change of thinking in state government circles that had grown out of the state's experiments:

> It is frequently argued that the removal of all interests intervening between the State and the tenant will increase the latter's incentive to obtain more yield from his land. This argument has no application in the circumstances prevailing in this State. . . . A more logical proposal is for State purchase of *all* private rights in land, and its distribution in equal portions among cultivating tenants, *bargadars*, and landless peasants. This is, however, impracticable, as there would not be enough land to go around. . . . It would be an utterly ruinous and retrograde measure in practice.[40]

State Ministers now came to argue that it was not land reform that would necessarily increase production or "revolutionize" the countryside, but rather the application of an im-

[39] The success of the Congress party in obtaining electoral support from rural landholders is pointed out in Myron Weiner, "Changing Patterns of Political Leadership in West Bengal," in *Political Change in South Asia*, pp. 177-227.

[40] Dey, *The Statesman* (Calcutta), August 5, 1952, p. 11. Compare this statement with Dey's evidence before the Land Revenue Commission in 1940, where he contended that "substantial advantages both social and economic may be claimed for any measure which eliminates all intermediate interests between the State and the actual cultivator." S. K. Dey, "Memorandum," in *Report of the Land Revenue Commission, Bengal*, v, 379.

proved technology in the villages, and the building of an industrial base in the urban areas. In the words of Development Commissioner Dey:

The real problem is the mounting demand for land. . . . There can be only one objective to reform all over the country, and that is to improve the productivity of land by its more economic utilisation. . . . This is a function of improved technology. Such technology can have profitable application only in a surplus, commercial farm. This is a matter of increasing the size of the holding. That is possible only when we have fewer people on the land. For this, we have to create new avenues of profitable living through continuing expansion of manufacturing enterprise, commercial undertakings and professional services.[41]

In this atmosphere, the land reform measures that were forthcoming, in 1953 and the years following, were not designed to alter radically the agrarian structure of West Bengal. They did indeed abolish the *zamindari* system created by the British, and they did result in state acquisition of some cultivable land which was redistributed. But the relationships obtaining between different agricultural groups and classes was not significantly changed; and the intermediaries were not eliminated from the hierarchical structure of land interests. The *barga* system of cultivation, and the large numbers of landless rural laborers remained in much the same positions that they had previously occupied.

The first piece of major land legislation, the Estates Acquisition (EA) Act of 1953, provided for state acquisition of lands belonging to intermediaries, and outlined the manner of assessment and the rates for paying compensation. Under the terms of this act, the state government was empowered to acquire the land of intermediaries, but with certain important exceptions: (1) intermediaries were allowed to retain *non-*

---

[41] Dey, *The Statesman* (Calcutta), August 5, 1952, p. 12.

agricultural land in their private (*khas*) possession up to as
much as twenty acres; (2) they were also allowed to retain
agricultural land in their private possession, up to as much as
twenty-five acres; (3) where an intermediary had his land
cultivated by *barga*, or where he sublet his lands, the state
was empowered to acquire his agricultural lands only in excess of thirty-three acres; (4) individuals could maintain their
"homesteads, *pucca* buildings, tea gardens, orchards, mills,
factories, and workshops"; and (5) the bill was not applicable
to the Calcutta municipal area.

Thus, from its very inception, the bill did not apply to all
intermediaries in West Bengal, or to all of the land held by
intermediaries. As S. K. Basu pointed out, the number of
families holding land in excess of twenty-five acres was estimated at only 40,000 (200,000 people or .8 per cent of the
population of the state) in 1953, and the amount of land held
by these people was an estimated 1,320,000 acres (or 10.3 per
cent of the cultivable land in the state). Allowing twenty-five
acres for each family in this category, the maximum amount
of agricultural land that the state could acquire under this
act was 320,000 acres or 1 and ½ per cent of the total cultivable land (12,850,000 acres) in the state.[42]

But even then, the legislation enacted by the state government did not assure state acquisition of this 320,000 acres, since
it was possible for holders of land in excess of twenty-five
acres to transfer a portion of their surplus land to relatives
(*benamdars*, the process of transferral being known as a *benami* transaction).[43] *Benami* transactions were made possible

[42] *West Bengal Legislative Council Debates*, III (November 30, 1953),
203-04. The speech by Land Revenue Minister S. K. Basu, which appears in the *Debates* (pp. 194-206), is a most useful summary of the
intentions and provisions of the Estates Acquisitions Act, 1953.

[43] That *benami* transactions were allowed by the government bill
was admitted by Minister S. K. Basu in a speech before the state legislature. See *West Bengal Legislative Assembly Debates*, IX (February
22, 1954), 468.

through the following devices. (1) The bill was brought forward without having first brought rural records of rights up to date, thus making it possible for large landholders to record *benami* transactions and back-date them *before* the government investigated their property claims. (2) The bill restricted government enquiries regarding *benami* transfers to those transactions made after May 5, 1953 (the day the EA bill was introduced in the legislature), thus legitimizing those transfers made in anticipation of the bill. (3) The bill placed a ceiling on *individual* holdings rather than *family* holdings, thus permitting numerous individuals within each family to hold property in amounts consistent with the ceiling limits.[44] As a result, it was estimated in a study financed by the Planning Commission, that "not less than 105,600 acres of agricultural land was transferred . . . [to relatives] . . . for the purpose of evading the ceiling legislation,"[45] and the government ultimately was able to take possession of only 211,000 acres of cultivable land, a mere 1.64 per cent of the total land in the state.[46]

As compensation for this land, the government guaranteed payments computed on the basis of a sliding scale, devised in terms of the net income that had been earned from the land in the past (see Table 2). As the government Land Minister, who introduced the EA bill in the Legislative Assembly, admitted, the system of sliding scales was drawn up in order that the "middle classes" would "get somewhat liberal compensation," while large landholders would "have to make some sacrifice."[47] But even then, the sacrifice expected of large landholders was mild when it is considered that the landholder could deduct from his gross income three substantial

[44] An excellent discussion of the effects of *benami* transactions, and the manner in which they were executed, is contained in Basu and Bhattacharya, pp. 90-91.

[45] See *ibid.*, p. 90.   [46] *Ibid.*

[47] *The Statesman* (Calcutta), May 8, 1953, p. 1. Quoted from a speech given by S. K. Basu, Land Revenue Minister.

amounts: (1) the sum payable by him in the previous agricultural year as land revenue, cesses, or rents; (2) his average annual expenditure on maintenance of the property; and (3)

TABLE 2

RATES OF COMPENSATION, WEST BENGAL
ESTATES ACQUISITION ACT, 1953

Net Annual Income	Amount of Compensation
First 1,000 rupees or less	15 times the net income
Next 1,000 "	13 " " " "
" 5,000 "	11 " " " "
" 10,000 "	9 " " " "
" 25,000 "	7 " " " "
" 50,000 "	5 " " " "
Balance	4 " " " "

SOURCE: H. D. Malaviya, "Highlights of West Bengal Estates Acquisition Bill," *AICC Economic Review*, v, No. 2 (May 15, 1953), 8.

his costs in collecting rents.[48] As a result of these liberal compensation allowances, the government estimated that it would pay more than 700 million rupees compensation for lands acquired by it, or an average of 3,163 rupees per acre.[49]

Finally, further concessions were made to rural supporters of the Congress party through a number of later additions and amendments to the 1953 EA Act. First, it was discovered in 1954 that a number of peasants were not paying their rents to the *Zamindars*, on the assumption that the *zamindari* estates had already been "abolished" (in actual fact the date of state acquisition was set for April 15, 1955, according to the 1953 legislation). In order to protect the property of landholders, the state thus promulgated an ordinance in July 1954, provid-

[48] This is pointed out in H. D. Malaviya, "Highlights of West Bengal Estates Acquisition Bill," *AICC Economic Review*, v, No. 2 (May 15, 1953), 8.

[49] *The Statesman* (Calcutta), February 8, 1958, p. 1.

ing that no *zamindar* could be deprived of his holding by government for nonpayment of rents prior to the planned date of transfer (April 15, 1955).[50] Second, when it was learned that an estimated 100,000 lower middle-class clerks and accountants were to be rendered unemployed by the EA Act, the state government agreed to hire these former *Zamindari* employees for the purpose of collecting state land revenue and for otherwise managing its newly acquired property;[51] and it agreed to pay them a monthly allowance of 27 rupees plus a commission ranging from 2 and ½ per cent to 4 per cent on the amount of revenue they collected from tenants.[52] Finally, on the ground that the EA Act had taken away a source of income from rural religious and charitable institutions, the government agreed, in a 1960 amendment to the original bill, to provide for payment of perpetual annuities to such institutions, in the amounts previously received from former intermediaries.[53]

As a result of the EA Act, then, a small portion of the landlords of West Bengal (those with holdings in excess of twenty-five acres of agricultural land) were forced to relinquish some of their lands in excess of twenty-five acres. They could of course choose that portion which they wished to retain, and they were allowed to transfer other portions to relatives. In addition, they were required to farm the twenty-five acres of agricultural land which they kept in their private (*khas*) possession for "personal cultivation," but absentee landlordism was still allowed by the provision in the law which defined "personal cultivation." In the words of the EA Act, "personal cultivation" meant: ". . . cultivation by a person of his own land on his own account by his own labour or by the labour of any member of his family *or* by servants or labourers on wages payable in cash or in kind or both."[54] Under the terms

---

[50] *Ibid.*, July 16, 1954, p. 8.　　[51] *Ibid.*, December 28, 1954, p. 8.
[52] *Ibid.*, May 28, 1957, p. 10.　　[53] *Ibid.*, December 7, 1960, p. 9.
[54] Jamini Mohan Ghosh, *The West Bengal Land Reforms Act, 1955* (Calcutta: Eastern Law House Private Ltd., 1956), p. 4 (italics mine).

of this provision, of course, a landholder could continue to farm his land by hiring *bargadars* or cultivating laborers and, insofar as this was done, the existing landlord-tenant relationships remained the same throughout the state.

In fact, by the enactment of its second piece of major reform legislation, the Land Reforms Act (LRA) of 1955, the state legislature reinforced the legal rights of those landlords and working peasants already existing, and consciously preserved the system of crop-sharing and wage labor. Under the terms of this act, "the right of ownership" was "conferred on the *raiyat* in respect of his holding,"[55] and every *raiyat*[56] was granted the right to transfer his property, or to pass it on to his beneficiaries, subject only to two conditions imposed by the state. One of these provided that he could not partition his holding below a certain minimum level, such level to be set by the state on the basis of the different conditions prevailing in "different localities and for different classes of land."[57] Second, he would be required to pay a "revenue rate" to the government, this rate again to be determined by government revenue officers on the basis of several local and particular factors (nature of soil and productivity of the land; average yield per acre; average market price during the preceding twenty years; and the market value of the land).[58] Again, the state government made concessions to its rural supporters, since it fixed surprisingly low maximum limits for the revenue rate to be

This volume and another with an identical title, D. P. Chatterjee, *The West Bengal Land Reforms Act, 1955* (Calcutta: A. Mukherjee and Co., 1956), both give legal commentaries on land reform legislation in West Bengal.

[55] Quoted from the speech by S. K. Basu introducing the LRA, 1955, *West Bengal Legislative Assembly Debates*, xii, No. 4 (September 27, 1955), 33.

[56] With the "abolition" of intermediaries, the term *raiyat* came to be applied by government personnel to both former intermediaries and working peasants, or, in the definition of Minister Basu, to those with "the right of ownership." *Ibid.*

[57] *Ibid.*, 34.   [58] *Ibid.*, 35.

collected. Land Revenue Minister S. K. Basu summarized the provisions of the LRA revenue sections as follows: "The revenue rate for any class of land shall not exceed, in the case of land growing paddy, one-fifth of the value of the yield per acre, and in the case of lands growing other crops one-tenth of the value of the yield per acre, while in respect of lands not used for growing any crop, the maximum revenue will be 2 per centum of the market value of such land."[59]

Finally, the LRA preserved the status of the *bargadars* and wage laborers in the countryside by providing for legal definitions of their rights relative to the owners of land. As Basu explained:

> . . . it has not been found possible to do away with the *barga* or share-cropping system of cultivation. If the *bargadars* were declared to be owners outright or were allowed to purchase such right by instalments, it would deprive an equal number of persons of their right of ownership, who in most cases are as much dependent on the produce of the lands as the *bargadars* themselves. On the other hand, if the owners were given a free hand to oust the *bargadars* at their will, the inevitable result would be an increase in the number of the landless. In such a situation there could be no alternative but to maintain the *barga* system.[60]

The *bargadar* was therefore defined by the act as one who "cultivates the land of another person on condition of delivering share of the produce of such land to that person," and the act merely went on to prescribe a legal system for sharing produce and for governing sharecropping arrangements. In dividing produce, the law required that it be shared between

[59] *Ibid.* Land revenue rates in West Bengal are so low, as a result of this legislation, that a West Bengal Finance Minister (Sankar Das Banerjee) once suggested that they be abolished entirely on the ground that it was uneconomic for the state to collect them. See *The Statesman* (Calcutta), March 1, 1960, p. 9; March 15, 1960, p. 9.

[60] *West Bengal Legislative Assembly Debates,* XII, No. 4 (September 27, 1955), 33.

owner and *bargadar* in the proportion of 50:50 where the *bargadar* furnished the seeds, manure, and cattle, and in the proportion 60 (for the landlord):40 (for the *bargadar*) where the landlord furnished these farming implements. The act thus reaffirmed the most prevalent system in this respect, and in others as well. It permitted the owner to resume cultivation of land under *barga* by evicting the *bargadar*, subject only to the provision that the owner must then "personally cultivate" the land. But, as was mentioned above, this meant only that the owner could hire agricultural laborers, or other *bargadars*, and did not necessarily imply that he cultivate the land himself.[61]

The LRA also worked against the interests of the *bargadars* and agricultural laborers in that it provided for the formation of Cooperative Societies, not among the landless, but only among those already established as owners (*raiyats*).[62] Moreover, since the surplus land that was acquired by the state was to be distributed primarily through Cooperative Societies,[63] this meant that the land was redistributed primarily among those with ownership rights, and not among the wage laborers and *bargadars*. Even when a deputation of peasant leaders appeared before the state Agricultural Minister in 1955, requesting that the land reforms bill be amended in favor of the *bargadars*, the state continued to insist that its legislation was "in the best interests of the state."[64]

[61] *Ibid.*, 34-35.   [62] *Ibid.*, 35.

[63] This was made clear by Land Revenue Minister Basu's successor, Bimal Chandra Sinha, in an announcement in March 1959. See *The Statesman* (Calcutta), March 7, 1959, p. 7.

[64] The *bargadars*, although they are not well organized, have continually made two demands on government. One of these calls for the *tebhaga* system of sharing the produce from land (under which system the *bargadar* receives two-thirds of the produce and the landlord one-third); and the other, for a redistribution of surplus government lands to Cooperatives of *bargadars* rather than to Cooperative Societies composed only of landlords and *raiyats*. See *ibid.*, September 9, 1955, p. 1. See also Sisir Kumar Das, "Agrarian Unrest in West Bengal," *ibid.*, March 21, 1959, p. 6.

State Resistance to Central Persuasion

Because West Bengal's land reforms were framed with an eye to the state government's conception of its own interests, they were in only some relatively minor ways in accord with the recommendations of the Planning Commission. As the PC itself pointed out, West Bengal's program *did conform* to the Plan's conception of a uniform policy in *some respects*—in the acquisition of the property of some intermediaries, and in the establishment of both a ceiling and a "floor"[65] for size of holdings—but the state government simultaneously ignored, or directly contradicted, much of what the Planning Commission had sought to effect.[66] In an assessment of the West Bengal reforms, written in 1958, the PC's Panel on Land Reforms in fact concluded that the legislation in West Bengal had, in many instances, "not been given effect to," and, in other areas, "failed to give the intended relief."[67]

In the face of state recalcitrance to conform to the recommendations of the Plan, however, many Indian central party and governmental leaders have not been wholly unsympathetic to state problems. Some Union personnel, faced with similar kinds of difficulties in their own states, have supported the position taken by West Bengal for this reason;[68] others have taken the position that West Bengal's reluctance to en-

[65] The term "floor" refers to the provision that holdings cannot be partitioned below a certain minimum level, a provision facilitating the Plan's program for consolidating holdings. See *West Bengal Legislative Assembly Debates*, xii, No. 4 (September 27, 1955), 33.

[66] West Bengal was classified by the Planning Commission in the late 1950's as one of the "areas of least change," insofar as land reforms were concerned. See Government of India, Planning Commission, *Second Five-Year Plan Progress Report, 1958-59* (New Delhi: Manager of Publications, 1960), p. 192.

[67] Government of India, Planning Commission, *Reports of the Committees of the Panel on Land Reforms* (New Delhi: Planning Commission, 1959), p. 36.

[68] This was the position of Govind Ballabhai Pant, who was concerned with a similar bill passed earlier in the U.P.; for Pant's position, see *The Statesman* (Calcutta), March 20, 1955, p. 1.

act radical reforms is the only sensible response possible at the present stage of India's social and economic development.[69] Where central leaders have sought a more rapid and far-reaching reform in West Bengal, they have acted in a manner consistent with the approach envisaged in the Constitution and the First Five-Year Plan. They have been unwilling or unable to use either coercion or party discipline in dealing with the state, and have preferred instead to attempt persuasion of the state through a variety of devices.

One of the means by which central personnel attempted to persuade state policy-makers is that suggested in the First Plan recommendation for elaborate and detailed surveys of India's agrarian structure. Pursuing this recommendation, the Ministry of Food and Agriculture, in cooperation with the PC and the Central Statistical Organization, requested each state in India (in January 1954), to cooperate in a national census of landholdings. In addition, the PC and the Working Committee of the Congress Party both appointed subcommittees (in the period after most states had enacted land legislation) and charged them with the task of tracing the impact of the new reform measures.[70] Finally, the PC has kept a running account of legislation in the states, on the basis of which it has made comparisons of the progress in each state toward an agrarian structure envisaged in the Plans. These research activities have clearly been intended by central personnel as a factor contributing to the evolution of a uniform land policy. In the words of a PC publication, ". . . detailed and reliable

[69] See, for example, D. R. Gadgil's description of the reaction among some central party leaders to the ARC Report. Gadgil argues that a number of party leaders felt that reforms could not be forced by governmental action, but rather had to come in response to movements by the rural populace. D. R. Gadgil, "Presidential Address: Land Reform," *Indian Journal of Agricultural Economics*, x (1955), 18ff.

[70] *The Statesman* (Calcutta), October 19, 1957, p. 4; July 14, 1958, p. 5. The PC's subcommittee was appointed by the Standing Committee of the PC's Research Programs Committee on October 18, 1957; the WC's subcommittee was appointed on July 13, 1958.

data regarding land holdings is necessary both for taking policy decisions with regard to land reforms as well as for implementing the decisions that may be reached."[71]

Second, both the Ministry of Food and Agriculture and the Planning Commission have sought to influence state government and party policy-makers through personal appeals made in the states. During the period when the West Bengal Land Reforms Act (1955) was being drafted, for example, a senior adviser to the Planning Commission (P. N. Thapar) was assigned to West Bengal, for the purpose of placing the views of the Planning Commission personally before the state government;[72] PC officials have made similar appearances in West Bengal, before both governmental and party organs, at which times they have not hesitated to state their own views and those of the organizations which they represent. In March 1958, for example, Union Food Minister A. P. Jain spoke before the West Bengal PCC and the state Congress Peasants Conference (meeting together at Kakdwip), and told the state party bluntly: ". . . while some other State Governments have taken steps to satisfy farmers, West Bengal has not properly implemented the provisions of the Bargadar Act . . . unless farmers can feel secure in their rights on land, agriculture cannot develop, and food production cannot increase."[73]

The point is, however, that the state of West Bengal has not been persuaded to change its basic pattern of agrarian legislation, despite the activities of Union leaders. The state has refused to undertake a census of landholdings on the ground that the present level of information obtaining in the state is sufficient for the purposes of its enacted reforms;[74] and the state government has also refuted vociferously those Union leaders who have appeared before party and governmental

---

[71] *Progress of Land Reforms,* 1963, p. 101.

[72] *The Statesman* (Calcutta), November 3, 1954, p. 1.

[73] *Ibid.,* March 3, 1958, p. 5.

[74] *Progress of Land Reforms,* 1963, p. 105.

organs within the state.[75] More so than in the previous case studies, it is clear that central party and governmental leaders were unable to influence in any significant way the state party government and state legislature because of their inability to unite in significant numbers or with sufficient organizational strength to devise a strategy designed to gain greater degrees of influence (in land reform matters, of course, the center did lack the constitutional powers that were available to it in the other case studies).

As in the other case studies, then, the state party government devised its own program, relatively independent of influence from central party and governmental leaders. Initially uncertain about the nature of the conflicts within the state on the land reform issue, the state government postponed significant reforms until such time that it could test the relative strength of various economic groups. When it became obvious that the leftist parties would not be able to mobilize the population behind a slogan of radical reform, and when there seemed to be a minimal consensus within the party in support of a moderate reform program, the state government was able to proceed with legislation. Here, too, the success of the state in pursuing its own conceptions of its own interests was largely a result of the ability of the state party unit to attain a high degree of cohesion behind a policy that benefited those of its supporters that were highly mobilized for political action.

[75] In reply to A. P. Jain's speech at Kakdwip, for example, the state government issued a press release which concluded: "To say that West Bengal's difficulties would be solved considerably if tenancy rights were given to *bargadars* is an oversimplification of the problem." See *The Statesman* (Calcutta), March 5, 1958, p. 7.

·VIII·

Party Government and Center-State Relations

WHILE federalism is not mentioned specifically in the Indian Constitution, it is clear that India's constitution-makers envisaged a series of federal institutions that would be appropriate to their political environment. As Austin has recently pointed out, the framers took cognizance of the recent thinking on "cooperative federalism," which presumes that neither the general or regional governments of a federal union can in reality be completely independent.[1] They assumed from the beginning that a successful Indian Union would necessitate a bargaining process between central and state leaders, one in which experiment, cooperation, persuasion, and conciliation could describe both the generally accepted norms and the usual procedural patterns of intergovernmental relations.[2] It was certainly intended that there would be a "strong, central or general, government," but the constitution-makers sought to insure that this would "not necessarily result in weak provincial governments that are largely administrative agencies for central policies."[3]

In the Indian Constitution, there are a number of provisions that are intended to promote a federalizing process. A central Parliament, state legislatures, and other assemblies were intended to serve as forums for the negotiation of political bargains between states and localities;[4] neutral high-level com-

[1] Granville Austin, *The Indian Constitution: Cornerstone of a Nation* (New York: Oxford University Press, 1966), p. 187. For a discussion of "cooperative federalism," see F. G. Carnell, "Political Implications of Federalism in New States," in *Federalism and Economic Growth in Underdeveloped Countries*, Leverhulme Trust, ed. Ursula K. Hicks (London: George Allen and Unwin, 1961), pp. 20, 38, 55.

[2] W. H. Morris-Jones, *The Government and Politics of India* (London: Hutchinson University Library, 1964), pp. 141ff.

[3] Austin, p. 186.   [4] *Ibid.*, pp. 144ff.

missions (such as the Finance Commission) were created by
the Constitution to deal with center-state disputes on a permanent basis;[5] and a great deal of flexibility was preserved
throughout the Constitution in an effort to permit experimentation with a variety of federal arrangements and devices.[6] Perhaps more important, the extraordinarily complex financial
provisions of the Constitution envisage a situation in center-
state relations in which mutually interdependent central and
state leadership groups are necessarily brought together.[7]

[5] The Constitution itself was drafted and accepted by a Constituent
Assembly that made frequent use of a number of high-level commissions, both permanent and temporary, which were created for the specific purpose of reconciling diverse and conflicting interests. These included the Central Pay Commission (1947), the Committee on Hyderabad (1948), the Linguistic Provinces Commission (1948), the Finance
Enquiry Committee (1949), and numerous others. For a discussion of
the role of high-level commissions in Indian politics see Norman D.
Palmer, *The Indian Political System* (Boston: Houghton Mifflin,
1961), p. 170.

[6] The Constitution allows, for example, for the transfer of Union
powers to the states under certain circumstances (in Article 258) and
it simultaneously vests in the states the power to entrust state functions
to the Union in certain instances (Article 258A). The constitutional
provisions require that the consent of both states and center be obtained in those matters that are fundamental to a federal balance, and
the amendment procedure requires that constitutional amendments concerned with federal topics be ratified by a majority of the states. Thus,
a state legislature can amend a federal statute, but it must have the
consent of the central Parliament; and the central legislature can
legislate in fields reserved to the states, but it must have the consent of
the state Legislative Assembly. On the flexibility of the Indian Constitution with regard to federal matters see Austin, pp. 262-64.

[7] Professor A. H. Birch and others have defined "cooperative fed-
eralism" almost solely in terms of the financial provisions of a consti-
tution. See A. H. Birch, *Federalism, Finance, and Social Legislation in
Canada, Australia, and the United States* (London: Oxford University
Press, 1955), p. 305. For an analysis of the federal features of the finan-
cial provisions of India's Constitution, see Austin, p. 187; see also
Charles Henry Alexandrowicz, *Constitutional Development in India*
(Bombay: Oxford University Press, 1957), pp. 193ff.

The preceding case studies indicate some of the ways in which these constitutional provisions and devices were used in the negotiation of federal disputes in West Bengal. In the states reorganization case, for example, it was the state Congress Parliamentary parties that ultimately carried the wishes of the state legislatures and the state party organizations to the central Parliament where a final solution was negotiated, and it was a Parliamentary subcommittee (heavily representing people from West Bengal and Bihar) that finally worked out a solution that was acceptable to both the state governments and the Union Parliament. Similarly in the case of the Damodar Valley Corporation. When it was determined in 1948 that a river valley development corporation was to be established, a Parliamentary subcommittee (of the Constituent Assembly, which was then acting as a legislative and constitution-making body) was immediately brought into being, and it was within this committee, again heavily representing Bihari and Bengali MP's, that a reconciliation of various state interests was effected and decisions made as to the distribution of benefits and costs.

The case studies are also replete with examples of the use to which independent high-level commissions can be put in the pursuit of intergovernmental negotiation. In the case of land reform, where the center had little or no influence in state legislation, the Planning Commission acted merely to keep central leaders informed and to use mild persuasive tactics in the hope of evolving a nationally standardized policy. In the DVC case, a number of commissions were either created or used, and for a variety of purposes. The Voorduin Commission (appointed by the Central Technical Power Board) was charged with the task of devising a plan that was in keeping with the highest technical standards, but which did not neglect the interests of the states of Bihar and West Bengal. When it was decided that a reorganization of the DVC structure was necessary, the Rau Committee was appointed by the participating governments of the DVC, and charged with the responsibility of investigating "all aspects of the DVC organization." Throughout the development of the DVC case study, the Finance Commission was involved in the arbitration and mediation of disputes and in other aspects of the federalizing process which took place. Finally, in the case of states reorganization, both the Linguistic Provinces Commission and the States Reorganization Commission were responsible for sifting the large volume of evidence, and reconciling the numerous arguments, which resulted from the boundary disputes that occurred throughout India after Independence. As the case study points out, the SRC was especially successful in postponing the reorganization issue for a number of years, while laying the basis for the negotiations that ultimately resulted in a final solution for West Bengal.

Other aspects of constitutional design also played a part in bringing together political leaders from the center and the states for the purpose of resolving conflicts. In the DVC case, for example, negotiations were brought about when the Constitution easily made possible a sharing of powers by both central and state governments in a river valley development corporation, and the necessity for reaching agreement through negotiations was a result of those constitutional provisions which required that both state legislatures ratify the Union bill creating the corporation. This case also provides some striking examples of the variety of intergovernmental negotiations involved in allocating alloted funds in a manner considered beneficial both by the state government and central leadership groups, and in allocating marginal funds for various projects through a variety of negotiating devices.

One conclusion that emerges from the case studies, however, is that India's institutionalized forms for the arbitration and mediation of disputes, while they might have facilitated in the evolution of some degree of cooperation, are not sufficient by themselves to explain the development of the federalizing experience of West Bengal. This is not to say that the Constitution was without effect, but simply to point to the role of a number of nonconstitutional factors when attempting to understand the kinds of political bargains that eventually evolved in the case studies. In fact, the framers themselves assumed that the Constitution would not initially be accepted as the sole source of governmental legitimacy in India, and many of them foresaw a very uneven development of relationships between the center and the various states of the Union.[8] Thus, while legislative organs, independent commissions of inquiry, and the other constitutional devices that encourage negotiations between the general and constituent governments were designed for use in all states, it was recognized that the ways in which they were used might differ significantly from state to state.

The State Congress Party

In West Bengal, the role of the Congress party becomes especially crucial for an understanding of the ways in which the federal Constitution was interpreted. For, in the cases, it was the Congress organization that led most of the intergovernmental negotiating that took place. Moreover, it was the leadership of the state party that was instrumental in securing support for the final solution that was decided upon in each of the cases.

In this context, it is significant that the coalition within the Congress party in West Bengal was able, after 1947, either to absorb or purge the urban coalition that dominated the Congress in Bengal throughout the nationalist movement. The pre-Independence urban coalition, under the leadership of C. R. Das and Subhas Bose, was almost constantly opposed to Gandhi and the central leadership of the party right up until Independence. But the present leader of the party, Atulya Ghosh, actually voted against Bose in his contests for party president during the late 1930's, and did not join the boycotts of Gandhi during the Mahatma's trips to Bengal just prior to

[8] Austin, p. 231.

Independence.[9] Ghosh's support of Gandhism is not unqualified, but is considerably more conducive to center-state cooperation than was the attitude of Bose.[10]

As a result of the hegemony of the Ghosh coalition after Independence, the leadership of the Congress party at both the state and central levels, during the period covered by the case studies, was a leadership that had worked together throughout the freedom movement to oppose the British. Representative of the closeness between state and central leaders in West Bengal during this period was the working relationship between Chief Minister B. C. Roy in Calcutta and Prime Minister Nehru in New Delhi. One observer, for example, stated in 1956 that ". . . apart from Maulana Azad, Dr. Roy is perhaps the only active politician in India whose relations with the Prime Minister are conducted on a basis of comradely equality."[11] This warm, personal relationship between Chief Minister Roy and Prime Minister Nehru was paralleled at other levels of the party and governmental hierarchy as well,[12] with the result that center-state relations did not change significantly with the death of B. C. Roy in mid-1962. In fact, in the only post-Roy case study elaborated here—the DVC case—negotiations between central and state leadership groups continued in much the same manner as before the death of Roy.[13]

[9] Related to the author by Atulya Ghosh in interviews conducted in 1963 and 1964.

[10] For a detailed explanation of Ghosh's position, see Atulya Ghosh, *Ahimsa and Gandhi* (Calcutta: Prabhat Basu, 1954); contrast this with Subhas Chandra Bose, *The Indian Struggle: 1935-42* (Calcutta: Chakerverty, Chatterjee, 1952).

[11] Vedette (pseud.), "Merger Issue Kept Alive by Dr. Roy," *The Statesman* (Calcutta), April 1, 1956, p. 8.

[12] This was pointed out by the Calcutta correspondent for *The Economic Weekly* when writing about the death of B. C. Roy in 1962. See "Dr. B. C. Roy," *The Economic Weekly*, xiv (July 7, 1962), 1035.

[13] It should also be pointed out that Bengalis frequently chided B. C. Roy for his inability to "use" his relationship with Prime Minister

There were a number of other factors obtaining within the state of West Bengal that affected the way in which the Congress party conducted center-state relations in the case studies. Many of these involved the presence of a strong party opposition within the state. Unlike most other parts of India, a tradition of Marxist leftism is well-established in Bengal, with the result that the leftist opposition is extremely influential. In response to an environment in which it is seriously challenged, the state Congress party structure has evolved in a manner unlike that found in some other areas where no serious challenge has confronted the party.

The extent to which the Communist and leftist parties do dominate the opposition in West Bengal can be seen from the results of three post-Independence elections. As is indicated in Table 3, the Communist party has steadily increased the number of seats it holds in the Legislative Assembly since Independence, and the percentage of the vote it has received has also constantly risen (from 10.8 per cent for its Legislative Assembly candidates in 1952, to 17.8 per cent in 1957, to 25.2 per cent in 1962). Moreover, the Communist party has been able to unite, at least for electoral purposes, with other leftist groups to form electoral fronts which have increased the electoral efficiency of the opposition.

But the strength of the opposition parties cannot be adequately assessed by reference to electoral statistics alone. For the influence of these parties also rests on their success in pursuing two nonelectoral political strategies; described by party mem-

Nehru to obtain special concessions for Bengal. Typical of such chiding is the following remark, made by a Bengali leftist politician during the debate on states reorganization: "We . . . ask what were the West Bengal Government doing so long? Have they pointed out, before this, the utter incongruity of the whole situation to the Central Government? . . . Is this a sample of Dr. Roy's much-vaunted pull with the Centre? If so, God save us." (Speech by Haripada Chatterjee, *West Bengal Legislative Assembly Debates*, xv, No. 1 (July 5, 1956), 52.

TABLE 3

SEATS WON IN WEST BENGAL, 1952-62[a]

Party	Legislative Assembly			Lok Sabha		
	1952	1957	1962	1952	1957	1962
Congress Party	150	152	157	24	23	23
Communist Party	28	46	50	5	6	8
Forward Bloc (M)	14	8	13	2	2	1
Praja Socialist[b]	15	21	5	0	2	0
Jana Sangh	9	0	0	2	0	0
Hindu Mahasabha	4	0	0	0	0	0
Independents	18	25	26	1	3	3
Totals	238	252	251	34	36	35[c]

[a] Figures for the 1952 and 1957 elections are taken from the reports of the Election Commission; figures for 1962 are taken from *India: A Reference Annual, 1962* (New Delhi: Publications Division, Ministry of Information and Broadcasting, 1962).

[b] The Praja Socialist Party was not founded until 1953. Figures for 1952 are those of the Krishak Praja Mazdoor Party, which eventually merged with the KMPP and the Socialist Parties at the national level to form the Praja Socialist Party.

[c] There were thirty-six *Lok Sabha* seats filled in 1962; one was won by the Revolutionary Socialist Party.

bers as "revolutionary," and "protest."[14] The adoption of revolutionary and protest strategies has been in large part responsible for the success of the Communist and leftist groups in attracting a large section of the Bengali middle class, a class which has historically supported Marxist leftism. Middle-class trade unions are better organized than are other unions in West Bengal, and have secured the greatest concessions from

[14] For a description of these strategies, and a more elaborate analysis of the leftist opposition in West Bengal, see Marcus F. Franda, "The Politics of West Bengal," in *State Politics in India*, ed. Myron Weiner (Princeton: Princeton University Press, 1968). For the history of Marxist leftism in Bengal see Myron Weiner, *Party Politics in India* (Princeton: Princeton University Press, 1957), pp. 117-37.

both government and private industry; organized demonstrations have been the most violent and the most effective when they have involved the Bengali middle class (particularly students), and the Communist and leftist parties have gained their most sweeping electoral successes in areas of Calcutta populated by Bengali middle-class residents.

The widespread support of revolutionary and protest strategies on the part of the urban middle class stems both from the weakness of this class in the electoral process and from the nature of their political attitudes and interests. The introduction of adult franchise after Independence meant a shift of political power from the urban middle class to other groups and communities throughout the state, and the Congress party came to depend on the financial backing of business groups and rural votes for its electoral success.[15] As a result, the state government tended to undertake projects to benefit business and the rural areas, while it avoided or postponed large-scale undertakings in Calcutta, and the distribution of education, public health, and social welfare funds has gone largely to people and communities who are numerically superior to the urban middle class.

Confronted by a situation in which they secure fewer benefits because they are outnumbered, a large portion of the urban middle class has been alienated from the electoral process.[16]

[15] The electoral strategy of the Congress party in West Bengal is traced in "Calcutta: Politics of Patronage," an essay that is scheduled to appear in Myron Weiner, *Party Building in a New Nation: The Indian Congress Party* (Chicago: University of Chicago Press, forthcoming 1967).

[16] This, and the following paragraphs, stem from an unpublished study conducted by the author in 1963-64 in Calcutta, in which a sample of 102 graduates, selected at random from 20 colleges in West Bengal, were interviewed in depth. The purpose of the study was to determine those factors in the environment that would lead graduates either to be predisposed towards, or opposed to, what they perceived to be the structure of political authority in India. Although it would be im-

The present state and central governments are viewed by these people as being representative of a less cultured, less refined group of people than those who governed in Bengal before Independence, and certainly than those who should govern ideally, and the efforts of politicians to attract votes, to appeal to caste and communal ties during election campaigns, and to use patronage as a political weapon does not conform to their ideas of how a democracy should operate ideally or how it operates in some western countries. The electoral process is thus viewed as a sign of the "decadence" or the "backwardness" of those in power.

Because of the widespread acceptance of such attitudes, a considerable portion of the Bengali middle class has refused to partake in electoral politics, or, when they have joined in, they have done so largely in the spirit of protest. The Communist and leftist parties have encouraged these attitudes, and have given expression to them, by the tactics which they use and by the policies which they adopt.

In this atmosphere, the pursuance of a successful electoral strategy by the Congress often serves only to widen the communications gap that already exists between the government and these sectors of the populace. In fact, demonstrations, processions, strikes, riots, and boycotts have now become almost everyday occurrences in the city of Calcutta. Led by the urban middle classes, people have banded together to burn tramcars, to hold protest meetings, hunger strikes, and sit-down strikes, and to stage one and two-day *hartals* that still the city. Some members of the opposition have even thrown eggs or come to blows with Congressmen in the Legislative Assembly. These are all forms of protest that reflect the increasing inability of a

---

possible from such a small sample to generalize for all Bengali graduates, it is significant that, of 102 graduates interviewed, 36 indicated a predisposition to fundamentally alter the electoral process; 23 were in favor of abolishing elections entirely; and 13 were in favor of a restricted franchise, usually restricted on the basis of educational qualifications.

certain group of people to get what they want from government, and their increasing willingness to resort to tactics that will not assure them the sympathy of government.

Faced with these tactics, the Congress leadership has consciously created a close-knit party which is based on local (and especially rural) people of influence, in an effort to effect some kind of political stability within the state. The leader of the state party organization, Atulya Ghosh, thus admits that he heads an organization that has "become a place for spoils and gaining favors" but argues that this is necessary lest the Communists, and other opposition parties that believe in violence, are swept to power.[17] In Ghosh's words, the alternative to Congress in West Bengal is "mobocracy." It is on this basis too that Ghosh frequently speaks out against those, both inside the party and without, who argue that his organization is responsible for failures to effect rapid social and economic change in West Bengal. In response to one of these charges, for example, Ghosh wrote:

There is . . . no harm in pointing out weakness or corruption in any person or organisation.

But if, without any specific charge, workers are continuously denounced, demoralisation is bound to set in. The irony of it is that those who enjoy the benefits of the efforts of the ordinary party workers are the loudest in finding fault with their field-level associates.

Those who are in an advantageous position, and are enjoying some privileges, are in the habit of condemning those who have never received even a garland of recognition of their services.

The traditions of the Congress are deep-rooted and unshakable. Our workers are wonderful. That most of them continue to retain their zeal and sincerity, continue to have

[17] The role of Atulya Ghosh in the West Bengal political machine is analyzed in Marcus F. Franda, "The Political Idioms of Atulya Ghosh," *Asian Survey*, VI, No. 8 (August 1966), 420-33.

a confidence in the Congress traditions and ideals, despite the unwarranted apathy and unkindness meted out to them, is an evidence of their essential integrity and goodness. We have thus avoided a major debacle.[18]

While it would be impossible at this stage of research to say a great deal about the extent to which these ideas are accepted by other members of the organization, it is significant that Ghosh's closest associates in the Pradesh Congress Committee speak in similar terms. The Treasurer of the PCC for example argues that without the organization that Ghosh has effected, "there would be only chaos in West Bengal." In his eyes, the opposition parties are irresponsible, opposing only for the sake of opposition, and incapable of running a government. The slogan "Congress or chaos" is one frequently echoed by state Congress personnel.

The Congress party organization that has been developed in response to the ṣtate leftist opposition serves to shape center-state relations in West Bengal in a number of ways. To begin with, the fact that the party is admittedly organized in response to a serious challenge from the leftist opposition provides for a justification of the party organization in the eyes of many central and state leaders. Thus, while central party leadership is generally critical of "corruption and nepotism" within the party at the state and local levels, it will frequently admit (because of the leftist threat) that "extenuating circumstances" require the policies which are initiated and supported by the state party organization in West Bengal. In both the land reform and DVC cases, for example, the central party leadership continually made statements acknowledging their appreciation of the "difficult situation of the leaders of West Bengal." Because of their appreciation of the difficulties facing state party leaders, the central party leadership is frequently less adamant than they might otherwise be in pressing for

[18] Atulya Ghosh, "Administration: The Human Approach," *Amrita Bazaar Patriḳa* (Calcutta), January 1, 1964.

uniform policies that promise far-reaching economic and social change.

That this factor was operative in the case studies is indicated by the fact that the compromises which were effected required very restricted concessions from the state Congress party unit. Conscious of the difficulties facing West Bengal and the PCC, and conscious of the nature of the opposition in the state, the central leadership of the party purposely framed their demands in terms that were consistent with the electoral strategy being pursued by the state party. In the case of land reform, the center pressed most vociferously for legislation that would result in the acquisition of the property of some intermediaries, and for provisions in that legislation which would establish both a ceiling and a floor for the size of holdings. In other words, the center sought to effect those provisions which would be most in keeping with the uniform national policy that was being advocated, but it was insistent only when its own policy was commensurate with that policy that had been evolved by the state party in response to electoral realities. The central leadership did not attempt to press those demands which were interpreted as unreasonable by the state party organization; it did not, for example, pursue the proposal that the *bargadar* system in West Bengal be entirely revamped.

Similarly in the DVC case, the center did persuade the state government to effect a betterment levy in West Bengal for DVC irrigation water. But, when the imposition of the levy resulted in massive opposition throughout the state, the center was quick to suggest a compromise measure. To assist the West Bengal Government (and the state party) in its attempt to cope with the opposition, it was decided that water from the DVC system would be supplied free to those people living in a 150,000 acre area, most of which was located in Burdwan district. To fulfill the other part of the compromise, the West Bengal Government was required to pass legislation *enabling* the state government to collect a betterment levy. In effecting this compromise, the central leadership of the party was certainly not unsympathetic to the political situation obtaining within the state. Indeed, a complete concession was made to the electoral strategy of the state PCC by providing for the free distribution of irrigation water to Congress supporters, and by simultaneously requiring only that the party government pass *enabling* legislation, a concession which did not in any way interfere with the state's electoral situation.

If the presence of a strong and effective opposition within the state of West Bengal sometimes encourages the central leadership of the Congress party to cooperate with the state-based party unit, it also facilitates in producing a posture of cooperation, at least in some instances, on the part of the state party organization itself. For the presence of the leftist opposition, supported by a volatile middle class, frequently drives the state party government to the Union in a search for support and assistance in maintaining a stable and viable state political order. By way of example, the impetus for the desire on the part of the state government to find a solution to the reorganization dilemma in 1956 was the by-election of that year in which a Congress candidate was defeated. Subsequent to that election the state party organization in West Bengal came to realize the possible consequences that could stem from further agitation generated by the boundary dispute, and, as a result, the attention of the state party came to focus on the importance of finding a mutually satisfactory solution quickly, being channeled away from the expression of differences which had previously led so quickly to conflict with the center and with Bihar.

In the case studies, the structure of the West Bengal Congress party was especially important for a process of intergovernmental negotiations because the Congress party managed to maintain itself in power in the state. Under these circumstances, party leadership at both levels could draw on their long-standing history of successful negotiations for precedent and confidence, and they could share their common interests, beliefs, and desires when effecting a party structure capable of resisting the massive opposition that existed in the state. Because of these factors, party leadership at both levels was willing to take advantage of the instruments of negotiation that were provided by the constitutional arrangement in a way that might not have been possible given the existence of different parties at the two levels of government.

The Socioeconomic and Cultural Environment

Yet the economic dependence of West Bengal, taken alone, might easily have impelled any state government to seek a position of cooperation with the Indian Union. For, largely as a result of partition, the economy of West Bengal was virtually destroyed with the coming of Independence. Sources for procuring the vast bulk of its raw materials were entirely cut off; transportation and communications networks essential to industrial production were snapped; and the consumer economy of the state was faced with the enormous burden that resulted from the influx of millions of refugees. Calcutta especially, but also other parts of the state, was faced with economic problems that were unprecedented in India, and perhaps even in Asia: gross overpopulation; entirely inadequate housing facilities; extreme overcrowding in educational institutions; large-scale middle-class unemployment; a concentration of homeless refugees in almost all public places; a serious deficiency in sanitation and health facilities; inadequate transportation; and a lack of anything approaching sufficient public utilities.[19]

It is doubtful that any state government, in any part of the world, could cope with the enormous economic problems that

[19] Between 1951 and 1961 the population of West Bengal rose by 33 per cent, compared to an all-India average increase of only 21 per cent. For the consequences of this inordinately high rate of population growth, especially on the city of Calcutta, see Richard L. Park, "The Urban Challenge to Local and State Government: West Bengal, with Special Attention to Calcutta," in *India's Urban Future*, ed. Roy Turner (Bombay: Oxford University Press, 1962), pp. 382-96.

have confronted West Bengal since partition, and especially if it were dependent on its own resources. It is an obvious certainty that West Bengal has been unable to do so. To cite the estimates of one study, the state of West Bengal would have to spend more than the total amount provided in its third Five-Year Plan proposed budget if it were to undertake a project that would provide only adequate housing for Calcutta's population alone.[20] To cite another, it would take an estimated 225 crores of rupees, "the price of a steel plant," to undertake only stopgap measures designed to provide adequate systems of drainage, sewerage, garbage disposal, and drinking water supply in Calcutta alone.[21] That state political leaders are conscious of their economic dependence on the Union is indicated by their approach to the two principal problems with which they are confronted: the resettlement of refugees and the problems related to the improvement of conditions in Calcutta.

With regard to the city of Calcutta, state leaders constantly argue that the city's problems are not the problems of West Bengal, but rather that they are problems which were created by Union personnel and for which Union personnel must share the responsibility. The state party government has in fact left the development of the city of Calcutta entirely in the hands of the center and of international bodies.[22] Similarly, the vast majority of the schemes for refugee relief and rehabilitation have been undertaken with funds provided by the center, and the state is constantly seeking to increase its allotment for this purpose.[23]

[20] *Ibid.*, p. 338.

[21] This is the conclusion of the [Michael] Hoffman Report of the World Bank Mission; see "Calcutta and the World Bank Mission," *The Economic Weekly*, xii (October 1, 1960), 1468-74.

[22] This is stated openly in Bidhan Chandra Roy, "Paving the Way," in *West Bengal Today* (Calcutta: West Bengal Pradesh Congress Committee, 1956), p. 19.

[23] The central government has set up numerous refugee colonies outside of West Bengal (in some cases whole new townships) and has established colonies within the state as well. By 1957 it was estimated

But the difficulties involved in tackling the problems of West Bengal revolve not only around matters of economics. Some observers have argued, for example, that the amount of funds recommended by the reports of international agencies could be obtained from sources outside the state, but that the projects recommended in these reports, if left in the hands of the state administration, would still either be only ineffectively implemented or not implemented at all.[24] Even more fundamental obstacles to the implementation of plans in West Bengal stem from the nature of the administrative personnel in the state, and from the ties between the administration and the Congress party.

Although the administration of West Bengal has not been adequately researched, most observers agree that large segments of the present state bureaucracy are incapable of innovating policies of reform, or of implementing policy effectively across the state (and not only at the local level). The reasons for this appear to stem from a variety of factors. To begin with, the administration is to a large extent staffed with middle-class Bengalis who themselves have been alienated from the present structure of political authority. Although they seek positions as administrators and clerks in order to maintain their social positions, they do not identify very closely with the work that they do on behalf of the government. Many clerks even view the circumstances of their own positions—the low salaries, poor working conditions, and the corruption and nepotism which goes on around them (and in which they sometimes share)—as an affirmation of their view that the pres-

---

that the center had provided funds for the rehabilitation of 656,000 refugees, and in 1963 it was estimated that the state had received approximately 200 crores of rupees from the center for this purpose. See *India: A Reference Annual* (New Delhi: Publications Division, Ministry of Information and Broadcasting, Government of India, 1963), p. 114.

[24] This argument appears in "Greater Calcutta," *The Economic Weekly*, xii (November 19, 1960), 1668-69.

ent government is incapable of coping with the problems of the state. The level of morale within the administration is, therefore, extremely low. Moreover, the views of the middle class within the bureaucracy tend to discourage the willingness to innovate, a tendency that is reinforced by other factors in the society which mitigate against the production of innovating individuals. As Weiner has pointed out:

> Bengal is characterized by the existence of hierarchical and generally authoritarian patterns within all institutions, from the family to schools, universities, administration and government, which serve to inhibit the development of innovating individuals. Men in authority view innovations within their institutions as devices to threaten their positions; they also tend to view new ideas from underlings as intolerable threats to their status. As a result, men with ambition express fidelity and humility to authority. When they attack authority it is not one's personal superior, but rather impersonal institutions, such as government, and in impersonal ways as in the street demonstrations.
>
> Those who are on the top not only discourage innovation from below, but having themselves been nurtured by the system are often incapable of innovating. Furthermore, inaction by men in authority brings no punishment, while action often opens the possibility of antagonizing someone in a still higher position of authority. Action-mindedness therefore is a quality possessed by very few men.[25]

The dependence of West Bengal on its ties to the Union, which results from these administrative and economic realities, sometimes encourages the state to negotiate for benefits that it could not otherwise obtain. Its reliance on administrative personnel not associated with the state party government, for example, was instrumental in its original willingness to enter

[25] Myron Weiner, "Political Development in West Bengal," in *Political Change in South Asia*, ed. Myron Weiner (Calcutta: K. L. Mukhopadhyay, 1963), pp. 255-56.

into negotiations for creating the Damodar Valley Corporation, and its dependence on central government funds for development projects made a multipurpose river valley development corporation (with its principle of shared costs) appealing. At a later stage, the state was willing to bargain with the central government (and with Bihar) in the allocation of the electrical power supply of the DVC, primarily because the state's own power requirements necessitated the use of those people who had constructed the facilities of the Damodar Valley Corporation. Finally, the major compromise to which the government of West Bengal was a party (again in the DVC case) came about because of the threat from the central government that funds for a state-sponsored dam project, which was crucial to the future development of West Bengal, would be withheld.

The dependence of West Bengal on its ties to the Indian Union is also indicated by a number of other factors which are not illustrated in the case studies but which nevertheless impinge on center-state relations. The existence of a volatile middle class, and the nature of the opposition parties in the state, serve to increase the dependence of the state on central government funds, troops, and administrators for the control of violence and for development projects with which to meet middle-class demands. In addition, the state is able to use the national government (and the "great issues" of national politics) to deflect criticism and scorn that would ordinarily be directed against itself. In 1958, for example, the state government and state Congress party argued that it was the work of Nehru and the central government which had led to the Nehru-Noon agreement dividing Berubari Union between East Pakistan and West Bengal, even though state government officers had initially concurred with the boundary agreement.[26]

[26] See "Storm Over Berubari," *The Economic Weekly*, xii (December 10, 1960), 1785-86. The dispute over Berubari Union of Jalpaiguri district in Cooch-Behar arose because of a conflict between Indian and Pakistani maps. The Radcliffe Award had originally given Berubari

Again in 1962, the state government was able to shelve plans for a separate Ministry in charge of Calcutta, and to diminish its plan outlay for projects to be undertaken in the city of Calcutta (thus keeping its rural-oriented projects intact) with the plea that these measures had been necessitated by the Chinese invasion.[27]

West Bengal's ties with the Indian Union also lend to the state party government an air of legitimacy, and a continuity with the past, that the state government can use to its advantage, especially when confronting the Bengali middle class. An instance in which an appeal to national unity was clearly used to deflect middle-class agitation was provided in the case study of states reorganization, where the government consciously promulgated (and sustained) the merger issue in an

---

(an area of 8.75 square miles) to West Bengal, but the map annexed to the Radcliffe Report had placed Berubari in East Pakistan. As a result, both nations claimed Berubari until 1958, when an agreement (the Nehru-Noon agreement) was finally reached, dividing Berubari into two equal halves and distributing it between the two countries.

Although it was a small fragment of territory, the reaction of the Bengali middle class was immediate and intense. The opposition parties formed a "Berubari Defence Committee," and began holding mass protest meetings and demonstrations. Eventually this agitation was supported by the state Congress party, and a motion censuring the boundary agreement was passed in the Legislative Assembly with state Congress support. This was done despite the fact that state party government officials had initially concurred in the settlement.

[27] Shortly before the Chinese invasion, Chief Minister P. C. Sen had stated in a press conference that "Calcutta got nothing during the First Plan period and almost nothing during the Second. During the Third Plan we must do something for the city." He therefore promised that a Minister of State for Calcutta would be created after the Puja holidays, and that Third Plan funds would be allocated to Calcutta for a number of specific projects (*The Statesman*, September 20, 1962, p. 1). After the Chinese invasion, however, he announced that his plans for a separate Ministry of Calcutta were being dropped, and that West Bengal's reduction in plan outlay would necessitate the elimination of a number of projects *in Calcutta* (*ibid.*, November 14, 1962, p. 1).

effort to turn attention away from regional emotions and demands. Moreover, by emphasizing the ties between the Congress party government in West Bengal and the government at the center, the state government is able to sway middle-class residents in Calcutta on the basis of appeals to nationalist feelings (as it does, for example, when it stresses anti-Pakistan or anti-Chinese issues in Calcutta election campaigns).[28] By stressing the links of the West Bengal Pradesh Congress Committee (PCC) to the nationalist movement of pre-Independence days, the party government shares, at least to a certain extent, the admiration and awe that is reserved for the heroic leaders of India's past.

Because the state is so heavily dependent on its ties to the Indian Union, it obviously is encouraged to negotiate with the Union, and it would seem that it could even be compelled in some instances to submit to Union-supported compromises and forms of persuasion. But perhaps the most remarkable facet of center-state relations in West Bengal is the fact that the bargaining process which takes place is not typically characterized by "submission," or by authority relationships which directly result from the threats that the center can put forth as a result of the state's dependence. The case studies, in fact, supply impressive evidence of the unwillingness or inability of central government and party leaders to discipline West Bengal's political leadership, or to use fully the constitutional powers granted to central leadership groups. For a more complete understanding of the case studies, it is therefore essential to explore those factors in the political and social environment of West Bengal that give the state's political leadership a large measure of independence.

[28] The use of national issues in Calcutta election campaigns is discussed in Asok Mitra, "West Bengal Elections: A Further Note," *The Economic Weekly*, xiv (May 12, 1962), 781-87. See also "Election Prospects in West Bengal," *ibid.*, xiv (February 24, 1962), 367-70; and "Gains Cancelled by Losses," *ibid.*, xiv (March 10, 1962), 435-36.

Sources of State Independence

THERE were a number of compelling reasons for the framers of India's Constitution to think in terms of a centralized, co-operative federation immediately after Independence. It was obvious that the size and diversity of India would prevent the efficient working of a highly unified administration, and yet the massiveness of the problems that faced the new Indian leadership, combined with the enormity of the goals they had set for themselves, suggested the need for a central authority powerful enough to prevent disintegration and to offer direction in the changing world that was sure to come. Communalism, regionalism, economic imbalances, social revolutionary goals, all of these seemed to demand a formula of unity in diversity, which, when translated into a constitution, called for "federation with a strong centre."[1] Moreover, the Indian federation was brought into being by the devolution of powers from a strong, unified (British) administrative apparatus, first in the 1919 Government of India Act, later in the 1935 India Act, and finally in the Constituent Assembly of an independent India. This experience, which is so unlike that of the framers of the Constitution of the United States (who came together as representatives of separate states), indicates most clearly the reliance on central power in India's immediate past, as well as the fact that Indians had neither experienced nor participated in the working of a more traditional federal system like that of the United States or Australia.

As a result of these factors, the framers of the Indian Constitution adopted a number of provisions that would seem to weight the federal balance so much in favor of central dominance as to call into question the federal nature of the In-

[1] This is the phrase Nehru frequently used when describing the Constitution, quoted in Austin, *The Indian Constitution*, p. 196.

dian polity.[2] In Article 3, the central Parliament is authorized, presumably by a simple majority, to form new states or to alter the boundaries of any state, without obtaining the consent of the state or states concerned. Article 254 provides that, in any instance where a law passed by a state Legislative Assembly is repugnant to a statute of the federal Parliament, the latter shall prevail. Article 248 vests residual powers in the central government, and Article 249 provides that if two-thirds of the members of the Council of States approve, Parliament may "make laws with respect to any matter enumerated in the State List." Articles 352 to 360 contain the emergency provisions which empower the President to suspend the Constitution under certain circumstances and in certain prescribed ways, and to administer a state (or states) from New Delhi in those instances where he is convinced either that there is a threat to the security of the nation, that there is a financial "emergency," or that the constitutional machinery of government has broken down.

But while these constitutional provisions have been used in some states with great effectiveness, they have been used only sparingly in West Bengal. Indeed, the case studies (in which hard and sometimes brutal political decisions had to be made across the spectrum of public policy) point out most clearly that the central government has not been as strong or as forceful in its relationships with West Bengal as the thrust of the Constitution and the dependence of the state on the center would seem to make possible. Further analysis of the party structure and system in West Bengal, and the ability of the state party leadership to mobilize the population for electoral

[2] The first work to question the "federal principle" of the Indian Union was Kenneth Wheare, *Federal Government* (2d edn., London: Oxford University Press, 1951), p. 28. Since 1951, a number of other authors have adopted Wheare's description of the Indian Union as a "quasi-federation." See, for example, K. N. Sinha, "The Constitution of India: More Unitary than Federal," *The Modern Review*, xcviii (1955), 448-52.

and agitational purposes, is essential for an understanding of these developments.

Party Structure and System

The principal political factor operating to make West Bengal relatively independent in center-state relations during the period of the case studies was the existence of a state-based, close-knit Congress party organization that had been able to resist central party discipline and control. Since Independence, the Congress party of India had held power both in the central government and the state government in West Bengal (as well as in most local governments), and there had been an effective party discipline in the *Lok Sabha* and in the state Legislative Assembly. The state Congress party was defeated in the Legislative Assembly elections in 1967 by a coalition of opposition parties, but we cannot conclude (as Richard L. Park has recently done)[3] that the Congress party was "disciplined" or "centrally controlled" even during that period when the Congress dominated the state government. Indeed, it is clear in the case studies, not only that the party structure in West Bengal operated in such a way as to impede central decision-making, but also that this was the result of factors that were fundamental to the state political process. More succinctly, those aspects of the party structure and system that are most relevant for center-state relations in West Bengal are as follows: (1) the sources of party effectiveness are local and not national (that is, they derive from the socioeconomic and

---

[3] In Park's words: "India . . . has concentrated authority and power in the hands of the central government to bolster the country's sense of national unity. The result has been a tendency to impose authoritarian decisions upon resisting state and local governments. The Congress party, which controls almost every major governmental unit in the country, through its disciplined and centrally controlled party power, bypasses interparty compromises that might otherwise strengthen the position of leaders at state levels." Richard L. Park, "India," in Roy C. Macridis and Robert Ward, *Modern Political Systems: Asia* (Englewood Cliffs, New Jersey: Prentice-Hall, Inc., 1963), p. 293.

cultural environment of the state); (2) the electoral success of the state Congress party results as much from the ability of state party leaders to effect a close-knit party organization as it does from the connections of the state party to the Congress-dominated nationalist movement; (3) the state party is organized separately from the central party and is able effectively to repel attempts by central leaders to interfere in state party matters; and (4) because of these factors, the state party is able to pursue courses of action independent from (and often contradictory to) those of central party leaders.

These conclusions, while they are based solely on the experience of West Bengal, are not unsupported by data drawn from other parts of India. In contrast to Park's analysis, for example, Weiner's very recent study of the Congress party in a Mysore constituency concluded that the Congress was "non-ideological" and "aggregative," based "largely on those who wield local power" and on those who have wielded local power in the past.[4] This is precisely the kind of description that would apply to the party in West Bengal. The Congress party of West Bengal does characteristically refuse to adhere to the ideological positions of central leadership groups, and it certainly refuses to act on the basis of central programs that seek to change the existing structure of society. Instead, it attempts to attract supporters throughout the state from among those who are already influential in their own localities and on the basis of local issues.[5]

That the Congress party in the state should attempt to build

[4] Myron Weiner, "Traditional Role Performance and the Development of Modern Political Parties: The Indian Case," *Journal of Politics*, xxvi, No. 4 (November 1964), 849.

[5] Material for an analysis of the Congress party in West Bengal was gathered in West Bengal in 1963-64. For a more detailed statement of the conclusions stated here, see Franda, "The Politics of West Bengal," in *State Politics in India*. These conclusions are also consistent with Weiner's studies of West Bengal: see "Changing Patterns of Political Leadership in West Bengal" and "Notes on Political Development in West Bengal," in *Political Change in South Asia*, pp. 177-257.

this kind of organization is not surprising, especially in light of the existing social order. Like other areas of India, the social structure of West Bengal is extremely disjointed, conflict is generally pursued within geographically limited areas, and a pattern of hierarchical social relationships is widespread. What results is a situation in which some men have far more influence than would be possible in a nonhierarchically organized social system, at the same time that such influence is necessarily confined to small spatial and social areas. In every village, town, and neighborhood of West Bengal there are men who are known to be exceedingly influential ("big men" in the vernacular): landowners, on whom tenants and sharecroppers depend for their holdings; small tradesmen, who control credit supplies and who have the ability to foreclose; petty officials and land-settlement officers who determine how official documents will be recorded; managers of *bustees* or *dhobi khannas* (washermen compounds) in Calcutta who determine rent-rates and have the power to evict; and a number of other men who exercise a similar kind of control over the public and private facilities and services upon which large numbers of people depend for their livelihood.

The economic power of these men is often reinforced by elements of the social system. Especially in the rural areas, some men have influence over large numbers of people because they are members of a leading caste in their locality, or because they occupy hereditary positions of authority within their caste. In one village (Chandipur) studied by Nicholas, for example, it was found that "the dominant caste of a community initiates and controls many kinds of events in village life. Castes which are inferior in status must, for the most part, accept the initiative of the dominant group."[6] Even in the urban areas, the *sirdar* of a factory gang in Calcutta maintains authority over almost all spheres of the lives of those

[6] Ralph W. Nicholas, "Village Factions and Political Parties in Rural West Bengal," *Journal of Commonwealth Political Studies*, ii, No. 1 (November 1963), 19.

under his charge, which derives largely from his place in a village social structure.[7] A large measure of influence may also rest in men who are highly respected in their community: leaders of tribal and untouchable associations; members of the Bengali middle class who are deferred to because of their cultural attainments, or the cultural attainments of their family; leaders of the *para* (neighborhood) organizations who organize and provide funds for neighborhood *pujas* (religious festivals); and patrons of literature and the arts who provide facilities and funds for dramas and cultural events.

Because they hold positions in which they control the economic fortunes of a large sector of the local population, or because their positions of authority and respect command deference from a large number of people, these "key men"[8] are capable of swaying most, or frequently all, of their followers, clients, and dependents to vote for one political party or the other. But the fact that they stem from such varied and diverse social and economic backgrounds, and that their influence is confined to relatively small areas, is an indication of their relative lack of common interest or purpose. This means that, if these men are to be used for purposes of political organization, it would be difficult to attract them by the use of firm and consistent party stands on most issues.

But since the state Congress party is unfettered by strong ideological commitments, or by commitments to central government plans and programs, it can effect alliances with these "key men"—by striking bargains and compromises, and by offering rewards or punishments—with an eye only to local circumstances. In the Damodar Valley Corporation case,

[7] Asok Mitra, "West Bengal, Sikkim and Chandernagore," in *Census of India, 1951*, Vol. VI, Part I-A "Report" (Delhi: Manager of Publications, 1953), pp. 318-19.

[8] This is the phrase coined by Rajni Kothari, "Some Problems of Articulation in Indian Politics," paper prepared for the International Political Science Association, Bombay, January 1964, p. 2. (Mimeographed) It is also used by Nicholas, *Journal of Commonwealth Political Studies*, II, No. 1 (November 1963), 10.

for example, the West Bengal Congress party was able to aid in the distribution of irrigation water from channels of the DVC to those who saw it as being in their interest to pay the irrigation cess and gain the benefits therefrom. At the same time, in other areas, it was able to work for the noncollection of the irrigation cess from those who were unwilling to take DVC water from the regular channels and who preferred to take it surreptitiously. In this instance the party could side with those cultivators and landowners who argued that local improvements were more important than completion of the second stage of the DVC project, and could subsequently take on the character of a relief organization in the localities that were hard hit by the floods that came because the second stage was not undertaken. The party has a reputation for being susceptible to pressure from people who are considered "key men," and for being capable of resisting ideological orientations, and it is on this basis that it has effectively organized the state.

Especially important in the effective pursuit of this kind of political representation is the Congress organization that was developed after Independence, an organization which was largely the creation of Atulya Ghosh. When Ghosh was elected General-Secretary of the Pradesh Congress Committee (PCC) after Independence, he immediately proceeded to establish a number of centers—at Deulagara in Bankura district, at Arambagh in Hooghly, at Ghosh's home in Karballa Tank Lane in Calcutta, and elsewhere—in which political workers could live and work, or simply meet for discussion. In each of these centers live a number of young party workers who carry on constructive activities, keep themselves informed of local and district political affairs, maintain Congress files, and other such matters. Each of them is visited frequently by state party and governmental leaders who are passing through the district, and by political workers from the district who come to the party center regularly to secure information and make reports. The existence of these centers provides a network for the close intercommunication of political leadership with the rank-and-file; they are vehicles for the promulgation of particularistic policies downward and the communication of local and parochial demands and complaints to the upper echelons of the state Congress party. The closeness of the relationships between people involved with these networks and centers is indicated by the frequent use of affectionate terms between them (Ghosh himself is known as *borababu*—an affectionate word for boss—or as Atulya *da*—elder brother). The effectiveness of the organization is indicated by the fact that the vast majority of the numerous factions which dominated Bengali politics before Independence (when the leadership of the state party was indeed ideologically oriented) have been either eliminated or absorbed.

The independence of the state Congress party from influence by central party leaders rests not only on the state-based, close-knit organization that has been created, it is also encouraged by the formal structure of the party itself. As can be seen in Figure 6, the pivotal group within the Congress party organization has been, since the 1920's, the Pradesh Congress Committee (PCC), which generally organized the party within state or provincial boundaries. The PCC determines the number of local district and *mandal* Congress committees that shall be organized within the state, and it is almost solely responsible for bringing these locally organized units together. Control of local units obviously gives the state party leadership a great deal of influence with party membership, and, as a result, an important role in the maintenance of the electoral position of the state ministries and the central Parliament. The importance of the state Congress party leadership is also enhanced by a number of other factors. Since the constitution of the Congress party forbids the same man to hold the positions of Chief Minister and PCC president simultaneously, the ministry cannot readily capture and control the party organization, and the Chief Minister is thus often forced to acknowledge in concrete ways his dependence on the political machine that

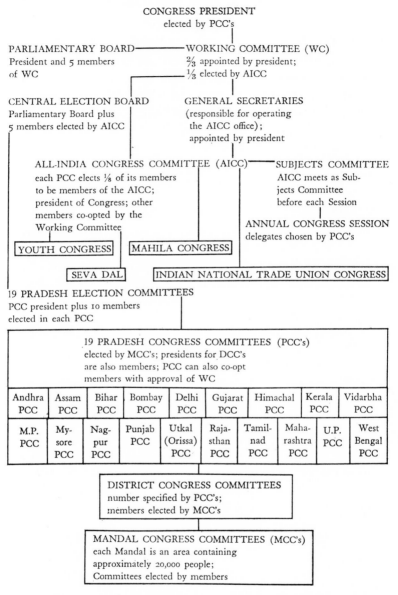

CONGRESS PRESIDENT
elected by PCC's

PARLIAMENTARY BOARD————WORKING COMMITTEE (WC)
President and 5 members   ⅔ appointed by president;
of WC   ⅓ elected by AICC

CENTRAL ELECTION BOARD   GENERAL SECRETARIES
Parliamentary Board plus   (responsible for operating
5 members elected by AICC   the AICC office);
                                appointed by president

ALL-INDIA CONGRESS COMMITTEE (AICC)————SUBJECTS COMMITTEE
each PCC elects ⅛ of its members   AICC meets as Sub-
to be members of the AICC;   jects Committee
president of Congress; other   before each Session
members co-opted by the
Working Committee   ANNUAL CONGRESS SESSION
                                delegates chosen by PCC's

| YOUTH CONGRESS | | MAHILA CONGRESS |

| SEVA DAL | | INDIAN NATIONAL TRADE UNION CONGRESS |

19 PRADESH ELECTION COMMITTEES
PCC president plus 10 members
elected in each PCC

19 PRADESH CONGRESS COMMITTEES (PCC's)
elected by MCC's; presidents for DCC's
are also members; PCC can also co-opt
members with approval of WC

Andhra PCC	Assam PCC	Bihar PCC	Bombay PCC	Delhi PCC	Gujarat PCC	Himachal PCC	Kerala PCC	Vidarbha PCC
M.P. PCC	Mysore PCC	Nagpur PCC	Punjab PCC	Utkal (Orissa) PCC	Rajasthan PCC	Tamilnad PCC	Maharashtra PCC	U.P. PCC	West Bengal PCC

DISTRICT CONGRESS COMMITTEES
number specified by PCC's;
members elected by MCC's

MANDAL CONGRESS COMMITTEES (MCC's)
each Mandal is an area containing
approximately 20,000 people;
Committees elected by members

Fig. 6. The Structure of the Congress Party According to the
Party Constitution (March 1962)

keeps him in office. Moreover, the party chief controls the party finances in the state and is a major figure in the collection of campaign contributions for the Congress coffers.[9] Because of these forms of control, the state PCC is frequently able to gain a great deal of autonomy within the state it organizes.

Because the Congress party in West Bengal is a close-knit organization, deriving its strength from local sources independent of the national party, it has been able to effectively repel those attempts by central party personnel to interfere in state party matters. Indeed, central party leaders have at times sought to control district and local party units in West Bengal from New Delhi, they have attempted to impose candidates favorable to central party leaders on the state organization, and they have even sided with dissidents who sought to oust the present state party leadership. But the effectiveness of the state party in resisting the directives of the central leadership groups has been proven on a number of occasions.

The first post-Independence attempt by central party leaders to control the West Bengal Congress organization came immediately after Independence had been achieved in 1947, at a time when the state of West Bengal was in the throes of a serious political crisis. At this time the urban coalition that had dominated the Congress party in West Bengal throughout the nationalist movement was no longer intact, largely as a result of the defection of its leader Subhas Bose. A number of the Congress supporters had followed Bose out of the Congress during the war and joined the leftist parties; a number of Congress strongholds had been cut off by partition, and the party faced the prospect of contesting elections in an area where a Muslim Ministry had been in power before Independence. With no single group in control of either the Assembly or the Bengal PCC, the Congress high command decided to support Prafulla Ghosh, a member of the Congress Working

---

[9] Marcus F. Franda, "The Organizational Development of India's Congress Party," *Pacific Affairs*, xxxv, No. 3 (Fall 1962), 253.

Committee and an ardent supporter of Gandhi. But Ghosh lacked political backing within West Bengal: he was the leader of a Gandhian group centered in the *Abhoy Ashram* at Comilla (in East Bengal) and without a large following in West Bengal. His support dwindled, the Legislative Assembly party did not support him, and he was ultimately forced to resign at the insistence of state politicians.

The instigation for the present Congress organization in West Bengal therefore came from the state itself and not from the center.[10] In January 1948, the Congress members of the state Legislative Assembly party threw their support to Bidhan Chandra Roy, a respected doctor from Calcutta, and Roy quickly turned for support to the organized groups and factions centered in West Bengal. Prafulla Sen, the leader of the Arambagh group, was appointed to a Ministry in the Roy government (he later became Chief Minister), and members of the Hooghly group were similarly placed in a number of ministerial posts. Atulya Ghosh, then a prominent leader in Hooghly district politics, became the party secretary. In addition, a number of important Ministries were either kept in Roy's personal hands or turned over to Roy's supporters and associates from Calcutta.

The state-based coalition that took power in West Bengal in 1948 has remained remarkably stable, and it has been able to thwart any renewed attempts by central personnel to influence directly state organizational affairs. This can be seen from the way in which the party dealt with a factional dispute which developed in mid-1952 within the South Calcutta District Congress Committee (DCC), the dispute being related to the kind of organization that was being created at that time. In mid-1952, a large number of the members of the South Calcutta DCC were in favor of a more ideologically oriented party than that which Ghosh had brought into being, a party which the dissidents thought would be more capable of promoting rapid and

[10] K. P. Thomas, *Dr. B. C. Roy* (Calcutta: West Bengal Pradesh Congress Committee, 1955), p. 225.

revolutionary changes in the social and economic sphere.[11] While this faction was out of power within its own District Congress Committee at the time, it was felt that the majority of the members of the DCC were in favor of a revision of the DCC organization, and that the dissidents would be able to win a fresh party election. The dissidents thus appealed to the Congress Working Committee, asking that it arrange for fresh DCC elections, and the Working Committee immediately called for fresh elections in South Calcutta. The secretary of the PCC, Bejoy Singh Nahar, did state that fresh elections to the South Calcutta DCC would be held (on May 24, 1952), but five days before the elections were to take place the unit was completely revamped. Instead of carrying out the orders of the Working Committee, the state Congress party president (then Atulya Ghosh) dissolved the constituent unit, and directed Nahar to "take charge of and deal with all matters relating to the South Calcutta District Congress Committee."[12] The state party then worked to draw in enough new members to outvote the dissidents within the South Calcutta unit, and was ultimately able to purge the dissidents from the state party organization. The point is that all of this was done against the orders of the central party organ.[13]

[11] Some of the leading Congressmen most recently associated with this faction in West Bengal are Prafulla Banerjee, Naren Sen, Jehangir Kabir, Mrs. Maitreyee Bose, Aurobindo Bose, Kanailal Goswami, and Asoke Sen. Members of this faction commonly believe that Congressmen intent upon securing a political base from which to promote greater influence by the center in state party matters have frequently been nominated by the state party organization for especially difficult contested seats. In the states reorganization study this was certainly the case; Asoke Sen, nominated by the party to run on the unpopular Bengal-Bihar merger issue, is a major leader of the dissidents in West Bengal, and was a close friend of the late Prime Minister Nehru.

[12] *The Statesman* (Calcutta), June 18, 1952, p. 5.

[13] When members of the South Calcutta DCC appealed to the Working Committee to reconstitute the DCC at a later date, on the ground that the state PCC had not conformed to the Working Committee's

A second major attempt by the Congress high command to interfere in the affairs of the state party organization came in 1958, just prior to the 1958 elections to the West Bengal Pradesh Congress Committee. At that time a number of West Bengal Congressmen organized an *ad hoc* committee to work for the election of Saila Kumar Mukherjee, a respected Calcuttan, former speaker of the Legislative Assembly, and a man in favor of adherence by the state to central government plans, programs, and policies. Initially the "ginger group," as it was called, appealed to Nehru, asking him to request the resignation of Ghosh as party president. Nehru refused to request the resignation of Ghosh, stating: "I have a high opinion of the work done by Mr. Ghosh in the Congress organization in West Bengal. He is a fine organizer and has served the Congress well. . . . It is not for me to impose leadership or anything else on West Bengal. I am interested in effective work by Congressmen."[14] At the same time, however, Nehru encouraged the dissidents by adding that "as a matter of principle it was good to have a rotating system of office-bearers in Congress committees."[15]

Soon after Nehru's statement, the Working Committee of the Congress Party issued a directive, instructing all Members of Parliament who were also Pradesh Congress Committee executives to resign one position or the other. Since Atulya Ghosh was simultaneously an MP and West Bengal PCC President, he was instructed by the central Parliamentary Board of the party to resign his chairmanship of the PCC on

---

previous directive, a WC subcommittee, composed of Desai, N. V. Gadgil, and Pant, dismissed the charges as being "too vague." See *ibid.*, January 13, 1953, p. 5.

[14] *Ibid.*, July 25, 1958, p. 1.

[15] For evidence that this was taken as encouragement by the "ginger group," see *ibid.*, p. 5. A number of dissidents also stated in interviews that they had been encouraged by Nehru to proceed with their plans in private meetings.

the ground that he was valuable to the party as a Member of Parliament (in reality he had attended meetings of the *Lok Sabha* on only three occasions prior to this time, even though he had been an MP for six years). While Ghosh and his followers viewed this as an instance of unwarranted interference by the center in state affairs,[16] they were able to comply with the instructions of the central party organs and to maintain control of the organization at the same time. On October 31, 1958, Atulya Ghosh resigned as president of the Pradesh Congress Committee and on the following day all other officers of the PCC submitted their own resignations. Two days later they met for (supposedly) the last time as the Executive Council, and voted in favor of their own dissolution. At the same time they arranged for a meeting of the whole of the Pradesh Congress Committee (some six hundred-odd members) at which meeting a new Executive Council would be elected.

The dissidents of West Bengal immediately appealed to both Nehru and U. N. Dhebar (Congress president) to set up an *ad hoc* committee to run Pradesh Congress Committee affairs, on the presupposition that pro-Ghosh people would be reelected if the scheduled PCC meeting were allowed to take place. And they proposed the name of Saila Mukherjee as temporary chairman of this *ad hoc* committee.[17] But Mukherjee refused to consent without the support of Chief Minister B. C. Roy,[18] and ultimately Roy refused to support the dissidents against Ghosh and the group that had kept his government in power. As a result, a 72-year-old Congressman, Jadavendra Nath Panja from Ghosh's own constituency, was proposed as president by the pro-Ghosh group (P. C. Sen himself proposed the name) and was subsequently elected by a considerable margin at the PCC meeting. Panja immediately named as his aides the same people who had made up the Executive Council of the PCC before the election, with the

[16] Stated by Ghosh in an interview, April 16, 1964.

[17] *The Statesman* (Calcutta), November 14, 1958, p. 1.

[18] *Ibid.*, November 24, 1958, p. 1.

exception of some of those people who had sided with the dissidents. Ghosh also remained on the Executive Council and a number of other important PCC committees when committee members who had been named by Panja resigned voluntarily and themselves nominated Ghosh. The result, of course, was that the dissidents were either persuaded to accept the leadership of Ghosh and his organization, or they were purged from the party. In a statement after the PCC election, they stated that what had taken place was a "mere shuffle of the cards," and that they were even more powerless now than they had been previously.[19]

It may be that the Congress party in other areas of India is "disciplined" and "centrally controlled" in the way that Park has indicated. But the inability of central party leadership to discipline the West Bengal PCC reflects at once the strength of the Congress party organization in West Bengal and the dependence of the all-India Congress party on that organization. Because it is able effectively to repel attempts by central party personnel to influence directly state party affairs, the state PCC need have no qualms about pursuing independent courses of action. And because of their inability to discipline the PCC, leaders of the all-India Congress party are dependent on state leaders for votes, for party finances, and for an electoral organization.

That this kind of party structure acts as an impediment to centralized decision-making is clearly indicated in the case studies. In the DVC case, for example, the state Congress party sided with those cultivators who took water surreptitiously from DVC channels, and against central party directives that condemned this kind of behavior. And, despite this, the central government granted almost all of the demands of state leaders (who were pursuing a course of action independent of the center) because the state party argued that this was necessary for its survival. Similarly, in the states reorganization case, the government was forced to make concessions to

[19] *Ibid.*, November 26, 1958, p. 7.

the state party when the PCC threatened nonviolent demonstrations after the publication of the initial report of the States Reorganization Commission; and the center was unable to prevent the state party from working against the government proposal to merge West Bengal and Bihar. Finally, in the case of land reform, state leaders argued that legislation which favored the rural gentry was necessary for the maintenance of the party organization in the state, and central party personnel who thought differently were unwilling to make their opposition felt lest they risk their electoral position in the state.

Political Mobilization

It could be argued, however, that a number of other Indian states exhibit similar state Congress party structures, and that the party system functions in much the same way in these states as it does in West Bengal, but with different results for center-state relations. The Madhya PCC to take an obvious example, has the same structural arrangements with the central organs of the party as the PCC in West Bengal, but because of the low levels of political participation obtaining in Madhya Pradesh, and because of the inability of state politicians to mobilize the populace on center-state issues, the state has been subject to a great deal of control from New Delhi. It is in this context that the high rate of politicization obtaining in West Bengal becomes important. For it is clear that the population of West Bengal is as highly mobilized as that found in any other Indian state, and that a large segment of the population is particularly susceptible to being mobilized on center-state issues very quickly.

The high rate of politicization in Bengal is a result, both of the colonial history of the region and its post-Independence experience. Bengal was one of the first areas to be colonized by the British in India, and was the center of a great many attempts by the British to devise methods for governing and for social change of the entire subcontinent. Throughout the 19th century especially, British land reform measures, educational policy, industrial and commercial policy, and many other experiments were first tried in Bengal and only later extended to the other provinces.[20] Not surprisingly, a consciousness of things political grew up in Bengal (especially in the area surrounding Calcutta), and Bengalis were soon at the forefront of a number of national political movements. The first Congress president was a Bengali, as were a number of prominent moderates who led the Congress in its early stages. Bengalis were also instrumental in the rise of the terrorist agitation and revolutionary violence that appeared in India in the early part of this century; the earliest terrorist organizations (Jugantar and Anushilan Samiti) were founded in Bengal, as were most of the Marxist left parties that came to life in India after the Russian revolution. Indeed, Bengal's prominence in the nationalist movement did not recede until the third decade of this century, with the rise of Gandhi and a new national leadership.

In this century, then, Bengalis have been subject to a series of events that have served to intensify political awareness in the region. While Bengalis were experiencing the decline of the cultural and political hegemony of their province in this century, they also found themselves involved very heavily in a major famine (1943); the Allied military operations in and around Calcutta during World War II; the partition of the subcontinent in 1947 and the rioting that accompanied partition; and an independent India in which the rate of change was increasing rapidly. The Bengali middle class met with a high degree of frustration and hardship during those years when it was trying to maintain its cultural "superiority" over the rest of India. Educated unemployment, common in India, was augmented in West Bengal by the dislocations of the economy resulting from partition, and by the rapid expansion of the middle class as a result of educational and land reform

---

[20] The growth of political consciousness in Bengal in the 19th century is traced out in Namai Sadhan Bose, *The Indian Awakening and Bengal* (Calcutta: Firma K. L. Mukhopadhyay, 1960), pp. 152ff.

policies. The struggle for middle-class jobs, educational opportunities, and housing became seriously acute when the size of the middle class was considerably enlarged by the influx of refugees from East Pakistan, and by the abolition of *zamindari* rights for 1.3 million intermediaries. Since Independence, the economic position of the urban middle class has further deteriorated with the rising cost of living, and with the neglect of the mounting problems of the city of Calcutta as a result of electoral realities. At the same time, the dislocations of Bengal, combined with the heavy demand for education, has created an educational system which is far from adequate to maintain the same level of cultural activities that once attained in the province.

It is commonplace, of course, to say that the numerous "regions" of India each has its own distinctive language, social structure, caste system, cultural traditions, and its own pattern of economic distribution and structure. It has also been said many times that Bengal has very seldom in its history been subordinated to Delhi, and even when it has, its ties to a central empire have usually been temporary and loose. But however commonplace it may be to speak of India's diversity, it is at the same time necessary to point out the ways in which diversity, when coupled with other factors, has affected the thoughts and emotions of Indians, and the consequences which this has for center-state relations in different areas.

In the case of Bengal, a high degree of politicization has combined with regional tradition to produce a situation in which a large segment of the population is highly conscious (and extremely jealous) of the separate cultural identity of Bengalis. Most Bengalis consider their language to be the most highly developed of all of India's languages; Bengali literature, art, drama, and films are considered to be far superior to those of other regions; and Bengalis consider it a result of the Bengali "genius" that Tagore has been the only Indian to win a Nobel prize, that the Presidency college was once called "the Harvard of India," and that Gokhale once said, "What

Bengal thinks today, India thinks tomorrow."[21] The Bengalis still attach great importance to cultural achievements and intellectual and educational attainments which are in keeping with the Bengali tradition, and the majority of the middle-class families insist on activities and customs which have been pursued for centuries by the Bengali *bhadralok* ("gentleman" or a "man of good breeding") class.

In response to the events of this century a wide section of the urban middle class has thus come to interpret almost all political events in terms of conspirational activities on the part of the British government, the state and central governments, and the non-Bengali and foreign businessmen. And this feeling, that "a conspiracy is threatening the soil of Bengal," frequently results in an emotionally charged campaign against actions that are interpreted as central dominance, or as "Hindi imperialism," or as other forms of federal control. Indeed, a large portion of the Bengali middle class blames Gandhi and the central leadership of the party for partition and its consequences,[22] accuses Nehru of a "cold and brutal disregard" of Bengali interests in accepting the Nehru-Noon agreement to divide Berubari Union equally between Pakistan and India, and accuses the central government of being "unsympathetic or unconcerned" with Bengal on a number of other issues. In their campaigns to "right these wrongs" the Bengali middle class has not been hesitant to launch mass

[21] A number of Bengalis feel that Bengal's cultural "genius" is inherent in the Bengali people. Three "theories" that attempt to account for this genius are especially prevalent: one attributes it to the fertility of the land, which allowed Bengalis to spend more time on the luxuries of life; another attributes it to the climate, which encouraged the pursuit of leisure; and a third attributes it to the racial composition of the Bengali people.

[22] The attitude of Bengalis toward Gandhi is summarized in a paper by Leonard A. Gordon, "Bengal's Gandhi: A Study in Modern Indian Regionalism, Politics and Thought," unpublished paper prepared for the Second Annual Conference on Bengali Studies, University of Missouri, Columbia, Missouri, May 13-15, 1966.

movements and *hartals* designed to recruit the entire Bengali population, they have sought to exert tremendous pressures on the state party and the state government in defense of their demands, and they have on numerous occasions taken to the streets.[23]

That such feelings, and the possibilities for political mobilization that exist in such a milieu, can inhibit the ability of the central government to make decisions from Delhi is clearly indicated in the case studies. In the states reorganization case, for example, the central Working Committee did vote to accept a solution which it saw as a compromise between West Bengal and Bihar, but without consulting the state Congress parties or the state governments. And this was a sphere in which the central government clearly had the constitutional authority to make a decision. But the mere rumor that the center had arrived at a decision without consulting state leaders led to massive opposition within the state. Large-scale protest organizations grew up overnight, mass demonstrations were almost immediately held throughout the state, violence was threatened, and even the state Congress party was convinced of the necessity of joining those in protest. When such opposition as this was generated against central decision-making, central government and party leaders quickly backed down.

But the local and regional traditions that have grown up in Bengal serve to provide opportunities for mobilization against central decision-making in still another, perhaps less obvious, way. As Cohn has pointed out, it is possible analytically to differentiate at least four levels of the political system that have existed independently throughout India's history: the imperial, the secondary, the regional, and the local.[24] And, again

[23] The tactics pursued by the middle class in Calcutta are traced in Myron Weiner, "Violence and Politics in Calcutta," *Journal of Asian Studies*, xx, No. 3 (May 1961), 275-81. See also Myron Weiner, "Student Problem in India," *The Statesman* (Calcutta), May 26, 1954, p. 6.

[24] Bernard S. Cohn, "Political Systems in Eighteenth Century India:

throughout India's history, it is possible to say something of the stability of each of these levels. The imperial and secondary levels have changed drastically in the course of time, sometimes encompassing the whole of the subcontinent or large portions thereof, sometimes almost disappearing from sight. But the regional, and more especially the local systems, while changing in some respects and in certain periods, exhibit more continuity—in terms both of their functioning and their personnel—than do the others. In Cohn's words, a tradition had developed by the 18th century in which "lineages, families or (local) leaders directly controlled the local peasants, merchants and artisans and collected from them cash or a share of the crop, in return for which they offered some protection from outside interference."[25]

We are not trying to argue that Bengal villages or local governments are "unchanging," but it is important to note in the present context the importance of a tradition of strong local rule. For the success of the present party system, and the ability of the state party government to resist central coercion, rests (at least in West Bengal) on the mobilization by the present state party leaders of this stratum of local rulers. Nicholas has shown that many of the *zamindars* of West Bengal, and all of the "headmen" in the villages he studied, "supported the British and, more or less successfully, managed to hold their rural dependents in the pro-British camp," but when Independence became a certainty, "most of these elements abruptly switched their support to the Congress."[26] The actions of the leaders of the local political levels in West Bengal in this instance is not fundamentally different from the actions of local leaders throughout Bengal's history. In the

---

The Benaras Region," *Journal of the American Oriental Society*, LXXXII, No. 3 (July-September 1962), 312-20.

[25] *Ibid.*, p. 314.

[26] Ralph W. Nicholas and Tarashish Mukhopadhyay, "Politics and Law in Two West Bengal Villages," *Bulletin of the Anthropological Survey of India*, xv (1964), 36-37.

face of a central control that has been constantly changing, Bengal's local leaders have in fact shown a remarkable consistency in allying themselves with whomever appears to be the stronger of the contenders for occupying positions at the regional and secondary levels.[27]

In basing their electoral organization on these local systems, moreover, the state Congress party of Bengal fills a number of traditional roles. As Weiner has pointed out, the Congress typically acts as "expeditor" (linking the administration to the people); as "mediator" (in settling disputes between different local peoples); and as "constructive worker" (providing charity and social services to local areas).[28] In these actions the state Congress party is merely adapting to roles that have been filled for centuries by the regional and local authorities.

The presence of a local tradition, and the ability of the Congress party at the state level to mobilize supporters within that tradition, served to make a decentralized party system work, and to impede central decision-making in the cases studied. For, while the system of close ties between the state party and the local political level made for a viable party government in the state, it also inhibited the effectiveness of any attempts at reform by the central administration or government. The implementation of policy in this system was influenced as much by the party representative, who had to please those who wanted to preserve the existing state of affairs, as it was by the central administrator, who was often charged with the responsibility of reforming the existing state of affairs. The central (or even the state) government could thus enact legislation and policy decisions which promised desired change, but the negation of many government policies was subsequently encouraged by the provision of regularized channels for canceling out those aspects of a policy that were unde-

[27] This was also the conclusion of Nirmal Kumar Bose, *Modern Bengal* (Calcutta: Vidyodaya Library, 1959), pp. 20ff.

[28] Weiner, *Journal of Politics*, 832ff.

sirable to those people who were established in the social and political structure.[29] In both the DVC and land reform case studies, it was the local notables, in control of the traditional local political level, that were eventually able to shape the course of those policies that affected their own localities. The central government and central wings of the party were unable to control either the state Congress or local power-holders, and, as a consequence, were relatively ineffectual.

Conclusions

The case studies indicate that a number of factors—the structure of political parties at the state level, the nature of the party system at the state level, social class composition, economic distribution, and political culture—are closely related to the working of India's federal Constitution in West Bengal. At the same time, if only because India is a nation where these factors differ so markedly from state to state, the case studies raise a number of questions, and the answers to these questions require comparative analytical studies of other

[29] Numerous examples of the way in which this system operates in West Bengal are available: the processing, distribution, and transportation of food grown in the state are all subject to government regulations, but law enforcement and administrative agencies are often reluctant to prosecute those who illegally hoard food, or those who misuse government permits to run price-controlled food shops; the Congress government has established elaborate licensing procedures to control the private sector, but it simultaneously negates the effect of many of these procedures by failing to enforce them effectively, and by establishing bodies designed to mitigate against their effectiveness; a city ordinance requires that all cows in Calcutta be kept in government-licensed sheds, a state law makes it illegal for nonlicensed book dealers to sell government textbooks, and state building regulations demand that certain housing requirements be met by landlords, but at the same time the system of close party-administrator-constituent ties makes it possible for some people to break all of these laws almost at will. See Frank J. Tysen, *District Administration in Metropolitan Calcutta* (Calcutta: Institute of Public Administration, 1964); see also Franda, in *State Politics in India.*

states. What is the effect of India's one-party dominant system on a cooperative federal constitution? How is a process of rapid political mobilization related to the maintenance of a federal balance? What is the relationship, if any, between federalism and a politics of scarcity, the emergence of new groups into politics, or a rapidly increasing articulation of demands? How consequential is a cooperative federal constitution in a society of extreme pluralism, with a population whose most basic attachments are to primordial ties?

These are questions that can only be answered when a number of studies of center-state relations in various states are available. The present study indicates, however, that two factors—the cohesion and strength of state party units (at least where the dominant party is in power in the state) and the degree to which the populace can be mobilized for political action—play a large part in determining the nature of center-state relations in India. One might even conceive of a "market situation," in which the degree of state party cohesion and strength, coupled with the willingness and ability of state populations to mobilize for political action, would provide the principal sources of state independence relative to the system's central allocating institutions. In these terms, party cohesion, the presence of a highly politicized populace, and the ability of state political parties to mobilize the population in pursuit of state goals, each of these would represent "assets" that could be used to enhance the ability of state politicians to act independently of central government and party leaders. The lack of party cohesion and strength, the lack of viable state parties, or the absence of a state population that can be mobilized for political action, these could be viewed as "liabilities" diminishing the effectiveness of state leaders in attaining independence in center-state affairs.

In testing these and other generalizations that emerge from the present study, it is essential to contrast findings in West Bengal with comparable data drawn from other areas of India. It would be especially valuable to compare West Bengal with Andhra, where decisions would seem to be influenced by regional (especially caste) factors. Equally valuable would be a contrast with Keral, or even with West Bengal after the 1967 elections, areas in which there has been Congress party splintering and in which the Congress opposition has succeeded in attaining power. Contrasts with Madhya Pradesh, where the populace is not readily mobilized for political action at the state level, or with Maharashtra, where the populace is highly mobilized but without a strong leftist orientation, would also be useful. Comparative studies of center-state relations in different parts of India would not only point up more clearly the relative importance of a number of factors that impinge on center-state decisions, it would also allow us to make some estimate of the relationship between various patterns of center-state relations and the larger problem of political integration.

Bibliography

I. Federalism and Indian Politics

BOOKS

Alexandrowicz, Charles Henry. *Constitutional Development in India*. Bombay: Oxford University Press, 1957.

Austin, Granville. *The Indian Constitution: Cornerstone of a Nation*. Oxford: Clarendon Press, 1966.

Bailey, F. G. *Politics and Social Change: Orissa in 1959*. Berkeley: University of California Press, 1963.

———. *Tribe, Caste, and Nation: A Study of Political Activity and Political Change in Highland Orissa*. Manchester: Manchester University Press, 1960.

Bhargava, Rajendra N. *The Theory and Working of Union Finance in India*. London: George Allen and Unwin, 1956.

Bondurant, Joan V. *Regionalism Versus Provincialism: A Study in Problems of National Unity*. Berkeley: University of California Press, 1958.

Brass, Paul R. *Factional Politics in an Indian State: The Congress Party in Uttar Pradesh*. Berkeley: University of California Press, 1965.

Brecher, Michael. *Nehru: A Political Biography*. London: Oxford University Press, 1959.

Chanda, Asok. *Aspects of Audit Control*. New York: Asia Publishing House, 1960.

———. *Federalism in India: A Study of Union-State Relations*. London: George Allen and Unwin, 1965.

Gadgil, Dhananjaya Ramchandra. *The Federal Problem in India*. Poona: Gokhale Institute of Politics and Economics, 1947.

Harrison, Selig S. *India: The Most Dangerous Decades*. Princeton: Princeton University Press, 1960.

Indian Institute of Public Administration. *The Organization of the Government of India*. New York: Asia Publishing House, 1958.

Keith, A. Berriedale. *A Constitutional History of India, 1600-1935.* 2d edn. London: Methuen, 1936.

Leonard, T. J. *The Federal System in India: Nation and State in an Eastern Republic.* Tempe: Arizona State University Press, 1963.

Leverhulme Trust. *Federalism and Economic Growth in Underdeveloped Countries.* Edited by Ursula K. Hicks. London: George Allen and Unwin, 1961.

Macmahon, Arthur W. *Federalism: Mature and Emergent.* New York: Doubleday, 1955.

Mahajan, Vidya Dhar. *The Constitution of India.* 4th edn. Lucknow: Eastern Book Company, 1963.

Morris-Jones, W. H. *The Government and Politics of India.* London: Hutchinson University Library, 1964.

———. *Parliament in India.* Philadelphia: University of Pennsylvania Press, 1956.

Nair, Kusum. *Blossoms in the Dust.* London: Gerald Duckworth and Co., 1961.

Nayar, Baldev Raj. *Minority Politics in the Punjab.* Princeton: Princeton University Press, 1966.

Nandi, Amar. *The Constitution of India.* 8th edn. Calcutta: Bookland Private Ltd., 1962.

Palmer, Norman D. *The Indian Political System.* London: George Allen and Unwin, 1961.

Prasad, Bisheswar. *The Origins of Provincial Autonomy.* Allahabad: Kitabistan, 1941.

Pylee, M. V. *India's Constitution.* New York: Asia Publishing House, 1962.

Roy, Naresh Chandra. *Federalism and Linguistic States.* Calcutta: Firma K. L. Mukhopadhyay, 1962.

Santhanam, K. *Planning and Plain Thinking.* Madras: Higginbothams, 1958.

———. *Union-State Relations in India.* London: Asia Publishing House, 1960.

Sharma, Sri Ram. *A Constitutional History of India, 1765-1954.* London: Macmillan and Co., 1955.

Sharp, Henry. *Good-bye India.* London: Oxford University Press, 1964.

Sinha, Bimal Chandra. *Changing World and Other Essays.* Calcutta: Prakashani Publishers, 1940.

Tinker, Hugh. *India and Pakistan: A Political Analysis.* New York: Praeger, 1962.

Tope, T. K. *The Constitution of India.* Bombay: Popular Prakashan, 1963.

Weiner, Myron. *Party Politics in India.* Princeton: Princeton University Press, 1957.

――――. *Political Change in South Asia.* Calcutta: Firma K. L. Mukhopadhyay, 1963.

――――. *The Politics of Scarcity: Public Pressure and Political Response in India.* Chicago: University of Chicago Press, 1962.

―――― (editor). *State Politics in India.* Princeton: Princeton University Press, 1968.

Wheare, Kenneth C. *Federal Government.* 2d edn. London: Oxford University Press, 1951. Also 4th edn. London: Oxford University Press, 1964.

ARTICLES

Bombwall, K. R. "The Finance Commission and Union-State Relations in India," *The Indian Journal of Public Administration,* x, No. 2 (April-June 1964), 278-90.

Carnell, F. G. "Political Implications of Federalism in New States," in *Federalism and Economic Growth in Underdeveloped Countries.* Edited by Ursula K. Hicks. London: George Allen and Unwin, 1961. Pp. 16-69.

Chandavarkar, A. G. "Finance of State Governments," *Bulletin of the Reserve Bank of India,* xi (August 1957), 732-50.

Chandra, Mahesh. "The Arbitrariness of Chief Ministers," *The Statesman* (Calcutta), November 17, 1961, p. 6.

Chaudhuri, Nirad C. "Independence and the Indian Mind," *The Statesman* (Calcutta), August 15, 1953, Sec. ii, p. 1.

Chaudhuri, P. K. "Balanced Regional Growth," *The Economic Weekly*, XII (1960), 1501-04.

"Congress High Command and the States," *The Statesman* (Calcutta), July 6, 1962, p. 6.

Das, N. "Federal and Regional Autonomy," *The Statesman* (Calcutta), August 15, 1956, p. 6.

Dash, S. C. "Emergency Provisions and Union-State Relations in India," *The Indian Journal of Political Science*, XXII, Nos. 1 and 2 (January-June 1961), 53-63.

Datta, S. K. "New Training Programmes for Central and State Government Employees," *The Indian Journal of Public Administration*, IX, No. 3 (July-September 1963), Supplement, 125-43.

Deutsch, Karl. "The Growth of Nations: Some Recurrent Patterns of Political and Social Integration," *World Politics*, V (1953), 168-81.

Dwivedi, M. L. "Distinctive Federalism of the Indian Republic," *The AICC Economic Review*, VI, No. 13 (November 1, 1954), 7-10.

Ebb, Lawrence Forrest. "Inter-State Preferences and Discrimination in a Federal System," in *Public Law Problems in India: A Survey*. Edited by Lawrence Ebb. Stanford: Stanford University Press, 1957.

Friedman, Harry J. "Indian Federalism and Industrial Development," *Far Eastern Survey*, XXVII (March 1958), 33-41.

Gangal, S. C. "An Approach to Indian Federalism," *Political Science Quarterly*, LXXVII (June 1962), 248-53.

Ghosal, A. K. "Union-State Relations in India and National Solidarity," *The Indian Journal of Political Science*, XXII, Nos. 1 and 2 (January-June 1961), 159-67.

Jain, S. C. "The Working of Federal Finance in India," *The Statesman* (Calcutta), April 10, 1959, Sec. II, p. 1.

Khera, S. S. "District Administration," *The Indian Journal of Public Administration*, IX, No. 3 (July-September 1963), 465-68.

Leonard, T. J. "Federalism in India," in *Federalism in the Commonwealth*. Edited by William S. Livingstone. London: The Hansard Society, 1963. Pp. 87-145.

Lockwood, William W. "Adam Smith and Asia," *The Journal of Asian Studies*, XXIII, No. 3 (May 1964), 345-55.

"Political Commentary: Steady Decline in Central Authority," *The Statesman* (Calcutta), June 2, 1961, p. 6.

Rai, Haridwar. "The Changing Role of the District Officer (1860-1960), *The Indian Journal of Public Administration*, IX, No. 2 (April-June 1963), 238-57.

Ramaswamy, M. "The Indian Constitutional Amendments," in *The Indian Yearbook of International Affairs*, Vol. XII (1963). Edited by T. S. Rama Rao. Madras: University of Madras, 1963. Pp. 161-91.

Rangachari, K. "Relations Between States and Centre," *The Statesman* (Calcutta), January 26, 1964, Sec. II, p. 4.

Rudolph, Lloyd I., and Rudolph, Susanne Hoeber. "The Political Role of India's Caste Associations," *Pacific Affairs*, XXXIII, No. 1 (March 1960), 5-22.

Rudolph, Susanne Hoeber. "Consensus and Conflict in Indian Politics," *World Politics*, XIII (April 1961), 385-99.

Rusch, Thomas Alvin. "Decision-making in Underdeveloped Countries of Asia: India as a Case Study," *Western Political Quarterly*, X, No. 2 (June 1957), 456-57.

Santhanam, K. "The Changing Pattern of Union-State Relations in India," *The Indian Journal of Public Administration*, IX, No. 3 (July-September 1963), 457-64.

Schoenfeld, Benjamin. "Emergency Rule in India," *Pacific Affairs*, XXXVI, No. 3 (Fall 1963), 221-37.

———. "Federalism in India," *The Indian Journal of Political Science*, XX, No. 1 (January-March 1959), 52-62.

———. "Federalism in India—II," *The Indian Journal of Political Science*, XX, No. 3 (July-September 1959), 191-204.

Sinha, K. N. "The Constitution of India: More Unitary Than Federal," *The Modern Review*, XCVIII (1955), 448-52.

Srivastava, G. P. "Impact of Planning Union-State Relations in India," *The Indian Journal of Political Science*, XXII, Nos. 1 and 2 (January-June 1961), 27-34.

Tinker, Hugh. "Democratic Institutions in India and China," in *Democratic Institutions in the World Today*. Edited by Werner Burmeister. London: Stevens and Son, 1958. Pp. 117-50.

―――. "Tradition and Experiment in Forms of Government," in *Politics and Society in India*. Edited by C. H. Phillips. New York: Praeger, 1962. Pp. 155-87.

Varma, Vishwanath Prasad. "Towards Monistic Federalism in India," *The Indian Journal of Political Science*, XXII, Nos. 1 and 2 (January-June 1961), 35-42.

Weidner, Edward W. "Decision-making in a Federal System," in *Federalism: Mature and Emergent*. Edited by Arthur W. Macmahon. New York: Doubleday, 1955. Pp. 363-83.

Weiner, Myron. "India's Political Problems: The Longer View," *Western Political Quarterly*, IX (June 1956), 283-92.

―――. "The Politics of South Asia," in G. Almond and J. S. Coleman, *The Politics of the Developing Areas*. Princeton: Princeton University Press, 1960.

GOVERNMENT DOCUMENTS

India (Dominion). Constituent Assembly. *Debates* (1947-50).

India (Great Britain). *Report of the Royal Commission on Decentralisation in India*. C. E. H. Hobhouse, Chairman. 3 vols. Cd. 4360-69 (1908).

II. STATES REORGANIZATION AND WEST BENGAL

BOOKS

Basu Chandranatha. *The Partition Agitation Explained*. Calcutta: n.p., 1906.

Gupta, Atul Chandra. *Presidential Address to the All Bengal Linguistic States Re-distribution Conference*. Calcutta: Mohit K. Moitra, 1952.

Indian National Congress. All-India Congress Committee. *Bengali-Bihari Question: Report of the Rajendra Prasad Together with the Resolutions of the Working Committee.* Allahabad: All-India Congress Committee, 1939.

──────. All-India Congress Committee. *Report of the Committee Appointed by the All-Parties Conference to Determine the Principles of the Constitution for India.* Allahabad: General Secretary, All-India Congress Committee, 1928.

──────. *Report of the Linguistic Provinces Committee.* New Delhi: All-India Congress Committee, 1949.

──────. West Bengal Pradesh Congress Committee. *Recommendations of the West Bengal Pradesh Congress Committee Before the States Re-organisation Commission.* Calcutta: West Bengal Pradesh Congress Committee, 1954.

──────. West Bengal Pradesh Congress Committee. South Calcutta District Congress Committee. *Some Correspondence on Re-adjustment of Provincial Boundaries Between West Bengal and Bihar.* Calcutta: West Bengal Pradesh Congress Committee, 1949.

Narayana, Mahesa and Sachichidananda Sinha. *The Partition of Bengal or the Separation of Bihar?* Allahabad: Indian Press, 1906.

Roy, Naresh Chandra. *Federalism and Linguistic States.* Calcutta: Firma K. L. Mukhopadhyay, 1962.

ARTICLES

"Agitational Approach to S. R. C. in Bengal and Bihar," *Thought* (Delhi Weekly), VIII, No. 3 (January 21, 1956), 5-7.

Alexandrowicz, Charles Henry. "India Before and After Reorganization," *Yearbook of World Affairs*, XII (1958), 133-55.

Arora, S. K. "The States After Re-organization," *Indian Affairs Record*, II, No. 12 (January 1957), 3-8.

"Bengal for Bengali," *The Economic Weekly*, VIII (1956), 1065-66.

Chandrasekhar, S. "The New Map of India," *Amrita Bazaar Patrika*, March 1957, p. 35.

Chatterji, M. N. "West Bengal-Bihar Merger: The Developments in Bihar," *Indian Affairs Record*, ii, No. 2 (March 1956), 4-7.

———. "West Bengal-Bihar Merger: The Developments in West Bengal," *Indian Affairs Record*, ii, No. 3 (April 1956), 4-7.

Chaudhuri, Nirad C. "The SRC Report as a Portent," *The Statesman* (Calcutta), December 13, 1955, p. 6.

Ghosh, Atulya. "Linguistic Affinity Conducive to India's Unity," in *West Bengal Today*. Calcutta: West Bengal Pradesh Congress Committee, 1956. Pp. 31-40.

Gupta, Sisir. "States Re-organization: The Latest Phase," *Indian Affairs Record*, ii, No. 1 (February 1956), 4-7.

Harrison, Selig S. "The Challenge to Indian Nationalism," *Foreign Affairs*, xxxiv, No. 4 (July 1956), 620-36.

Kothari, Rajni. "Form and Substance in Indian Politics: Union and State Relations," *The Economic Weekly*, xiii, Part i (April 29, 1961), 679-80; Part ii (May 6, 1961), 715-21.

Menon, V. P. "The New Map of India: Some Political and Economic Consequences of Reform," *The Statesman* (Calcutta), November 1, 1956, p. 6.

"Re-Union or Federation?" *Thought* (Delhi Weekly), viii, No. 5 (February 4, 1956), 2.

Sen, Khagendra Nath, "The Economic Implications of Merger," *The Statesman* (Calcutta), February 11, 1956, p. 6.

Sen, S. N. "Historical Background of the Merger," *The Statesman* (Calcutta), February 9, 1956, p. 6.

Sinha, B. U. P. "The Cultural Aspect of Merger," *The Statesman* (Calcutta), February 9, 1956, p. 6.

Sinha, Sasadhar. "Some Dangers of Regionalism," *The Statesman* (Calcutta), January 26, 1957, Sec. ii, p. 5.

Vedette [pseud.]. " 'Phased' Discussion of SRC Report," *The Statesman* (Calcutta), October 16, 1955, p. 10.

———. "SRC Report: Time Now for Firm Handling," *The Statesman* (Calcutta), November 27, 1955, p. 8.

———. "States Re-organization: Likely Shocks and Surprises," *The Statesman* (Calcutta), August 14, 1955, p. 8.

"West Bengal and the Merger Proposal," *Thought* (Delhi Weekly, VIII, No. 10 (March 10, 1956), 6-7.

"West Bengal Assembly's Autumn Session," *Thought* (Delhi Weekly), VIII, No. 36 (September 3, 1955), 18-19.

Windmiller, Marshall Louis. "Linguistic Regionalism in India," *Pacific Affairs*, XXVII (1954), 291-310.

Zinkin, Maurice. "Regionalism in India: An Outsider's Appreciation," *Poona University Journal*, IX (1958), 124-30.

"Zonal Councils in India," *Indian Affairs Record*, IV, No. 6 (July 1958), 129-40.

GOVERNMENT DOCUMENTS

India (Dominion). Linguistic Provinces Commission. *Report.* New Delhi: Manager of Publications, 1948.

India (Great Britain). Bengal Boundary Commission. *Report.* Cyril Radcliffe, Chairman. Delhi: Government of India, 1947.

———. Royal Commission on Decentralization in India. *Minutes of Evidence.* Calcutta: Bengal Secretariat Press, 1908.

India (Republic). States Re-organisation Commission. *Report.* New Delhi: Manager of Publications, 1955.

III. The Damodar Valley Corporation

BOOKS

Bose, S. C. *The Damodar Valley Project.* Calcutta: The Phoenix Press, 1948.

Ganguli, D. S. *Public Corporations in a National Economy.* Calcutta: Bookland Private Ltd., 1963.

Hart, Henry C. *Administrative Aspects of River Valley Development.* New York: Asia Publishing House, 1961.

Hart, Henry C. *New India's Rivers*. Calcutta: Orient Longmans, 1956.

National Council of Applied Economic Research. *Techno-Economic Survey of West Bengal*. New Delhi: NCAER, 1962.

ARTICLES

Aiyer, R. P. "Electricity and the Law," *The Statesman* (Calcutta), May 4, 1959, p. 6.

Banerjee, B. N. "Tubewell Irrigation in West Bengal," *The Statesman* (Calcutta), February 24, 1955, Sec. II, p. 1.

Bhattacharjee, Ajit. "Community Project," *The New Statesman*, XLVII (February 26, 1954), 247.

Bose, N. K. "DVC and the Hooghly," *The Statesman* (Calcutta), February 27, 1954, Sec. II, p. 1.

"Controversies Over Bengal's Power Needs," *The Statesman* (Calcutta), May 4, 1962, p. 6.

"The Damodar Valley Project," *Science and Culture*, April 1946.

"Dams, Dams, Dams, and Damodar," *The Economist,* CLXXXII (February 2, 1953), 393-94.

Datta, Manoranjan. "Electricity in the Development of Small-Scale Industries," *The Statesman* (Calcutta), February 14, 1959, p. 16.

————. "Power Development in India," *The Statesman* (Calcutta), April 30, 1957, Sec. II, p. 8.

————. "Progress of Electricity Supply in West Bengal," *The Statesman* (Calcutta), February 15, 1957, Sec. II, p. 4.

"Demands for Electric Power in the DVC System," *The Statesman* (Calcutta), February 21, 1953, Sec. II, p. 10.

Driver, D. C. "West Bengal's New Industrial Area: Immediate and Future Problems of Durgapur," *The Statesman* (Calcutta), March 14, 1959, p. 9.

"DVC's Predicament: Too Many Tasks to Perform," *The Statesman* (Calcutta), October 5, 1961, p. 8.

Dwarkadas, R. "TVA Administration and Its Lessons," *The*

Indian Journal of Political Science, xx, No. 2 (April-June 1959), 155-62.

Ganguly, A. B. "A New Era in Agricultural History," *The Statesman* (Calcutta), August 9, 1955, Sec. ii, p. 1.

Hull, W. W. "Group Action in Damodar Valley," *Soil Conservation*, xxiii (September 1957), 27-34.

"Irrigation and Food Supply," *The Statesman* (Calcutta), September 26, 1957, p. 4.

James, A. "Damodar Valley Project," *Eastern World* (August 1953), 43-44.

Kapp, K. William. "River Valley Projects in India," *Economic Development and Cultural Change*, viii (1959), 24-47.

Malkani, N. R. "The DVC As I Saw It," *AICC Economic Review*, vi, No. 10 (September 15, 1954), 5-6.

Mazumdar, D. L. "Multi-Purpose River Valley Projects," *Indian Finance Annual* (1948), 61-72.

Morgan, L. "River Development in India," *Far Eastern Survey*, xxi (May 1952), 82.

"Multi-Purpose River Projects," *Eastern Economist*, viii (February 21, 1947), 366-67.

"Nature Turns the Wheels," *The New Statesman*, liv (October 19, 1957), 479.

"No Early End to West Bengal's Power Shortage," *The Statesman* (Calcutta), May 3, 1962, p. 6.

"Operation of DVC Reservoirs: A Brief Review," *Indian Journal of Power and River Valley Development*, xi, No. 1 (January 1961), 25-29.

"Power for Industry: DVC's Contribution," *The Statesman* (Calcutta), June 30, 1958, p. 19.

"Power Needs of West Bengal and Bihar During Third Plan," *Indian Journal of Power and River Valley Development*, xii, No. 4 (April 1962), 19-24.

"Power Shortage in West Bengal: An Analysis and Some Suggestions," *The Statesman* (Calcutta), April 27, 1961, p. 8.

Rau, P. S. "DVC As a Measure of Advance," *The Statesman* (Calcutta), February 15, 1957, Sec. ii, p. 1.

Rau, P. S. "A New Approach to the DVC," *The Statesman* (Calcutta), October 15, 1955, Sec. II, p. 1.

———. "The Role of the DVC in Railway Electrification," *The Statesman* (Calcutta), December 14, 1957, Sec. II, p. 6.

———. "Working of the DVC: The Real Picture," *AICC Economic Review*, VI, No. 11 (October 1, 1954), 7-10.

Ray Chaudhury, Nirmal Chandra Basu. "Problems of the Damodar Valley Corporation," in *Problems of Public Administration in India.* Edited by B. B. Majumdar. Patna: Bharati Bhawan for the Indian Political Science Association, 1953. Pp. 107-16.

"Rivers of Sorrow," *The Economic Weekly*, VI (August 28, 1954), 939-40.

Roy, Kamalesh. "Flood Control Given Low Priority in Projects," *The Statesman* (Calcutta), September 27, 1961, p. 6.

Sahay, M. B. "River Valley Projects of Bihar," *Indian Journal of Power and River Valley Development*, XII, No. 8 (September 1962), 5-9.

Schoenfeld, Benjamin N. "Planning Power Development in India," *The Indian Journal of Public Administration*, IX, No. 4 (October-December 1963), 669-79.

Sen, Sudhir. "We Need More River Valley Authorities in India," *Indian Journal of Power and River Valley Development*, Second Annual Number (1953), 53-89.

Sood, M. L. "River Valley Projects in India," *Eastern World*, (May 1950), 33-35.

Subramanium, T. A. "Men and Motives Behind the Durgapur Project," *The Statesman* (Calcutta), August 1, 1959, p. 6.

Summers, W. C. "India's Unfinished Business," *Reclamation Era*, XXXII (December 1946), 275-78.

GOVERNMENT DOCUMENTS

Government of Bengal. *Report of the Damodar Flood Enquiry Committee, 1944.* Alipore: Bengal Secretariat Press, 1945.

———. Bengal Public Works Department. *Selections from the*

Minutes of the Bengal Secretariat on Damodar River Embankments. 3 vols. Alipore: Bengal Secretariat Press, 1943.

India (Dominion). National Planning Committee. *River Training and Irrigation.* Edited by K. T. Shah. Bombay: Vora and Co., 1948.

India (Great Britain). Central Technical Power Board. *Preliminary Memorandum on the Unified Development of the Damodar River.* Calcutta: West Bengal Government, 1946.

———. Famine Inquiry Commission. *Final Report.* Delhi: Manager of Publications, 1945.

———. Famine Inquiry Commission. *Report on Bengal.* Delhi: Manager of Publications, 1945.

India (Republic). Damodar Valley Corporation. *Annual Reports* (1948-63). Calcutta: Damodar Valley Corporation, 1949-64.

———. Damodar Valley Corporation. *Audit Reports* (1948-63). Calcutta: Damodar Valley Corporation, 1949-64.

———. Damodar Valley Corporation. *Committee of Enquiry Report.* P. S. Rau, Chairman. New Delhi: Manager of Publications, 1953.

———. Damodar Valley Corporation. *The Damodar Valley Corporation Act, 1948.* New Delhi: Government of India, 1948.

———. Damodar Valley Corporation. *The Damodar Valley Corporation Amendment Act, 1957.* New Delhi: Manager of Publications, 1957.

———. Damodar Valley Corporation. *The Damodar Valley Project: Revised Estimates for First Phase with Economic and Financial Justification.* Calcutta: Damodar Valley Corporation, 1951.

———. Damodar Valley Corporation. *DVC at a Glance.* Calcutta: Damodar Valley Corporation, 1955.

———. Damodar Valley Corporation. *DVC in Prospect and Retrospect.* Calcutta: Damodar Valley Corporation, 1958.

———. Damodar Valley Corporation. *The First Eight Years of DVC.* Calcutta: Damodar Valley Corporation, 1956.

India (Republic). Damodar Valley Corporation. *Reports of the Board of Consultants* (1950-55). Calcutta: Damodar Valley Corporation, 1951-56.

————. Ministry of Irrigation and Power. *Report of an Inquiry into the Damodar Valley Floods of 1959.* S. D. Khungar, Chairman. New Delhi: Government of India, 1960.

————. Ministry of Irrigation and Power. *Report of the Committee to Enquire into the Causes of Recent Failure of Power Supply in West Bengal and Bihar.* M. R. Sachdev, Chairman. New Delhi: September 1961.

————. Planning Commission. *Major Water and Power Projects of India.* New Delhi: Planning Commission, 1957.

————. Planning Commission. *Report on the Efficient Conduct of State Enterprises.* A. D. Gorwala. New Delhi: Manager of Publications, 1951.

West Bengal. Ministry of Irrigation. Flood Enquiry Commission. *Report on the Damodar Valley Flood of 1959.* Sardar Mansingh. Calcutta: West Bengal Government Press, 1960.

JOURNALS

Bhagirath (1957-1960).
Indian Journal of Power and River Valley Development (1950-1964).

IV. Land Reform and West Bengal

BOOKS

Basu, S. K. and Bhattacharya, S. K. *Land Reform in West Bengal: A Study of Implementation.* Calcutta: Oxford University Press, 1963.

Chatterjee, D. P. *The West Bengal Land Reforms Act, 1955.* Calcutta: A. Mukherjee and Co., 1956.

Dey, Sushil Kumar. *Cooperative Farming: The Theory and Practice of a Scheme Being Tried in a Bengal District.* Nadia: I. Dey, 1940.

Ghosh, Jamini Mohan. *The West Bengal Land Reforms Act, 1955*. Calcutta: Eastern Law House, 1956.

Indian National Congress. Agrarian Reforms Committee. *Report*. New Delhi: All-India Congress Committee, 1949.

Jain, Sharad Chandra. *Problems and Policies of Indian Agriculture*. Allahabad: Kitab Mahal, 1963.

Malaviya, H. D. *Land Reforms in India*. New Delhi: All-India Congress Committee, 1954.

Mukerji, Karuna. *Land Reforms*. Calcutta: H. Chatterjee and Co., 1952.

——. *The Problems of Land Transfer: A Study of the Problems of Land Alienation in Bengal*. Santiniketan: Santiniketan Press, 1957.

Mookerji, Radha Kumud. *Indian Land System: Ancient, Medieval and Modern (With Special Reference to Bengal)*. Alipore: West Bengal Government Press, 1958.

Patel, G. D. *The Indian Land Problem and Legislation*. Bombay: N. M. Tripathi and Co., 1954.

Roy, Naresh Chandra. *Rural Self-Government in Bengal*. Calcutta: University of Calcutta, 1936.

Rudolph, Susanne Hoeber. *Some Aspects of Congress Land Reform Policy*. Cambridge: Center for International Studies, Massachusetts Institute of Technology, 1957.

Sen, Bhowani. *Indian Land System and Land Reforms*. New Delhi: People's Publishing House, 1955.

Sen, S. R. *The Strategy for Agricultural Development*. Calcutta: Asia Publishing House, 1962.

Thorner, Daniel. *The Agrarian Prospect in India*. New Delhi: Delhi University Press, 1956.

Thorner, Daniel and Thorner, Alice. *Land and Labour in India*. Calcutta: Asia Publishing House, 1962.

ARTICLES

Alexander, Horace, "India Re-visited," *Contemporary Review*, cxciv (July 1958), 9-12.

Baines, Frank. "A Real Life for the Cultivator—and Hopes for Mr. Ghosh Too," *The Statesman* (Calcutta), August 15, 1954, Sec. ii, p. 4.

Bekker, Konrad. "Land Reform Legislation in India," *Middle East Journal*, v, No. 3 (Summer 1951), 319-36.

Bose, Nirmal Kumar. "Types of Villages in West Bengal: A Study in Social Change," *The Economic Weekly*, x (January 1958), 149-52.

Chaudhuri, Ranjit. "Pattern of Leadership in a West Bengal Village," *The Economic Weekly*, xvi (April 4, 1964), 641-44.

Choudhury, Binodebehari. "Effects of the Abolition of Zamindari in West Bengal," *The Economic Weekly*, vi (November 13, 1954), 1275-76.

Cohn, Bernard S. "From Indian Status to British Contract," *Journal of Economic History*, xxi (December 1961), 613-28.

Cousins, William J. "Community Development in West Bengal," *The Statesman* (Calcutta), August 15, 1958, Sec. ii, p. 6.

Dantwala, M. L. "India's Progress in Agrarian Reforms," *Far Eastern Survey*, xix, No. 22 (December 1950), 239-43.

———. "Land Reforms in India," *International Labour Review*, lxvi (July-December 1952), 419-43.

Das, Sisir Kumar. "Agrarian Unrest in West Bengal," *The Statesman* (Calcutta), March 21, 1959, p. 6.

Dey, S. K. "The Perspective of Land Reform," *The Statesman* (Calcutta), August 5, 1952, p. 11.

———. "Progress of a Village," *The Statesman* (Calcutta), January 26, 1955, Sec. ii, p. 2.

D'Souza, Victor. "Rural Change in Bengal," *The Economic Weekly*, xvi (February 29, 1964), 439-40.

Gadgil, D. R. "Land Reform," *Indian Journal of Agricultural Economics*, x (1955), 10-33.

"Indian Villages in Trust," *The Economist*, clxxxiv (September 28, 1957), 1037.

"India's Socialist Property Owners," *The Economist*, clxxv (May 14, 1955), 584.

Krishnamachari, V. T. "Land Reforms in the Five-Year Plan," *AICC Economic Review*, v, No. 1 (May 1, 1953), 5-7.

Kulkarni, N. K. "Land Tenures and Their Reforms," *The Modern Review*, xciv (1953), 21.

"Land For the Little Man," *The Economist*, cxc (February 14, 1959), 582-83.

"Land Gift Movement in India: Vinoba Bhave," *World Today*, xiv (November 1958), 487-95.

Levai, Blaise. "India on the March," *International Review of Missions*, xlvi (April 1957), 191-96.

Malaviya, H. D. "Congress Agrarian Policy," *AICC Economic Review*, v, Nos. 18-19 (January 22, 1954), 20-23.

———. "Highlights of West Bengal Estates Acquisition Bill," *AICC Economic Review*, v, No. 2 (May 15, 1953), 7-10.

Moore, Frank J. "Land Reform and Social Justice in India," *Far Eastern Survey*, xxiv, No. 8 (August 1955), 124-28.

Morse, Richard. "Agrarian Reform in India: India's Progress," *Far Eastern Survey*, xix, No. 22 (December 1950), 233-39.

Mukherjee, Amar. "Socio-Economic Survey of Some Bengal Villages," *The Economic Weekly*, vi (October 2, 1954), 1095-98.

Mukherjee, Ramkrishna. "The Economic Structure and Social Life in Six Villages of Bengal," *American Sociological Review*, xiv (1949), 415-25.

———. "Economic Structure of Rural Bengal: A Survey of Six Villages," *American Sociological Review*, xiii (December 1948), 660-72.

Nanda, Gulzari Lal. "Progress of Land Reform in India," *AICC Economic Review*, ix, No. 10 (1957), 12-20.

Patil, R. V. "All Land to the Tiller: The Problem of Land Reform in India," *Economic Development and Cultural Change*, iii (July 1955), 374-80.

Sarma, Jyotirmoyee. "A Village in West Bengal," *India's Villages*. Edited by M. N. Srinivas. Calcutta: Development Department, West Bengal, 1960. Pp. 161-79.

Sen, Sachin. "The Fourth Amendment," *The Statesman* (Calcutta), March 17, 1955, p. 6.

Shea, Thomas. "Agrarian Unrest and Reform in South India," *Far Eastern Survey*, Vol. XXIII, No. 6 (June 1954).

———. "Implementing Land Reform in India," *Far Eastern Survey*, XXV, No. 1 (January 1956), 1-8.

Singh, V. B. "Land Tenure in an Indian State," *Science and Society*, XIX (Fall 1955), 303-19.

Sivaswamy, K. G. "Indian Agriculture: Problems and Programs," *Pacific Affairs*, XXIII (December 1950), 356-70.

Smith, Marian W. "Village Notes from Bengal," *American Anthropologist*, XLVIII (1946), 574-92.

"Towards the Socialist Patterns," *The New Statesman*, XLIX (May 28, 1955), 737.

Vij, A. N. "Financial Aspects of the Abolition of Zamindari," *Reserve Bank of India Bulletin*, IV (June 1950).

Weiner, Myron. "Political Parties and Panchayati Raj," *The Indian Journal of Public Administration*, VIII, No. 4 (October-December 1962), 623-29.

GOVERNMENT DOCUMENTS

Bengal. Land Revenue Commission. *Report.* 5 vols. Alipore: Bengal Government Press, 1940-41.

India (Dominion). Famine Inquiry Commission. *Land Tenures in India.* Bombay: Vora, 1946.

India (Republic). Directorate of Economics and Statistics. Ministry of Food and Agriculture. Agricultural Legislation. Vol. IV. "Land Reform: Abolition of Intermediaries (1953)"; Vol. VI. "Land Reforms: Reforms in Tenancy (1955)."

———. Ministry of Labour. *Agricultural Wages in India.* 2 vols. New Delhi: Manager of Publications, 1952-53.

———. Ministry of Labour. *Report on an Enquiry into the Conditions of Agricultural Workers in Villages.* New Delhi: Manager of Publications, 1951.

———. Planning Commission. *First Five-Year Plan Progress*

Reports, 1953-57. New Delhi: Manager of Publications, 1954-58.

————. Planning Commission. *The New India: Progress Through Democracy*. New York: Macmillan, 1958.

————. Planning Commission. *Reports of the Committee on the Panel on Land Reform*. New Delhi: Planning Commission, 1959.

————. Planning Commission. *Second Five-Year Plan Progress Reports, 1958-62*. New Delhi: Manager of Publications, 1959-63.

JOURNALS

Indian Journal of Agricultural Economics, III (1953). Special Number on "The Implementation of Land Reforms in the States."

UNPUBLISHED MATERIAL

Nayar, Baldev Raj. "Impact of the Community Development Program on Rural Voting Behavior in India." Unpublished Master's dissertation, University of Chicago, 1959.

V. POLITICS IN WEST BENGAL

BOOKS

Ashraf, Ali. *The City Government of Calcutta: A Study of Inertia*. New York: Asia Publishing House, 1967.

Beames, John. *Memoirs of a Bengal Civilian*. London: Chatto and Windus, 1961.

Bose, Nemai Sadhan. *The Indian Awakening and Bengal*. Calcutta: Firma K. L. Mukhopadhyay, 1960.

Bose, Nirmal Kumar. *Modern Bengal*. Vidyodaya: Library Private Ltd., 1959.

Bose, Subhas Chandra. *The Indian Struggle, 1920-42*. Calcutta: Asia Publishing House, 1964.

Calcutta Metropolitan Planning Organization. *First Report, 1962*. Calcutta: Calcutta Metropolitan Planning Organization, 1963.

Chakrabartty, Syamal. *Housing Conditions in Calcutta*. Calcutta: Bookland Private Ltd., 1959.

Chaudhuri, Nirad C. *The Autobiography of an Unknown Indian*. London: Macmillan and Co., 1951.

Ghosh, Atulya. *Ahimsa and Gandhi*. Calcutta: Prabhat Basu, 1954.

Ghosh, Shishir Kumar. *Peasant Revolution in Bengal*. Edited by Jogesh Chandra Bagal. Calcutta: Bharati Library, 1953.

Gupta, Atul Chandra (editor). *Studies in the Bengal Renaissance*. Calcutta: National Council of Education of Bengal, 1958.

Mandal, G. C., and Sengupta, Sunil C. *Kashipur, West Bengal (1956-60): Studies in Rural Change*. Santiniketan: Agro-Economic Research Center, 1962.

O'Malley, Lewis Sydney Stewart. *History of Bengal, Bihar and Orissa Under British Rule*. Calcutta: Bengal Secretariat Book Depot, 1925.

Pal, Bipin Chandra. *Memories of My Life and Times*. 2 vols. Calcutta: Modern Book Agency, 1932-51.

Ray, Prithwis Chandra. *Life and Times of C. R. Das*. London: Oxford University Press, 1927.

Roy, Naresh Chandra. *A Critical Study of Some Aspects of Public Administration in Bengal*. Calcutta: University of Calcutta, 1945.

Sen, S. N. *The City of Calcutta*. Calcutta: Bookland Private Ltd., 1960.

Singh, M. M. *Municipal Government in the Calcutta Metropolitan District: A Preliminary Survey*. Calcutta: Institute of Public Administration, New York, 1963.

Sinha, Narendra Krishna. *The Economic History of Bengal*. 2 vols. Calcutta: Firma K. L. Mukhopadhyay, 1956.

Sur, A. K. *History and Culture of Bengal*. Calcutta: Chuckervertti, Chatterjee and Co., 1963.

Thomas, K. P. *Dr. B. C. Roy*. Calcutta: West Bengal Pradesh Congress Committee, 1955.

Tysen, Frank J. *District Administration in Metropolitan Calcutta.* New York: Institute of Public Administration, 1964.

ARTICLES

Aird, John. "Bengali Urban Growth and Village Life," in *Pakistan: Society and Culture.* Edited by Stanley Maron. New Haven: Human Relations Area Files, 1957.

Baines, Frank. "Wanted in Calcutta: A Ruling Class Quick," *Thought* (Delhi Weekly), vi, No. 47 (November 20, 1954), 7-8.

Banerjee, Debendra Nath. "The Last General Election in West Bengal," *Modern Review,* xciii (1953), 37-40.

———. "West Bengal," in S. V. Kogekar and Richard L. Park, *Reports on the Indian General Elections, 1951-52.* Bombay: Popular Book Depot, 1956. Pp. 167-76.

Basu, Santosh Kumar. "Recollections of Congress Sessions in Bengal," *The Statesman* (Calcutta), January 20, 1954, Sec. ii, p. 4.

———. "West Bengal Financial Corporation: An Appraisal of Its Working," *The Statesman* (Calcutta), February 14, 1959, p. 11.

Bey, Hamdi. "Job Charnock and After: Thoughts on Asia's Most Controversial City," *The Statesman* (Calcutta), August 24, 1959, p. 6.

Bose, Nirmal Kumar. "Culture Zones of India," *Geographical Review of India,* xviii, No. 4 (December 1956), 1-12.

———. "East and West in Bengal," *Man in India,* xxxviii, No. 3 (July-September 1958), 157-75.

———. "The Effect of Urbanization on Work and Leisure," *Man in India,* xxxvii, No. 1 (January-March 1957), 1-9.

———. "Modern Bengal," *Man in India,* xxxviii, No. 4 (October-December 1958), 229-95.

———. "Social and Cultural Life of Calcutta," *Geographical Review of India,* xx (December 1958), 1-46.

———. "Some Aspects of Caste in Bengal," *Journal of Amer-*

ican Folklore, Vol. LXXI, No. 281 (July-September 1958), 191-206. Issue edited by Milton Singer, "Traditional India: Structure and Change."

————. "Some Aspects of Caste in Bengal," *Man in India,* XXXVIII (1958), 73-97.

————. "Some Aspects of Culture Change in Modern Bengal," *Man in India*, XXXII (October-December 1952), 189-97.

————. "Some Problems of Urbanization," *Man in India*, XLII, No. 4 (October-December 1962), 255-63.

————. "Types of Villages in West Bengal: A Study in Social Change," *The Economic Weekly*, X (February 1958), 149-52.

"Calcutta and the World Bank Mission," *The Economic Weekly*, XII (October 1960), 1469-74.

"Calcutta Scheme 'Under Consideration,'" *The Economic Weekly*, XII (November 26, 1960), 1711.

Chakravarti, Robi. "The Decline of the Left in Calcutta: Muchipara Constituency," *The Economic Weekly*, XIV (August 25, 1962), 1381-86.

Chanda, S. M. "Portrait of a Bengali," *The Statesman* (Calcutta), June 29, 1958, Sec. II, p. 1.

Chatterjee, Prabuddha Nath. "A Plea for Municipal Self-Government in Calcutta," *The Modern Review*, CIV, No. 5 (November 1958), 396-99.

Chattopadhyay, K. P., Bose, K. K., and Chatterji, A. "Undergraduate Students in Calcutta: How They Live and Work," *The Calcutta Review*, CXXXII, No. 1 (July 1954), 1-42.

Chaudhuri, Nirad C. "Subhas Chandra Bose: His Legacy and Legend," *Pacific Affairs*, XXVI, No. 4 (December 1953), 349-57.

————. "Tagore: A Rebellious Liberal," *The Statesman* (Calcutta), August 5, 1956, Sec. II, p. 1.

Chaudhuri, Ranjit. "Pattern of Leadership in a West Bengal Village," *The Economic Weekly*, XVI (April 4, 1964), 641-44.

"Congress May Lose West Bengal—If Refugees Remain Unsettled," *The Economic Weekly*, VI (July 10, 1954), 763-64.

"Congress Organization," *Indian Affairs,* 1 (October 1948-January 1949), 12-13, 77-82.

Datta, Jatindra Mohan. "Urbanization in Bengal," *The Geographical Review of India,* xviii, No. 4 (December 1956), 19-23.

Datta, Sudhin. "The World's Cities: Calcutta," *Encounter,* viii, No. 6 (June 1957), 35-45.

Datta Choudhury, R. "Joint Family System: Its Present and Future," *The Economic Weekly,* ix (September 21, 1957), 1233-36.

"Development of Calcutta," *The Economic Weekly,* xiii (January 14, 1961), 41-42.

Dotson, Arch. "Delhi and Other Cities: Comparative Study in Government," *The Statesman* (Calcutta), April 8, 1958, p. 8.

D'Souza, Victor. "Rural Change in Bengal," *The Economic Weekly,* xvi (February 29, 1964), 439-40.

"Election Prospect in West Bengal," *The Economic Weekly,* xiv (February 24, 1962), 367-70.

Flibbertigibbet [Niranjan Majumdar]. "A Big Man Goes," *The Economic Weekly,* xiv (July 7, 1962), 1034.

———. "Democracy, Their Democracy," *The Economic Weekly,* xvi (January 4, 1964), 11-12.

———. "The Euthanasia of English," *The Economic Weekly,* xv (May 18, 1963), 807.

———. "A Phoenix Too Frequent," *The Economic Weekly,* xvi (January 25, 1964), 113-15.

———. "Profile of a Bengali Businessman," *The Economic Weekly,* x (January 1958), 105-07.

———. "The Uncleared Garbage: Calcutta Corporation," *The Economic Weekly,* xv (June 1, 1963), 879-80.

"Gains Cancelled by Losses," *The Economic Weekly,* xiv (March 10, 1962), 435-36.

Ghosal, A. K. "Second General Elections in West Bengal: An Analysis," *The Modern Review,* ciii (May 1958), 374-80.

Ghose, Benoy. "The Colonial Beginnings of Calcutta: Urbanization without Industrialization," *The Economic Weekly*, XII (August 13, 1960), 1255-60.

———. "Crisis of Bengali Gentility in Calcutta," *The Economic Weekly*, IX (July 6, 1957), 821-26.

———. "Town Improvement in Old Calcutta: Its Impact on Property Owners," *The Economic Weekly*, X (July 1958), 873-76.

Ghosh, Atulya. "Administration: The Human Approach," *Amrita Bazaar Patrika* (Calcutta), January 1, 1964.

———. "P. C. Sen: A Life Career Sketch," *Amrita Bazaar Patrika* (Calcutta), April 10, 1964.

Ghosh, Kedar. "How the Army Restored Order in Calcutta," *The Statesman* (Calcutta), March 14, 1964, p. 6.

———. "Parliamentary Life in West Bengal," *The Statesman* (Calcutta), January 26, 1957, pp. 1, 3.

———. "Stocktaking in West Bengal [Review of West Bengal Five-Year Plans]," *The Statesman* (Calcutta), January 26, 1959, p. 8.

Ghosh, Sadhan Kumar. "Middle Class Revolution," *The Statesman* (Calcutta), August 23, 1953, Sec. II, p. 1.

Gorwala, A. D. "New Characters in the Drama of Modern Bengal," *The Statesman* (Calcutta), February 23, 1954, p. 4.

———. "A Study of Calcutta Today," *The Statesman* (Calcutta), October 19, 1953, p. 4.

"Greater Calcutta," *The Economic Weekly*, XII (November 19, 1960), 1668-69.

Guha, Arun Chandra. "Rehabilitation of East Bengal Refugees," *Indian Affairs Record*, III, No. 4 (May 1957), 71-74.

Guha, Meera. "Urban Regions of West Bengal: A Few Examples," *Geographical Review of India*, XIX, No. 3 (July-October 1956), 31-44.

Mahanti, P. C. "The Human Geography of Calcutta," *The Statesman* (Calcutta), April 6, 1954, p. 4.

Mandal, Gobinda Chandra. "A Socio-Economic Survey of the Students in a College in a Rural Area of West Bengal," *The Modern Review* (Calcutta), CI (February 1957), 125-27.

Mitra, Asok. "West Bengal Elections," *The Economic Weekly*, xiv (February 1962), 155-62.

——. "West Bengal Elections: A Further Note," *The Economic Weekly*, xiv (May 12, 1962), 781-87.

Mukherjee, Asok Kumar. "The Nyaya Panchayat in West Bengal," *The Indian Journal of Political Science*, xxv, Nos. 3 and 4 (July-December 1964), 357-64.

Mukherjee, Bhusan. "Urbanization in Burdwan Division," *Calcutta Statistical Association Bulletin*, vi, No. 21 (March 1955), 1-16.

Mukherjee, Sailas Kumar. "Last General Election in West Bengal, 1957," *Calcutta Review*, cxlvi (February 1958), 134-46.

Narad [pseud.]. "On Bengal: A Post-Mortem," *The Economic Weekly*, iv (August 15, 1952), 818-21.

Nicholas, Ralph W. "Ecology and Village Structure in Deltaic West Bengal," *The Economic Weekly*, xv (July 1963), 1185-96.

——. "Village Factions and Political Parties in West Bengal," *Journal of Commonwealth Political Studies*, ii, No. 1 (November 1963), 19.

——. and Tarashish Mukhopadhyay. "Politics and Law in Two West Bengal Villages," *Bulletin of the Anthropological Survey of India*, Vol. xv (1964).

Park, Richard L. "Congress Defeat in West Bengal," *Far Eastern Survey*, xviii (July 1949), 178-79.

——. "The Urban Challenge to Local and State Government: West Bengal, With Special Attention to Calcutta," in *India's Urban Future*. Edited by Roy Turner. Bombay: Oxford University Press, 1962. Pp. 382-96.

"Perks Will Out [Middle-Class Images of Politicians in India]," *The Economist* (London), ccvi (March 23, 1963), 1100.

"Politics of Rehabilitation," *The Economic Weekly*, x (April 19, 1958), 522-23.

"Profile of West Bengal," *The Economic Weekly*, VIII (September 15, 1956), 1095-97.

Purkayastha, K. M. "States' Share of Federal Funds: West Bengal's Grievances," *The Statesman* (Calcutta), November 26, 1959, p. 6.

Ray, Sibnarayan. "Decline of the Indian Intellectuals," *The Radical Humanist*, XXII (October 19, 1958), 503-04, 513-14.

Roy, Basanta Koomar. "The New Soul of India," *Open Court* (Chicago), XXXI (August 17, 1919), 504-08.

Roy, Ranajit. "Congress Work for the Peasantry," *The Statesman* (Calcutta), January 20, 1954, Sec. II, p. 9.

Roy, S. N. "The Decline of the Left in a Calcutta Suburb: Behala Constituency," *The Economic Weekly,* XIV (September 1, 1962), 1413-17.

Sarkar, Sasanka Sekher. "The Tribal Population in West Bengal," *Man in India*, XXXVIII (January-March 1958), 60-64.

Sarma, Jyotirmoyee. "Formal and Informal Relations in the Hindu Joint Household in Bengal," *Man in India,* XXXI (1951), 51-71.

———. "Social Change in Bengal in the Latter Half of the Nineteenth Century," *Man in India*, XXXIII (1953), 104-26.

Sen, A. K. "Bankura: A Study of the Cultural Landscape of an Urban Area," *Geographical Review of India*, XVIII (March 1956), 1-14.

Sen, S. N. "Calcutta's Lonely Crowd," *The Economic Weekly*, XI (February 21, 1959), 282-84.

Sengupta, D. N. "The Hooghly River," *The Modern Review*, CIV, No. 3 (September 1958), 201-05.

Sengupta, J. K. "The Employment Target of Our Second Plan," *The Modern Review*, C (August 1956), 109-11.

Sengupta, Sunil. "Family Organization in West Bengal: Its Nature and Dynamics," *The Economic Weekly*, X (March 15, 1958), 384-89.

Sharma, Ram. "The Party, The Government, and The Administration," *Calcutta Review*, CVII (June 1948), 130-34.

Sinha, K. K. "West Bengal: A Political Report," *Thought* (Delhi Weekly), xi, No. 33 (August 15, 1959), 28.

———. "West Bengal: Problems and Prospects," *Freedom First*, No. 80 (January 1959), pp. 5-6.

Sinha, Sasadhar. "What Is Wrong With Us Bengalis?" *The Statesman* (Calcutta), November 8, 1956, p. 6.

Smith, Marian W. "Village Notes from Bengal," *American Anthropologist*, xlviii (1946), 574-92.

"Southeast Calcutta," *The Economic Weekly*, v (November 28, 1953), 1309-1310.

Spate, O. H. K. "The Partition of the Punjab and Bengal," *Geographical Journal*, cx (1947), 201-22.

"Squatters Colonies," *The Economic Weekly*, vi (June 5, 1954), 631-33.

Thapar, S. D. "The Dandakaranya Project: Failure of an Ambitious Scheme," *The Economic Weekly*, xv (March 2, 1963), 401-04.

"To Save Calcutta," *The Economic Weekly*, xiii (April 29, 1961), 663-64.

"Unemployment in West Bengal," *Thought* (Delhi Weekly), vii, No. 37 (September 10, 1955), 17.

Vedette [pseud.]. "Calcutta Incidents Viewed from Delhi," *The Statesman* (Calcutta), February 21, 1954, p. 8.

Weiner, Myron. "Changing Patterns of Political Leadership in West Bengal," *Pacific Affairs*, xxxii (September 1959), 277-87.

———. "Political Leadership in West Bengal: The Implications of Its Changing Pattern for Economic Planning," *The Economic Weekly*, xi (July 1959), 925-32.

———. "Student Problem in India," *The Statesman* (Calcutta), May 26, 1954, p. 6.

———. "Violence and Politics in Calcutta," *Journal of Asian Studies*, xx, No. 3 (May 1961), 275-81.

"West Bengal's Middle Class," *The Economic Weekly*, vi (July 31, 1954), 847-48.

"West Bengal's Prohibition Policy," *Thought* (Delhi Weekly), VIII, No. 47 (November 19, 1955), 18.

"West Bengal's Second Plan," *Thought* (Delhi Weekly), VII, No. 41 (October 1955), 16-17.

"Why West Bengal Is a Problem State," *The Economic Weekly*, VI (September 5, 1954), 884-85.

GOVERNMENT DOCUMENTS

India (Great Britain). Census Commissioner. *Census of India, 1931.* Vol. v. "Bengal and Sikkim."

———. Sedition Committee, 1918. *Report.* Calcutta: Superintendent Government Printing, 1918.

India (Republic). Census Commissioner. *Census of India, 1951.* Vol. vi. "West Bengal, Sikkim and Chandernagore."

West Bengal, 1954. Alipore: Director of Publicity, West Bengal, 1954.

UNPUBLISHED MATERIAL

Bhattacharya, N. C. "Leadership Problems in the Communist Party of India, With Special Reference to West Bengal." Paper Prepared for the International Political Science Association, Bombay, January 1964.

Goldsmith, Ernest Harold. "Municipal Government in Calcutta: The Calcutta Corporation." Unpublished Master's dissertation, University of California, 1957.

Indin, Ronald B. "The Localization of the Hindu Elite of Bengal and Its Effects on the Polity of the Southeastern Bengal Chiefdoms." Unpublished Master's dissertation, University of Chicago, 1963.

Park, Richard Leonard. "The Rise of Militant Nationalism in Bengal: A Regional Study of Indian Nationalism." Unpublished Ph.D. dissertation. Harvard, 1950.

Sarma, Jyotirmoyee. "The Hindu System of Caste in the Province of Bengal in India." Unpublished Master's dissertation, University of Chicago, 1942.

Index

te Due